'As a former ESL teacher and workshop leader, I
agreement page after page of this important and v
authors expose the truth that many internationa
even deliberately, disregard the crucial role that ɛ
ESL and mother tongue programme plays in promoting the language
rights of all students and allowing access to the school's curriculum to
help nurture each student's true potential. It is a compelling argument.'

Victor Ferreira, IBDP Coordinator, American School of The Hague

'This straightforward and ferociously honest study provides vital and
attainable suggestions for creating an effective, inclusive ESL programme
for international schools. A must-read for teachers and leaders whose goal
is to set students up for future academic success.'

Melanie Sanchez, TheLanguageContinuum.com

'This is a great book, offering a clear vision. It gives international
schools compelling ammunition to steer away from an ESL "support"
model and create truly equitable multilingual schools in which ESL and
mother-tongue centres of expertise provide complementary professional
programmes for students, teachers and parents.'

**Joris van den Bosch, Secondary EAL teacher,
The British School of Brussels, Belgium**

Second Language Learners in International Schools

Second Language Learners in International Schools

Maurice Carder

with Patricia Mertin and Sarah Porter

 is an imprint of

First published in 2018 by the UCL Institute of Education Press, University College London, 20 Bedford Way, London WC1H 0AL

www.ucl-ioe-press.com

British Library Cataloguing in Publication Data:
A catalogue record for this publication is available from the British Library

ISBNs
978-1-85856-859-1 (paperback)
978-1-85856-884-3 (PDF eBook)
978-1-85856-885-0 (ePub eBook)
978-1-85856-886-7 (Kindle eBook)

Typeset by Quadrant Infotech (India) Pvt Ltd
Printed by CPI Group (UK) Ltd, Croydon, CR0 4YY

Cover image © Aflo Co., Ltd./Alamy Stock Photo

Contents

Part 2 Bilingualism and second language acquisition: Developments in theory and research

Part 3 The human factor

Part 4 The role of external curriculum and accreditation bodies: Pitfalls and alternatives

Part 5 The current situation in an international school

The authors

Maurice Carder graduated with a BA honours degree in Spanish in 1967 (Bristol); he followed a PGCE with a special focus on ESL in 1970 (London, Institute of Education) and an MA in Linguistics for English Language Teaching in 1979 (Lancaster), and completed an EdD (International) on 'Challenging the English-only orthodoxy: Linguistic pluralism, recognition and diversity rather than assimilation' in 2010 (University College London, Institute of Education). From 1967 to 1981 he taught English in various parts of the world in universities, institutes and schools, and from 1981 to 2009 headed the ESL and Mother Tongue department at the Vienna International School, Secondary. He worked closely with the IB on developing language A2 in the Diploma Programme, and on the *Language B Guide* and the *Second Language Acquisition and Mother Tongue Development Guide* for the IBMYP. He was an examiner for the International Baccalaureate IBDP language A2 and a moderator for language B in the IBMYP. He has served on many CIS accreditation teams around the world, co-chairing them at times. He chaired the ECIS ESL and Mother Tongue Committee for many years, and organized several conferences. He has given workshops on ESL and mother tongue issues at international schools worldwide, including teaching 'ESL in the Mainstream'. His book *Bilingualism in International Schools* (2007) gives comprehensive details of a successful model for second language learners. Visit www.mauricecarder.net (accessed 13 February 2018).

Patricia Mertin began her career in education at Goldsmith's College, London University, by completing her teacher training in 1969, after which she taught in London and in Germany with the British Forces Education Services. Subsequently she taught English as a foreign language in a German state school and various further education establishments, teaching both children and adults. She completed an external BA in Old High German Literature with London University, and an MA in TESOL with Sheffield Hallam University. In 1993 she joined the faculty of the International School of Düsseldorf, where she taught ESL for twenty years. She became department chair in 2003, and also developed the mother tongue department. In 2006 she completed a PhD on the topic of 'The role of culture in second language acquisition' with Goldsmith's College. She served on the ECIS ESL and MT committee as a member and as its chair, and hosted the 2011 ESL and MT conference in Düsseldorf, which had over four hundred participants. She is an IBDP English B examiner. She also serves on accreditation teams for the CIS and is a CIS Affiliated Consultant for ESL.

Sarah Porter first taught ESL at the 'Palace of Pioneers and Schoolchildren' in Krasnoyarsk, Russia, before qualifying as a teacher of Russian, French and German in 1999. After teaching modern languages at a state school in north London, she completed a master's degree in Russian in 2001. Her next post was teaching primary French at St Aubyn's Preparatory School in Woodford Green, Essex. She moved to Bucharest with her husband and three children in August 2013 and has taught in the British School of Bucharest (BSB) secondary EAL department since then, becoming EAL co-ordinator in September 2017. She has begun a master's degree in applied linguistics and TESOL.

Foreword

Virginia P. Collier

Professor Emerita of Bilingual/Multicultural/ESL Education
George Mason University

International schools provide a unique and important context for schooling diverse students whose parents serve in occupations that require them to live in multiple locations around the world. As global citizenship and multilingualism become more common, these schools are multiplying rapidly throughout the world; it is predicted that within two years there will be at least 10,000 international schools, serving over 5 million students (see the Introduction). This book is a timely and much-needed resource for the administrators and teachers who serve these schools. As experienced teachers in international school settings, its authors provide challenging perspectives as they examine in depth the research and writings that inform international school educators' decisions.

The unique process that students experience in international schools provides a powerful context for transforming schooling that might be applied to other multilingual settings in education, but these schools have not yet reached their transformational potential. Most of them follow Western curricula and Western ways of learning and teach the curriculum mostly in English. As stated by Dr Carder in Chapter 3, the student population of these schools typically consists of about 25 per cent native speakers of English, 25 per cent speakers of the host-country language, and 50 per cent speakers of other languages. Since the language of the curriculum is usually English, this means that around 75 per cent of the students receive their curricular subjects through their second language, not the language(s) spoken to them as young children by their family. This raises the interesting possibility, as proposed by the authors of this book, of transforming the way second language schooling is carried out in international schools, thus making them a model for global schooling designed to meet the needs of the twenty-first century. These schools have enormous potential when the multilingual communities who participate in this school context are viewed as an immense resource.

Now what does this mean? What does the research tell us? The authors of this book go in depth into the research that informs the field of education regarding the schooling of second language learners. Most important is, first, to understand the crucial importance of the mother tongue in the student's cognitive development. From hundreds of research studies of the relationship between students' mother tongue and cognition, we know that children must develop cognitively in their mother tongue until at least age 12 in order to be successful in curricular mastery in their second language. For example, our longitudinal research findings from the analysis of over 7.5 million student records from 36 school districts in 16 US states (summarized in Collier and Thomas, 2017; Thomas and Collier, 2017) show that English learners who do not continue to study school subjects in their mother tongue are typically two to four grades behind students who attend dual-language classes. In the US, dual-language schooling typically integrates the two language groups, so that the students acquire the curriculum through both their languages, and leads to above-grade-level achievement for all groups, in both English and the partner language (the home language of the English language learners).

In a multilingual context such as that of international schools, parents are important partners with the school in continuing mother-tongue development. In Chapter 4, Dr Carder states that, often, international school parents 'focus principally on their children becoming fluent in English, while not considering what might happen to their children's own language and identity'. Parents must assume responsibility for continuing the non-stop cognitive development of their children's mother tongue(s), including literacy skills, but this book illustrates that international schools also need to provide mother tongue curricular support when possible. The goal of all international schools should be to graduate bilingual/multilingual students academically proficient in their mother tongue and English, with the possibility of adding the host-country language as a third language of instruction, as well as other languages.

A major new research finding with implications for international schools comes from one of our latest research studies, which analyses statewide data from North Carolina on dual-language schools: innovations from second language teaching strategies help *all* students do better in school, not only second language learners. We found that students who in the US are considered most 'at risk' benefit greatly from second language teaching strategies – specifically, students of low-income background, including African Americans and Caucasian Americans, and students with special education needs, as well as English language learners. Our analyses of 3.3 million student records over a six-year period (grades 3–8) show that after several years of instruction in both English and the partner language, at-risk dual-language students' gains were two to four years greater than those of peers of the same background not in dual-language classes (Thomas and Collier, 2014, 2017). From interviews with administrators of these schools, we found they were convinced that courses that prepare second language teachers to teach the curriculum through students' second language lead to strategies for teaching that benefit all students, especially in diverse contexts. These school principals insist that all their school staff must use the innovative teaching strategies of second language teachers, and they provide ongoing staff development, given by those trained in these strategies, to support all staff. Second language teaching strategies include scaffolding supports, collaborative learning, real-world problem solving across the curriculum, varied student work groupings, sensitivity to cross-cultural issues, emotional support for all, and intentional and explicit non-verbal and verbal clues to meaning for both content and language.

This means that, in international schools, ESL teachers certified to teach academic content (not just language) are the best prepared to bring about academic success with very diverse classes, and these staff should provide ongoing staff development for the whole school. Dual certification should be required of all teachers, so that they get thorough training in second language teaching techniques *and* the standard coursework for the age group and curricular subject(s) to be taught. In dual-language schools in the US, typically two teachers team together, one teaching the curriculum through English and the other teaching the curriculum through the English learners' home language, working with two classes and trading the classes back and forth. The authors of this book illustrate many ways in which mother tongue and ESL teaching methodologies can be used effectively in international school settings. ESL teaching has formerly been viewed as an additional support for students, provided separately from the mainstream. Now it is clear from the research that second language teaching strategies benefit all students.

Preface

This book came about as a result of a conference in Amsterdam in 2014. Patricia Mertin and I were both scheduled as consultants at the ECIS ESL and Mother Tongue Conference there in the early spring, attended by some five hundred participants. We were each allocated a room, and ESL and mother-tongue teachers could sign up to discuss their professional concerns. We had met sporadically in recent years and were aware of our common interest in promoting the linguistic potential of SL learners, and that we were both living and raising children in multilingual families. Over coffee one morning we began to recount the issues that teachers were bringing to us. It turned out that we were both overwhelmed by the number of distressing issues that were being raised: how ESL programmes were being downgraded and teachers' status reduced, and how directors were dictating policy on how ESL should be taught, allowing no input from the professionals concerned.

Coincidentally, we had pursued very similar career paths. We both had an initial degree in languages, and had followed a teaching certificate, done a master's in matters relating to linguistics, and ended our teaching careers with a doctorate on second language/mother tongue issues. We had also each headed a secondary department with the title 'ESL and Mother Tongue' in a large international school. As the conference progressed, and the enormity of the situation facing the teachers and students of English as a second language continued to emerge, we resolved to write about the matters being raised in order to make quite clear to those responsible what the fundamental issues were, why SL instructional programmes were taking a wrong turn, and how to resolve those issues.

We are confident about our writing in this book: we have spent our professional lives in the classroom, at conferences and at workshops, writing programmes for international curricula, and taking part in international accreditation processes. We have studied in depth, and to the highest levels possible, the theory and intricacies of issues relating to SL acquisition and bilingualism.

Our hope is that those responsible for curricula, accreditation and programme implementation in international schools around the world will take note: that can only benefit all of those who make up the international school community.

List of abbreviations

AfL	Assessment for Learning
AGM	annual general meeting
BICS	basic interpersonal communication skills
CALP	cognitive and academic language proficiency
CELTA	Certificate in English Language Teaching to Adults
CIS	Council of International Schools
CLIL	content and language integrated learning
CPD	continuing professional development
EAL	English as an additional language
ECIS	Educational Collaborative for International Schools
ELL	English language learner
ELT	English language teaching
EMI	English as the medium of instruction
ESL	English as a second language
FL	foreign language
IATEFL	International Association of Teachers of English as a Foreign Language
IB	International Baccalaureate
IBDP	International Baccalaureate Diploma Programme
IBMYP	International Baccalaureate Middle Years Programme
IBPYP	International Baccalaureate Primary Years Programme
IELTS	International English Language Testing System
IGCSE	International General Certificate in Secondary Education
INSET	in-service training day

L1	first language
L2	second language
LOI	language of instruction
MT	mother tongue
NALDIC	National Association for Language Development in the Curriculum
NEASC	New England Association of Schools and Colleges
NNEST	non-native English-speaking teacher
NNS	non-native speaker
NS	native speaker
Ofsted	Office for Standards in Education
PE	physical education
PGCE	Postgraduate Certificate in Education
PISA	Programme for International Student Assessment
PTA	parent–teacher association
SEN	special educational needs
SFL	systemic functional linguistics
SIOP	Sheltered Instruction Observation Protocol
SL	second language
SLA	second language acquisition
SLIC	second language instructional competence
SLL	second language learner
TA	teaching assistant
TESMC	teaching ESL students in mainstream classrooms

Introduction

The number of international schools is set to rise rapidly in the near future. Whereas in 2000 there were 2,584 international schools worldwide with just under a million students, in 2013 there were 6,400 international schools, and by 2020 it is predicted that, worldwide, there will be over 10,000 international schools with over 5 million students (Brummitt and Keeling, 2013: 27–8).

This presents a huge challenge to those involved with international schools: curriculum providers, accreditation guide writers, school leaders, and teachers. In many of these schools, second language learners are a majority. Native speakers of the school language of instruction, which in 90 per cent of schools is English, thus represent a minority. Students learning English are described as ESL students.

A word on terminology is appropriate at this stage as, first, the field of linguistics and bilingualism is complex and, second, the provision for sound models of instruction has been heavily influenced by political rather than educational concerns, which have spread from national educational systems to the international sphere, where they should have no place.

The most often used terms the reader needs to be familiar with are 'second language', 'foreign language' and 'mother tongue'. It is essential to make a sharp distinction between *second* and *foreign* language. 'Second language' is the term used to describe the language students learn in order to follow the entire curriculum of the school. 'Foreign language' refers to a language learnt in the curriculum, often French or Spanish, for a fixed number of lessons per week, which is not generally used outside that classroom. For example, if English is the language of instruction in the school, students who are not able to work comfortably in English will need a comprehensive programme of instruction in English as a second language. 'Second' does not refer to a mathematical progression: that is, it is not necessarily students' second-best language; 'second language' is the standard linguistic terminology for a language learnt after the first language for everyday purposes and needs. It is useful to remember the expression 'second nature': if something is second nature to you, you have done it so much that you no longer think about it, and it seems as if it is part of your character. It is the same with a second language: you will develop such fluency in it that it will become part of your character. The term is based on the theory of second language acquisition.

In England and Wales in the 1980s, there was much politicization of the process of programme delivery, prompted by fears of racism, which tainted the models of delivery and the terminology, so that a new term was introduced, English as an additional language (EAL).

> [T]here is a proliferation of labels in the field internationally. For instance, in the USA, language minority students from non-English speaking communities who are learning English are now referred to as English Language Learners (ELLs; previously ESL, English as a Second Language, students). In England the teaching provision of English language to adult students is referred to as ESOL (English for Speakers of Other Languages); for school aged students the preferred and widely used term is EAL (English as an Additional Language, up until the mid-1990s it was known as ESL). The term 'second language' is used in many European contexts. ... [T]he different terminologies reflect the particular histories and experiences of the different countries.
>
> (Leung, 2013: 13)

The term EAL will not be used (except where it refers to writings, or situations in schools, that use the term), as it has come to be associated with the 'support' model for ESL students, which we regard as inadequate. Crawford and Krashen have written:

> [E]ducators must learn to cope with external pressures and become strong advocates for the programs that best serve ELLs [English language learners]. Perhaps no other area of education has been more politicized in recent years. Immigration has become a stormy controversy and language a frequent lightning rod.
>
> (Crawford and Krashen, 2007: 10)

They added:

> What are the worst mistakes that schools make in serving ELL students? Three common responses can be summed up as denial, delegating, and remediation. None of them is beneficial to ELLs.
>
> (ibid.: 14)

These are issues that we address throughout the book, and which underlie much of what has developed in second language issues in the international school sector.

Since the book is aimed at international schools worldwide, where English is not always the language of instruction (the IB offers its curriculum model in Chinese, French and Spanish, for example), the term used will often be second language learners (SLLs), that is, learners of any language of instruction in a school. However, since at present 'The British Council reckons that English is spoken at a useful level by some 1.75 billion people, a quarter of the world's population' (Ostler, 2018), the terms ESL students and EAL students appear more frequently when used by various writers to refer to those who require a dedicated programme of instruction in English which is relevant to their academic and social needs, a second language programme (SLP).

'Mother tongue' (MT) will be used to refer to the native language of students, and although there are many cases where students have more than one language in the family, or have imperfect knowledge of their mother tongue, the aim is to convey the sense of the student's home language(s). The focus in this book is on the middle and upper school, where the mastery of academic language is of overriding importance.

The book is divided into six parts and twelve chapters. Each chapter heading is followed in the Table of Contents by subheadings intended to guide the reader through the arguments developed in the book. The book begins with an overview of the international school and its essential differences from most national schools, and continues with the many factors that have influenced the development of programmes for SL learners; all the facts related are supported by research, the experience of the authors, and vignettes from teachers. Part 2 summarizes the theories behind the proposed models, and summarizes the writings of those who have influenced them. Part 3 delves into the complex aspects of teacher relationships, and investigates what is actually taking place in classrooms and across disciplines. Part 4 traces the development of provision for SL learners in particular curriculum agencies – the IB – and accreditation guides – the CIS. These are well-documented investigations that show how quickly better models for ESL students can be overtaken by political forces.

Part 5 brings the situation to life, with a description of a young teacher's direct experience of encountering the challenges faced by SL learners in an international school. It leads on to Part 6, in which the authors lay out their plans for building on the potential of SL learners. They include establishing a department of professional ESL staff, ensuring that all staff receive appropriate continuing professional development, and building up a system for maintaining students' mother tongues. Chapter 11 investigates how it is that, even after so much has been written about the importance of recognizing the potential of SL learners and what they can contribute, many international schools still provide what is essentially a monolingual programme based on that of national educational systems. The authors close in Chapter 12 with the hope that 'school heads and directors who are genuinely persuaded by the arguments in this book will need not only to set up the model advocated, but to back it all the way. This will mature into a lasting embedding of equitable and professional programmes for SL learners. Policies alone are not enough: they need consistent implementation.'

Part One

1

International schools
and influences on their
provision for second
language students: Islands of
language and a high socio-
economic base

Chapter 1

What second language learners bring to international schools

Patricia Mertin

How do we define an international school?

How do we arrive at a satisfactory definition of an 'international school'? State schools in Europe and other parts of the world where the rates of immigration are high could well claim the title 'international' if this simply meant that the students came from many different countries. Here we try to identify what makes an international school different, first looking at the features that international schools have in common, and then examining the diversity found in the sector. Finally, we consider the challenges faced by students, teachers and administrators in delivering effective education, and ask to what extent are international schools meeting these challenges?

What international schools have in common

International schools charge fees (see chapter 3 for a discussion by Maurice Carder). Langford (2001: 28–9) highlights other important commonalities among international schools, in addition to the multinational composition of the student body, such as high population turnover and international mobility. A consequence of parental career paths is the likelihood that students will not complete their education in the country in which the school is located, but will move on to another city or country, or repatriate to their passport country. The students will probably be influenced by the culture of the host country as well as by the cultures they themselves embody.

The teaching staff at international schools also share important characteristics. They fall into three main groups: host-country nationals, locally hired expatriates, and overseas-hired expatriates. The number of host-country teachers hired depends largely on the location of the school and the language of instruction. There are more possibilities for hiring host-country teachers for an English-medium school in Anglosphere countries (see below) than in countries where the language of the school is not the local language, as host-country teachers are likely to be hired to teach the host-country language classes.

(The Anglosphere comprises those English-speaking nations which have a similar cultural heritage, based on people originating from the nations of the British Isles (England, Wales, Scotland and Ireland), and which today maintain close political and military cooperation. The term does not usually include all the countries in which English is an official language, although the nations that are commonly included were all once part of the British Empire. In its most restricted sense, the term covers the United Kingdom, Ireland, the United States, Canada, Australia and New Zealand, which, post-British Empire, maintain a close affinity of cultural, familial and political links. See also 'Angloworld' in Belich (2011), and Kenny and Pearce (2015). A more specific definition has been given by James C. Bennett: 'This term, which can be defined briefly as the set of English-speaking, Common Law nations, implies far more than merely the sum of all persons who employ English as a first or second language. To be part of the Anglosphere requires adherence to the fundamental customs and values that form the core of English-speaking cultures. These include individualism, rule of law, honouring contracts and covenants, and the elevation of freedom to the first rank of political and cultural values' (www.theguardian.com/news/blog/2004/oct/28/explainingthe, accessed 13 February 2018).)

Locally hired expatriates tend to be the partners of host-country nationals or of expatriates employed in other work. A disadvantage is that they may leave abruptly if their partner's contract changes. On the other hand, locally hired expatriates who have lived in the host country for some years will bring valuable knowledge of the language, the culture and local resources and facilities, all of which contribute greatly to the school's international understanding.

Overseas-hired expatriates tend to be young and enthusiastic, but they seldom stay in a school for long. They make a valuable and interesting contribution to the faculty of any school. The younger teachers introduce a new dynamic to the school, often questioning the way things are done, introducing new ideas and adding valuable impetus to teaching and learning.

A final commonality relates to the administration of international schools. Administrators tend to come from anglophone countries and are often monolingual. It is unusual for them to learn the language of the host country. As Blandford and Shaw (2001: 14) point out, 'There is less security of tenure for a headteacher in an international school than in most national schools: being fired is a frequent occurrence.'

What makes international schools different

Although international schools share many characteristics, there are also important differences within the sector. In this regard, Murphy (2000, quoted in Hayden and Thompson, 2000: 1) asks not only 'What is an international school? but also 'What is an international education?' The answer to the first of these questions underlines the huge diversity observable in schools that include 'international' in their title. As Skelton (2002: 34) points out, '[we all] know that "The International School of X" may be a very, very different place from "The International School of Y"'.

Some schools have, for example, been established by small groups of parents to fulfil family needs; others have been set up by companies for profit or may even be part of a chain. International schools vary in size from fewer than 200 students to over 1,500. Some are well established, many are new: two of the longest-established international schools – Yokohama International School and the International School of Geneva – date back to 1927 (Hayden and Thompson, 2013: 3), whereas today 'international schools are being established across the world at an unprecedented pace' (Brummitt and Keeling, 2013: 27–8). In the start-up phase of a new school, the numbers will be low; they will also vary according to, for instance, the location of major companies.

The student population also varies considerably. Some schools have a large proportion of students from the host country whose parents want them to benefit from an international education. Some cap the number of host-country nationals in order to maintain the balance and nature of the school population. The other students may be from embassies and international companies in the area, and may come from any country in the world. It is not unusual for a school to have students of up to a hundred different nationalities, each with its own language and culture.

In most cases, one language is used as the main medium of instruction, usually English or French; occasionally, a policy of bilingualism is pursued. The predominant language and nationality of the students will depend on the school's geographical position, the population of the area it serves, and the location of international companies. If English is the language of instruction and also of the environment, both students and parents will feel comfortable. However, it may mean that the students have less opportunity to learn a further foreign language, and the dominance of English may make it harder for students to maintain their mother tongue. If the language of the environment is less accessible to parents and students, the school is likely to become a major social centre for the families.

Accreditation

The accreditation status of international schools varies: some are accredited, others are not. They may follow American or British school systems, with implications for the curriculum and examination system they follow. As Murphy observes:

> Maybe it is time ... to stop trying to organize the unorganizable by dint of words alone. ... We might want to accept, finally, that we do not, in this community, speak with one voice; that we are educators with different experiences and backgrounds working in many different kinds of schools for different reasons, and whose common enterprise reflects a rich variety of approaches; and that we may or may not eventually arrive at a point where we conform to a single vision.
>
> (Murphy, 2000, quoted in Hayden and Thompson, 2000: 1)

In answer to Murphy's second question – 'What is an international education?' – a useful starting place is 'international-mindedness'. This term is philosophically related to UNESCO's Aims of International Education, 1996, which are to develop:

- a sense of universal values for a culture of peace
- the ability to value freedom and the civic responsibility that goes with it
- intercultural understanding which encourages the convergence of ideas and solutions to strengthen peace
- skills of non-violent conflict resolution
- skills for making informed choices
- respect for cultural heritage and protection of the environment
- feelings of solidarity and equity at the national and international levels.

(Ellwood and Davis, 2009: 205)

The ultimate goal of any international school must be to provide an international education to students from a wide variety of different linguistic and cultural backgrounds. As Hayden and Thompson affirm:

> many students in international schools value interaction with those of other cultures as one of the fundamental characteristics of international education which promotes the development of an 'international attitude' .... The deliberate, planned interaction of students from different cultural backgrounds is widely regarded as a cornerstone of international education.
>
> (Hayden and Thompson, 2000: 3)

Although interactions of this kind contribute to an international education, three other dimensions are commonly recognized: a balanced formal curriculum, exposure to cultural diversity, and a range of appropriate administrative styles. As we will see, however, the extent to which international schools succeed in meeting these ideals varies.

The development of international-mindedness creates a need for an international curriculum. Hill (2000) lists four underlying principles for such curricula: that they contain course content that provides an international perspective, they recognize that the countries of the world are increasingly interdependent, they provide activities that bring students into contact with people of other cultures, and they create a context for world peace by providing opportunities for many cultures to learn together in mutual understanding and respect.

The most widely known example of an international curriculum framework is provided by the IB, with its emphasis on the attributes of the Learner Profile (International Baccalaureate Organization, 2006), which encourages children to become inquirers, thinkers, communicators, risk-takers, knowledgeable, principled, caring, open-minded, healthy and reflective. The Learner Profile is, however, strongly oriented to the West; many of the desired attributes, such as inquiring and risk taking, are not necessarily regarded as desirable attributes in other cultures.

Challenges for international schools

International schools face a number of challenges in delivering quality education, such as the culture shock experienced by new students and new teachers, the lack of initial training and continuing professional development (CPD) for teachers, and the difficulty of supporting students to maintain their mother tongues.

Culture shock

Teachers and students experience culture shock when they arrive. According to scholars (Fennes and Hapgood,1997; McCaig, 1994; Mertin, 2006; Storti, 1997; Useem and Downie, 1976, 1986) their acclimatization has three main phases. At first they feel excitement and anticipation: everything is new and wonderful. In the next phase, when the new and wonderful seems less wonderful, reality sets in and sometimes frustration and even anger are experienced, which are connected to a feeling of loss of identity and dissatisfaction. This is compounded when the language of the local environment is not spoken and the organizational systems both within the school and in the outside world are unfamiliar. The final phase of acclimatization is acceptance of the situation and appreciation of its positive features. Because of the turnover of teachers and students characteristic of international schools, this process is continuous.

Continuing teacher development

On top of the problems of adjusting to a new country, new teachers have seldom had much preparation for dealing with the complex needs of international school students and their families. As Cummins (2000: 13) explains, 'Pre-service teacher education programs across North America typically regard knowledge about linguistic and cultural diversity as appropriate for "additional qualification" courses rather than as part of the core knowledge base that all teachers should possess.' Neither are they familiar with the international curriculum taught in the school. Consequently, they require specific training, particularly for an IB school.

Teachers must be able to explain all aspects of the material they are using – the content, concepts and language. Academic demands increase as the students get older; they are not only learning a language, but learning through that language, and need to do it quickly. It is crucial that students are taught by teachers who understand the linguistic challenges they face. New teachers must learn to appreciate and value the many languages and cultures in their classroom and understand that they are a major resource. New teachers will find it valuable to learn the language of their new country, and that experience will give them some insight into the challenges that second language students face.

Maintaining and developing the mother tongue

English language learners studying in international schools will return to their home country at some stage and continue to study in their mother tongue. For them, maintaining and developing the mother tongue is vital. Furthermore, as Baker has shown, translanguaging supports students' second language development: it 'attempts to develop academic language skills in both languages[,] leading to a fuller bilingualism and biliteracy' (Baker, 2011: 290).

The question remains, however, as to how successful schools are in responding to these challenges. They will fail to meet the ideals of a truly international school if, for instance, students are expected to leave at the school gates not only their language but their culture and required to speak only English throughout the day, and mother tongues are banned. Or if the administrators and the majority of teachers are monolingual English speakers with experience only in their own national systems. Or if the only sign of internationalism is the ubiquitous collection of flags and a visitor walking through the school would only hear, see and read English. Or if the norms and philosophies of administration and teachers were completely Western.

The development of ESL instruction in international schools

In the 1970s and early 1980s the preferred model in many international schools was to pull ESL students out of classes and give them English language instruction in small groups. The focus was on the four skills – listening, speaking, reading and writing – plus grammar and spelling: a traditional approach. ESL teachers were seen largely as an adjunct to English departments, and peripheral to the traditional subjects taught by the main departments: maths, science, humanities, English, foreign languages, arts and PE.

At a conference organized by the ECIS ESL committee in 1987, Professor Jim Cummins talked to ESL teachers from many international schools about his research into the time students needed to learn English and the importance of maintaining literacy in the mother tongue, as skills learnt in the latter transfer to the second language. He distinguished between conversational English, learnt in two years or less, and academic English, which requires up to seven years. He stressed the importance of 'empowering' ESL students so that their sense of self-worth enhanced their progress.

The committee built on this breakthrough in 1989, when Professor Virginia Collier was the keynote speaker at the second ESL subject conference. She and Professor Wayne Thomas, both at George Mason University, described their massive project of number-crunching vast amounts of data about ESL students in the US (Thomas and Collier, 1997). Their research showed which types of programmes benefited students most. However, their work focused on the benefits of bilingual models, which in the USA implies English/Spanish. International schools generally have small groups of speakers of many different languages, so a bilingual model is not possible. Accordingly, Collier wrote the following specifically for the international schools context:

> When the demographics of a school population include a multilingual student group with small numbers of each language represented, then mother tongue literacy development for each language group, combined with ESL taught through academic content, may be the best choice for support of non-English-speakers' needs.
>
> (Collier, 2003: 8)

This statement from such a respected expert in the field affirmed the potential of ESL students to bring a great deal to international education, instead of being seen as a challenge. Certainly, we have found over many years that the second language students we taught were high fliers. This mirrors the view of Frank Monaghan of the Open University that 'some of the highest achieving pupils in British schools were those not having English as a first language' (quoted in Woolcock, 2014).

It is easy to see international schools, with their clientele of wealthy students and their spacious, well-equipped facilities, as a desirable model of education that attracts parents. However, our experience of visiting international schools throughout the world has shown us that second language students are often catered for in precisely the ways that researchers have shown to be inadequate: they have no mother tongue programme, their approach to pedagogy is not about encouraging critical, interactional teaching, and testing has become valued above all else, often disadvantaging the second language students in particular.

The cultural values of the predominant school nationalities, the culture of the school rules of discipline and expected behaviour, the cultural style and content of the lessons, and the teaching styles and attitudes of the staff, all construct a framework within which the non-dominant nationalities must interact. Matthews showed in his study (1989a, 1989b) that international school teachers are predominantly American or British, have little or no training in cross-cultural learning differences, and largely retain their national teaching style. These factors can impact negatively on the motivation of other national groups. As Hedges observes:

> Most elite schools ... do only a mediocre job of teaching students to question and think. ... They focus instead ... on creating hordes of competent systems managers. Responsibility for the collapse of the global economy runs in a direct line from the manicured quadrangles and academic halls ... to the financial and political centers of power.
>
> (Hedges, 2009: 89)

The heads of successful ESL departments in large international schools in various locations in Europe have commented on the failure of their directors to recognize the needs of second language students. As one told us, 'I have given up trying to persuade the director to always employ content teachers who have undertaken serious professional development in "linguistically responsive teaching"'. Another said – upon retiring – 'I couldn't face the thought of having to educate yet another director on how we successfully run ESL and mother tongue programmes here.'

There is clearly a need for strong, informed leadership to ensure a structured programme of second language instruction, and that it is given institutional back-up. But this is hard to establish when school leaders bring with them the outdated and inaccurate ideas about second language acquisition of their national systems – especially England's – and know little about the benefits of bilingualism. Many are wholly unaware of how poorly ESL students are served by the current models in their national systems. Frequently the result is *ad hoc* ESL and mother tongue provision, or none at all, which marginalizes both ESL students and their teachers. The only recourse for the teachers is to seek their own strategies for providing sound second language programmes.

However, given the hierarchical management structure of international schools, in which policies are determined from above and teachers' views are not necessarily given credence, and given that two principal educational agencies, the IB and the CIS, give ESL students peripheral status (support), the knowledge and advice of the ESL teachers may well be ignored. Yet the children of the international community live in a sociological bubble, an international space in which their individual personalities are shaped by linguistic factors (Carder, 2013a). They have no national identity to which they have to assimilate; they would benefit from a structured second language programme with a mother-tongue programme to back it up, so that their social, cognitive and intellectual potential can be fully developed. Only when there is equity of programme provision for ESL students will they receive the education they deserve.

Some international schools worked hard in the 1990s and 2000s to promote appropriate, meaningful in-service training for content teachers by adopting the 'ESL in the Mainstream' course and its successor 'TESMC – Teaching ESL students in mainstream classrooms'. However, even this modest step forward is being undermined by ESL teachers themselves. At a conference in January 2016 of the Association of German International Schools (AGIS), a new group, the English as an Additional Language Working Group, was formed. It decided that 'English in the Mainstream' (meaning in fact 'ESL in the Mainstream') was a comprehensive programme but could be costly to implement in terms of time, resources and money. So they designed, instead, a 5-hour professional development course to enable EAL teachers to take the training back to their schools and present it to teachers. We know from the experience of one of the authors of this book that this represented a huge step backwards, since he devoted much time in the 1980s and early 1990s to developing just such a course and producing a handbook on it for teachers and school leaders. When he was shown 'English in the Mainstream' he could see the massive difference in the quality and quantity of the material. His 'ESL in the Mainstream' was run at the school several times. It did take up time and cost money, of course, but such was its impact that it proved its worth. What the EAL teachers of the AGIS had done was to step back 25 years and confirm that they had the same low status as the ESL teachers of the 1980s: they were no more than supporting, peripheral staff in whom it was not worth investing time, resources and money.

The consequences of importing national models

Teaching staff and management cannot but bring from their own countries' systems the prejudices and lack of knowledge about the best way to nurture the potential of SL learners – emerging bilinguals. Most of the teachers have had no specific training, so they see ESL students as they did in their national systems, as peripheral, potential SEN students who have to be supported.

Pearce (2013: 61–2) sums up the pernicious consequences of such performance on the teaching of ESL in international schools thus: 'in general teachers have performed international education according to the national models in which they have been trained'. It may be possible to find teachers for international schools who have the appropriate knowledge in specialist areas such as maths and science – although these subject areas also have their own distinct languages – but different approaches are needed for teaching the social sciences, especially history. Foreign languages, surprisingly, do not need so much adaptation, except that foreign-language teachers coming from the Anglosphere may be surprised at the abilities of the students. But it is above all the approach, methodology, theory and practice of addressing the needs and seeing the potential of second language students that Anglosphere teachers and school leaders so urgently need to learn.

The culture of the student and the school

The wide range of students in any international school means a concomitant variety of cultural values, and this can affect a student's learning if there is a cultural clash between their behaviour and expectations and the teacher's. We seldom realize how our culture affects our ways of behaving, and it is this lack of awareness that causes us surprise when we encounter behaviour that differs from our own or from what we expect of students. Administrators, teachers, parents and students in the international community must take account of the variations in the students' cultures and the part they play in education. Culture must not be seen as just the 3 Fs – flags, festivals and food.

If we think of cultural differences as an iceberg, the part we see corresponds to the visual, easily recognizable aspects of culture – dress, language, traditions and so on. The larger part of the iceberg, which lies, invisible, underwater, corresponds to the significant, but often covert, aspects of culture – expectations, values, perceptions, norms, time orientation, learning styles, space and so on. The situation of students facing in school a culture very different from that of their home and their previous school is well researched, but it is seldom considered in international schools.

Hofstede (1980) identified four areas of deeper culture which can be compared across cultural groups: power distance, individualism versus collectivism, masculinity versus femininity, and uncertainty avoidance. He later added a fifth: long-term orientation. Three of these areas are relevant to international education, which sees in the classroom the meeting of minds from many diverse cultures.

It is helpful to our argument to consider *power distance*: the unequal distribution of power in society. In a high-power-distance culture the members are respectful of people in authority or who have seniority. Students from such cultures treat the teachers with great respect. They expect the teacher to know the correct answers, and would not argue or express contrary opinions as this would show a lack of respect. In low-power-distance cultures, the relationship between teachers and students can be much more informal, and in some ways equal. Alternative views are freely expressed and discussed. Students from a high-power-distance culture can find this atmosphere, the tone of discussions and the general air of equality confusing. Their families are probably accepting of authority too, are respectful of teachers and expect unquestioning respect from their children. The student who moves between differing cultures at home and school has to deal with two quite different ways of behaving and communicating.

ESL students generally learn after a while to copy the behaviour of their peers and this can cause difficulties if an ESL student hasn't learned the invisible boundaries of acceptable behaviour in the dominant culture. They see the other, predominantly Western, students discussing with and challenging their teachers in a way which would be found unacceptable in the ESL student in their home country. But when they try to behave in the same way, they don't know the accepted norms and limits the other students unconsciously follow and may appear to behave inappropriately. It is worth noting that many of the students in international schools have come from schools where they were accustomed to being academically successful; this too makes their situation as second language students more difficult. The previously successful student can find that their lack of proficiency in the language of instruction puts them in an almost unbearable situation.

After a strenuous school day speaking in a second language, learning in it, and always having to overcome challenges but never being the acknowledged expert, students can feel very frustrated. At home, they must revert to the accepted ways of behaving, however restrictive this now feels. Such constant readjustment imbues the ESL student's life with stress and tension, whereas the native speaker of English transfers from home to school with little need of linguistic or cultural adjustment.

This conflict of cultural beliefs, related to so many aspects of education, can also undermine the student's academic success. The ESL student from a high-power-distance culture expects their learning to be driven and controlled by their teachers; self-directed, independent learning is a new and alarming concept. The student assumes that the teacher will talk and the student will listen, but the teacher from a low-power-distance culture expects the students to express their views. The student from a high-power-distance culture expects their teachers to provide all the information they need to be successful and will be confused when other students ask questions or challenge their teachers. These differences in expectations need to be carefully explained to new students and, especially, to new teachers.

And this applies to other areas of cultural differences that may impact on the learning of students from other cultures, such as *individualism versus collectivism*. The Western, individualistic society encourages individuality, independence, self-fulfilment and standing out, whereas the collectivistic culture emphasizes group membership, interdependence, social responsibility and fitting in. A student from a mainly collectivistic culture may find it difficult to cope with being in a classroom in which their peers are from an individualistic culture. The Japanese have an expression, 'The nail which stands out will be hammered down'; this explains why many students from collectivist societies are unwilling to express personal opinions or speak in front of the whole class, or do anything which might disrupt harmony within the group.

In the common classroom situation in which students volunteer answers to the teacher's questions to the whole class, students from an individualistic culture will want to contribute and stand out, whereas students from a collectivistic culture will remain silent to avoid standing out at all costs. Teachers need to have a basic knowledge of such cultural differences.

Teachers also need to understand *uncertainty avoidance*, another of Hofstede's areas of cultural difference, which presents huge challenges for students from non-Western cultures. These students want clear guidelines and to have matters explained thoroughly. Moreover, they expect the teachers to have all the answers.

The philosophy of education in most international schools emphasizes cultural norms that are in radical contrast to some of the students' cultural values. This puts them in difficult situations when they can't recognize where the limits are in the new culture. At the same time, they must be able to adjust their behaviour in situations out of school in which their natural culture rules.

Several of the provisions in the IB Learner Profile (International Baccalaureate Organization, 2005–18) contrast greatly with important, desirable aspects of collectivist cultures. Clearly, it is not only the students, but also their parents, who need to be prepared for the culture and practices of any international school when it presents a direct contrast to the family's own opinions, behaviours and beliefs. And their teachers need to be sensitive to the students' conflicting views and values.

Ezra lists 16 recommendations to facilitate new students' entry to an international school, most of which concern culture shock as it affects both native English speakers and speakers of other languages. She sums up as follows:

> Since culture, language and personality are inextricably bound, teachers must develop awareness that the speed and ease with which children are successfully acculturated into a new English-medium environment are dependent on cultural values and traditions, the rate of English-language acquisition and differences of personality.
>
> (Ezra, 2003: 144)

Consequently, international schools need to provide teachers and administrators with CPD related to cultural differences, so that they can enable students to succeed academically and socially.

The benefits SLLs bring to international schools

In international school classrooms across the world, students from a wide variety of nations sit next to each other, work together, discuss and debate and, at the same time, learn from each other. Through this fruitful collaboration, the students learn to accept world views and opinions other than their own, and to develop new ways of looking at their own ideas. They are learning to be world citizens through the experiences gained by working closely with and learning from students from other nations and cultures. These interactions play a key role in the creation of truly international communities, but for a community to be truly international every member must be able to contribute equally, and every member must be heard.

When ESL students are not actively encouraged and empowered by the teachers and administration in international schools, the result, in Cummins's view, is a 'disabling' of the students. Cummins lists four organizational aspects of schooling that are affected by the administrator's or teacher's own attitudes to the education of multilingual, multicultural students. The first two of these are particularly relevant to this discussion:

- The extent to which students' language and cultural background are affirmed and promoted within the school; this includes the extent to which literacy instruction in school affirms, builds on, and extends the vernacular literacy practices that many culturally diverse students engage in outside the context of school.
- The extent to which culturally diverse communities are encouraged to participate as partners in their children's education and to contribute the 'funds of knowledge' that exist in their communities to this educational partnership.

(Cummins, 2000: 47)

The most important area of an international school for second language learners is the ESL department, which often provides a safe haven for those who find the culture of the school and the language used unfamiliar, strange or even frightening.

The benefits ESL parents can bring to international schools

The parents of English language learners in international schools share, of course, their children's mother tongues and cultural orientations. The parents themselves may come from different cultures and each have their own mother tongue, so the students may already be bilingual within their own family. Parents are an immense asset to any school, not only through sharing food, dress and other outward signs of culture, but also because they represent the international in the title 'international school'. So it is vital that their voices are heard, but this is not always the case in the school community. This may be partly because of linguistic challenges but can also be because they receive little encouragement or recognition from the administrators, who are often monolingual. And such are the cultural differences between these parents and those who are self-confident and assertive, and speak on equal terms to teachers and other parents, that their voices are unlikely to be heard. It is the responsibility of the administration and the teachers, and also the other parents, to be sensitive to cultural differences and to give equal recognition and equal attention to all the families within the school community.

Linguistic challenges

In any international school, parents who have the same mother tongue will naturally gather together. All parents need information about the school, not only the confident English speakers. The language challenges non-native speakers of English encounter often start during the admissions process, unless the school has culturally and linguistically aware admissions staff who have been trained to communicate effectively with people from different cultures and language backgrounds.

The admissions forms, school flyers, handbooks and other documents given to parents should be translated into all the languages of the school community. If the information is important enough to be handed out, it must be equally important to ensure that every parent can easily understand it. Translation can, for example, be made part of a community service project for senior school students.

Parents within school communities who share a mother tongue find each other quite quickly and are very helpful in welcoming new parents to their group, keeping them informed and encouraging the use of their mother tongue by both parents and children. Such social groups can be a lifeline for new parents who find themselves in a country where they cannot speak the language, dealing with a school in which a further language is used, and who may feel isolated when their partner works long hours or is frequently away, and the children are at school all day. The parent groups also play a key role in school-wide events such as international days at which attention is paid to their talents, languages and cultures.

The concept and practice of sharing and valuing other languages and cultures should, however, also be upheld when parent representatives are elected to school governing boards, on which the parents who don't speak the dominant language tend to be underrepresented. In a truly international school, all language groups should be represented so that the parents from various linguistic and cultural backgrounds can play an active role in the school, bringing their knowledge and experience to the table.

During the school year, parents receive information in the form of weekly bulletins, emails, notes home, invitations to parent conferences and of course report cards. These should be offered to the parents in their mother tongue whenever possible, to show them that their contributions are valued and their languages respected.

Some school administrators hold parent coffee meetings during the school year at which parents can ask questions and raise their concerns. Parents of second language learners may have many questions but not know how – or whom – to ask, and will be understandably hesitant, whereas a native speaker of English will often just find their way to the person who can help, or fire off an email whenever they wish.

As well as linguistic impediments, parents may have cultural issues which make communication with teachers or administrators difficult. A British or American parent can easily talk to a teacher on an equal basis. Teacher and parent have a common language in which to talk about education. Their previous experiences of education and school culture are generally similar, so any misunderstandings can be easily cleared up. However, a parent who has had quite different educational experiences and expectations won't easily find common ground in discussions with teachers. In addition, parents whose cultures are hugely respectful of teachers will be reluctant to question the way things are done in the school. The teachers and administrators must ensure that the educational philosophy of the school is clearly understood by the whole school community, so that no serious misunderstandings arise. If questions are left unasked, and so unanswered, and issues simmer unresolved, misunderstandings and further difficulties can quickly develop. So it is particularly important that the parents who don't speak the dominant language of the school have a forum for discussion in which a knowledgeable translator can assist the process of communication and effect clarity for all concerned.

To summarize, the students who don't speak the dominant language, and their parents, are what make the school international. They should be valued as a major resource, and provisions and practices should be in place to ensure that they receive all the advantages that the school affords the students and families of the dominant language group.

Chapter 2

Characterization of the international school clientele in language matters

Education must transform itself into sociology, that is, it must teach about the societal play of forces that operates beneath the surface of political forms.

(Adorno, 2005: 203)

An international space rather than assimilation

In international schools many students' language repertoires are central to their lives in ways that differ from those in national schools: these students can benefit from an enrichment of their language repertoires.

An assimilationist pedagogical ideology towards English is not appropriate for international school students, where English as an international language is but one part of their language repertoires, their mother tongue(s) maintaining a prominent position in their identities as regards sociocultural, cognitive and academic formation. A summary of the positions of assimilation and multiculturalism is given by Baker and Prys Jones:

> At the heart of the assimilationist ideology is the belief that an effective, harmonious, society can only be achieved if minority groups are absorbed into mainstream society. Harmony and equal opportunity depend on a shared language and culture. ... A multicultural viewpoint is partly based on the idea that an individual can successfully hold two or more identities.
>
> (Baker and Prys Jones, 1998: 299)

Some families realize too late the tragedy of children losing their mother tongue. Azadi tells of her brother leaving Iran to live in the USA:

> The shock of changing cultures so drastically ... caused him terrible psychological problems later. The hardest part was that he went to live with a family where no Persian was spoken .... One morning, about six months after moving there, he woke up

to find that he could neither speak nor understand Persian any longer. To this day, when Cyrus is at a family gathering, one of us has to translate for him when the conversation turns to Persian.

(Azadi, 1987: 43–4)

International school students live in an *international space*, having arrived with or without a knowledge of English, and much of their life will be lived in an international arena: their parents probably work in an international organization in which English is likely to be the medium. Their friends will be international school students, and they may be viewed by those not in this milieu as an elite: elite children, however, require as much understanding and attention to their linguistic, emotional and related profiles as any other children. Thus the model most applicable to such students is that of pluralism and multiculturalism. In international schools an assimilationist model is not appropriate as there are no political pressures for assimilation; there is no nation state to assimilate to, nor political measures to treat immigrants circumspectly: international school students are not immigrants. A model can and should be provided that promotes enrichment in each student's mother tongue while encouraging students to gain biliteracy in English. International schools provide a unique opportunity for a truly multicultural and multilingual teaching programme.

Pennycook (2003) proposed that the term *niche* should be applied to particular groups, networks, or communities of practice. Thus there will be a *niche* for international school students as a community of practice. (Those wishing to read more widely about the assimilationist policies of England and other Anglosphere countries are referred to Mohan *et al.*, 2001; Crawford, 2000; Leung and Franson, 2001a, 2001c; Monaghan, 2010: 15–31; Carder, 2008a, 2013a, 2013b, 2017a, 2017b.)

English can be culture-free

In an English-speaking environment with English as the medium of instruction (EMI) and teaching and administrative staff largely from the English-speaking world, it is frequently the case that there is a drift towards a naive acceptance by the teaching and administrative staff of 'getting by' in English without consulting the broad range of research now available. Interestingly, MacKenzie (2003) undertook a small research project which substantiated that parents overwhelmingly wanted their children to learn English at any cost – apparently including the loss of their mother tongue. This reflects the observation by Edwards in the context of South Africa, though applicable to our case:

> [t]here is a palpable tension between the perception of parents, on the one hand, that the surest route to upward mobility is through English-medium education and the firm belief of policymakers, on the other hand, that a strong foundation in the children's mother tongue will lead to more equitable outcomes.
>
> (V. Edwards, 2009: 44)

We should add to us the proviso that in international schools it is often dedicated practitioners rather than policymakers who advocate the importance of the mother tongue.

The world of international school students today therefore requires a relevant model from the IB, the ECIS, the CIS and all other curriculum providers and accrediting agencies for the best possible linguistic framework as opposed to one lifted from national systems in the Anglosphere.

Minority students as a majority

Students in international schools, as noted above, are rather in a bubble of internationalism where English is the language of the school for academic and social purposes, but not of the wider environment. The language of the host country can be anything from Italian to Indonesian and may be taught in the school if it is considered 'useful' for any future purpose; thus host-country languages such as Vietnamese or Mongolian are usually not taught, French or Spanish being preferred as a foreign language suitable for study. Students return to their own countries for frequent visits, and some continue their university studies in their own country (see the ECIS Directory for a list of international schools worldwide). It is clearly in students' interests to maintain fluency and literacy in their mother tongue.

On a visit to an international school where teachers had collected vignettes of students, I found that one was of an English student who 'had been at the school for 15 years but spoke not one word of the host-country language'. Such behaviour on the part of an immigrant would be lambasted by politicians and the press in many countries, but is accepted as perfectly normal in an international school, especially when the student involved is a native speaker of English. Discussion with another invited workshop leader revealed her experience in Asia, where she felt students were often totally isolated from the local community; she commented that some students lived in a 'bubble within a bubble', their wealthy parents ensuring that they 'floated above the daily lives of ordinary people, their feet literally hardly touching the ground as they were chauffeur-driven around and pampered'.

The situation of many educators and school leaders in international schools seems to be that of those in national systems: over time students will move away from native-language cultural maintenance and absorb majority English language and culture. Many parents see knowledge of the globally dominant language, English, as a safer guarantee of a secure future for their children than their native language (the children are unlikely to have a say in whether they move to a new school abroad), and globalization and technology may have added strength to their argument. This is often the non-specialist's view, unaware of the issues of additive and subtractive bilingualism.

The existence of a mother-tongue programme may be seen as a solution, and the mother-tongue teachers are certainly among the few professionals who understand the depth of the challenges faced. But the need for a solid core of ESL professionals to act as a central pivot in the middle school is overwhelming, and in the few international schools where there is an ESL department it does not have the influence, status or power to provide the guidance for the whole school that is necessary for successful outcomes for the majority of ESL students, and is under constant threat of having its staff reduced or forced into a support role.

Linguistic intolerance – linguicism – seen as acceptable

In 2004 workers at a branch of McDonald's were asked to speak English at all times, not only when serving customers but also in the staff room. The McDonald's staff sign said: 'Attention all staff. Due to the common language within the store, all staff members must use English at all times. This is in accordance to HQ.' It added: 'Warnings can be issued to anyone who doesn't follow this notice. Thank you.' Complaints by staff were made to Qassim Afzal, a former Manchester city councillor and member of the federal executive of the Liberal Democrat Party.

McDonald's issued a statement which said:

> Within McDonald's we specifically encourage teamwork and inclusivity, and this encompasses the language spoken. We have over 70,000 UK staff who speak many languages, representing a diverse, multi-ethnic workforce.

> We recognise, however, to ensure consistency that there is a need for a common language and in the UK this is English. There are many sensible benefits to having a common language, including consistency in customer service, food quality and safety. As a result, staff are encouraged to speak English when working

and when liaising with customers. Outside of these times we, of course, respect their right to converse in whichever language they choose.'

Employment law specialists said the 'English language only' rule could be discriminatory – because only someone of English origin could fully comply.

(http://news.bbc.co.uk/2/hi/uk_news/england/manchester/4022461.
stm; accessed 17 September 2018)

This example reveals the complexities involved wherever the languages being spoken come up against an institution or workplace, and the lack of clear, or indeed any, legislation on linguicism. This state of affairs makes it all the more important to make a determined effort to demystify bilingualism and consistently research for the best models. The German Chancellor, Angela Merkel, when congratulating Trump upon his election as US president, listed the values that bind Germany and the US together, offering cooperation only on the basis of these values: 'Democracy, freedom, as well as respect for the rule of law and the dignity of each and every person, regardless of their origin, skin colour, creed, gender, sexual orientation or political views' (www.theguardian.com/commentisfree/2016/nov/12/europe-trump-america-president, accessed 13 February 2018). The attributes that should not affect respect for the dignity of every person did not include language.

The term 'linguicism' was proposed by Tove Skutnabb-Kangas in 1986, and a full account of it is given in Skutnabb-Kangas (2000), where she defined it (p. 30) as 'Ideologies, structures, and practices which are used to legitimate, effectuate, regulate, and reproduce an unequal division of power and resources (both material and immaterial) between groups which are defined on the basis of language'. She comments: 'Ignorance about language(s) is not the main reason for the killing of languages, though – power relations, including structural forces, are. Formal education is, together with mass media, a main killer of languages' (ibid.: 29). Whereas in international schools we are talking about muting rather than 'killing' languages, there is a case for positing that formal education in English, parents' overwhelming desire to have their children become fluent in English, and school directors' (most of them monolingual in English) desire to please the clientele, all go a long way towards reducing children's ability to maintain literate fluency in their mother tongue.

Mission statements will routinely contain such aims as 'We do not tolerate any form of discrimination', but the realities of adhering to such a practice are rarely thought through. Skutnabb-Kangas outlines six classes of prejudice, namely racism, ethnicism, linguicism, sexism, classism and ageism, which she defines as follows:

> Ideologies, structures and practices which are used to legitimate, effectuate, regulate, and reproduce an unequal division of power and resources (both material and immaterial) between groups which are defined on the basis of:
>
> > Race (in biologically argued **racism**);
> >
> > Ethnicity and/or culture (in culturally argued racism, **ethnicism** ... or culturism);
> >
> > Language (in linguistically argued racism, **linguicism**);
> >
> > Gender (in **sexism**);
> >
> > Class or social group (in **classism**); or
> >
> > Age (in **ageism**).
>
> (Skutnabb-Kangas, ibid.: 369)

International schools have a responsibility to follow through in ensuring that four of these practices of discrimination are 'not tolerated'. Schools have students from the global mix of races, and racism becomes a non-issue. Gender and class fall in the same category. An interesting insight in this area was apparent at a CIS symposium at which a Mexican presenter, not familiar with international schools, was talking about her experience in the USA. She had been in contact by phone with various agencies about her willingness to talk to schools about her experiences of multicultural education. She spoke of the surprise of 'white' school principals when they met her, as although on the phone she sounded like 'an American', she looked 'like a Mexican'. In an international school such observations would not enter the radar: international school students are from all over the world and teachers soon learn not to categorize them by race or colour. An American colleague sitting next to me commented that 'in the USA, though, race is the determining factor'.

Age is not an issue in a school, which by definition is limited to young people. Efforts are made to accommodate the various cultural attributes of students and their families, though here the predominantly 'Western' culture of international school staff clearly has an overwhelming effect on the general school ambience. Cultural issues are usually, though not necessarily, closely linked to those of language, and linguicism is the issue that is the most difficult for schools to get to grips with. How can we provide an equitable pedagogical programme for children coming to an international school, possibly without their consent and not knowing the school's language of instruction, English, without committing linguicism? There is only one solution, and that is to ensure that parents are fully aware of the facts pertaining to studying in a second language: that it is crucial to maintain and develop the mother tongue throughout the child's study at the school, and that it is equally crucial to provide a comprehensive second-language-learning programme, in a school where all staff are trained in and aware of all that is involved in teaching emerging bilinguals.

An extreme version of linguicism was highlighted in the press when an Australian senator told another senator to 'learn to speak Australian' in the Australian Senate – the object of the criticism had a Scottish accent. The journalist writing about the incident recounted how, when she arrived from Scotland at school in Australia,

> It was made abundantly clear to me, from the first day at school, that I was different. For every child who found me to be a curiosity they wanted to strike a friendship with, there was another child telling me angrily and hatefully to go back to my own country. Telling me they couldn't understand my accent. Telling me to 'speak Australian'.

> (Duncan, 2015)

If this can happen to a fluent native speaker (of Scottish English), imagine the potential for the bullying of L2 speakers. In fact, since she was not speaking another language, but a dialect of English, this could be termed as 'dialectism'!

The need to inform parents in depth of the linguistic issues

It is a truism to say that parents are a major factor in how their children are educated. In international education, especially at international schools where there are large numbers of parents who work for international organizations such as the United Nations, international agencies, embassies and other prestigious bodies, parents have high expectations of the educational programme. As in any group of people, there is a variety of attitudes towards education, and clearly the cultural background of each family will influence its attitudes. As Baker says, when discussing bilingualism in Wales:

> There is a significant task in persuading parents to pass on the language to their children. Such persuasion is always going to be difficult. It is not easy to reach parents, nor is it easy to influence them.
>
> (C. Baker, 2003: 101)

Fishman, too, discusses the matter of parental involvement, and recommends that

> if intergenerational mother-tongue transmission is being aimed at, there is no parsimonious substitute for focusing on the home-family-neighbourhood-community processes which bind together adults and children ... in early bonds of intergenerational and spontaneous affect, intimacy, identity, and loyalty.
>
> (Fishman, 2004: 435)

At international schools, there are various parental groups which are official bodies, for example the Parent–Teacher Association (PTA), and an annual general meeting (AGM) at which parents elect a new board of governors. The PTA focuses largely on fund-raising and organizing such events as an annual bazaar; the AGM is mostly taken up with choosing new board members and the percentage increase of the fees. It is fair to say that a primary preoccupation of many parents is cost: international schools are private schools, and any additional costs such as mother-tongue classes will impact on each family in different ways. Attempts to make mother-tongue classes more inclusive by including them in the school fees are virtually unknown. International school parents are unwilling to become activists for a cause in the way that happens in some national contexts; they are middle-class professionals and many prefer to take their cause individually to the director. Since directors do not stay long at a school, such issues evaporate. Little in the literature on international schools reports on matters of parental activism for this cause. A further factor is that the parents, who are often highly qualified professionals in their own fields, are themselves often second language learners and are linguistically unable to defend their children. They also assume that the international schools have the experience and expertise to teach their children appropriately and so relinquish the responsibility to the school.

We are dealing here with language as a concept in itself, with many different languages and their cultural manifestations, with an international community and its many different languages, cultures, prejudices and aspirations, and with a phenomenon peculiar to this situation: the community believes itself to be privileged, but vital aspects of educational provision – the second language programme and the fact of students' mother tongues – are more often than not treated in a way that reflects the treatment usually allocated to a dominated section of society, that is, immigrants. This means that parents are thrust into a role with which they may feel uncomfortable. There is a parent body, some members of which have their own agendas, which is naturally concerned with getting the best academic, emotional and cultural provision for their children, and in addition has an interest in the financial aspects. Also involved is a body of teachers of different linguistic and cultural origins, who have financial as well as pedagogical concerns. On top of this there is the school management, which has to cater for a broad range of parental concerns in an environment of a perceived elite enrolment representing international organizations, possibly linked financially to the host-country government, perhaps through a subsidy. Finally, there is a board of governors, who may be unpredictable but are potentially ruthless towards any management that does not follow its views.

The myth of the native speaker

There are many myths about the desirability of having native English speakers as teachers in international schools in order to ensure the best quality. The research is clear about such views: 'there is a monolingual bias in research and practice on language learning and teaching which have deeply negative consequences' (Ortega, 2014: 32). In addition, there is a monolingual bias in the field of second language acquisition which has become unsustainable. Researchers believe that it is a fallacy to take L1 speakers as benchmarks to evaluate the learning success of L2 learners, and damaging deficit approaches become unwittingly entrenched in many practices found in classrooms and schools. Non-native speakers (NNS) are portrayed as having an 'approximative' kind of linguistic competence and native speakers (NS) are taken as the norm, the default. 'NNS are seen as subordinate, seen as having a less natural way of doing and knowing and learning a language than monolinguals; this is harmful from an ethical standpoint as it casts a deficit light on L2 users, who are seen as less legitimate and less pure' (ibid.: 35). This state of affairs has arisen because all SLA research is carried out by monolinguals trying to add on another monolingual command of the L2. This confirms the hypothesis that 'monolingualism is taken as the norm; the reality of bilingualism is thus made invisible; and linguistic ownership by birth and monolingualism are elevated to an inalienable right and advantage' (ibid.: 36). The result of this is that 'a subtractive bilingualism approach is uncritically embraced' (ibid.).

It would be more helpful if schools recognized that 'It is widely agreed that today there are more second language (L2) speakers of English than speakers of English as a first language (L1)' (Hu and McKay, 2014: 65), and 'today many speakers do not necessarily aspire to a native-speaker target but rather want to become intelligible speakers of English' (ibid.: 66). There would then be no such demands as the one imposed recently on all applicants for teaching posts at TH School in Hanoi, founded in 2016 (www.ticrecruitment.com/th-school/, accessed 13 February 2018), which states that 'First language should be English'. This will ensure a huge loss of potentially expert teachers and will be a negative influence on the many second language students, who will not see any bilingual teachers with English as their second language as role models. I have known countless first-class professionals whose mother tongue was not English, but who were excellent teachers in their chosen subjects; this applies especially to ESL teachers. There seems to be a particular problem surrounding the issue in Asian schools, researched in depth by Krashen (2006). The school mentioned above also claims to be encouraging bilingualism. A positive move on the part of school leaders would be to stop explaining why SL speakers are not native speakers and talk about the mechanisms of becoming bilingual.

For many years those directly involved in the teaching of second language learners have advocated more awareness among those responsible for curricula and accreditation processes, as well as for programme design in schools. In many ways little has been achieved at the institutional level; there may be a reluctance to make changes that conflict with perceived views in political circles in certain English-speaking countries, and finances also play a part.

Parents' views on mother-tongue instruction

In conversations with parents at a large international school, I garnered some useful insights into the status and procedure of mother tongue lessons. The question of when to have these lessons was important to parents, and they believed it was intertwined with the status of the programme: scheduling them after school placed the classes as supplementary, second-class, not as important as other school subjects. Parents suggested alternatives, but were not able to agree. They were frustrated that there could be an official school IBDP foreign-language class with three students in it, taking place in a classroom, while a mother-tongue IBDP class of five students had to have their lesson in a corridor. The point had been raised with the school management, which responded that the mother-tongue programme was extra-curricular and outsourced. In fact, there were a number of official foreign-language (French and Spanish) IBDP classes which had fewer students than, for example, mother-tongue Spanish and Russian classes. The former were taught in classrooms; the latter might have been taught in a classroom, if one was available, but were often taught in corridors, which sends a message to students and teachers that such classes are lower in status. These matters are written about by Cummins (2000) concerning power relations as they affect second language learners. Fishman (1966, quoted in V. Edwards, 2004: 121) 'comments that the only reason for reference to heritage language teaching schools in official documents is when they have been cited for lack of bathrooms, windows or fire escapes'. As regards status, Edwards notes that in the UK 'There was, until recently, no initial teacher training in community languages, thus perpetuating the underdog status of this group of teachers and, by extension, their languages' (V. Edwards, 2004: 124).

Mother tongues unrewarded and requiring extra payment

Parents agreed that matters such as payment and timing could be taken to the management, as there may be a chance of changing them. They appeared to believe that a matter such as giving mother tongues the same status in the IBMYP as in the Diploma Programme would be 'too difficult'. Having the programme made a part of the regular curriculum is to do with perception, on the part of both the school management and parents; for the latter, there is an unwillingness to be activists for a cause. The students who want to play football after school are understandably irked when, after being in the classroom all day, they have to spend another two hours learning their mother tongue while their peers are outside on the field.

The issue of the IBMYP is important from a motivational point of view. There is no doubt that the main reason that many students take their mother tongue in the IBDP is to get certification, an IB Diploma, for which a language is required. A standard issuing of similar certification in the MYP would be a major benefit and would surely increase the numbers of students taking mother-tongue classes. At present the procedures for gaining such certification are far from standard and present complex bureaucratic obstacles.

Students who did after-school activities gained points for the community service requirement of the MYP, whereas students who did mother-tongue classes after school every week, year after year, gained no points. Students gained points for such activities as sports of all kinds. Students who studied their mother tongue were giving up leisure time after school for more academic work, which was tiring, especially for younger ones; in addition, their parents were paying for these classes. They were thus disadvantaged in two respects: the programme was not part of the core programme, and neither was it acknowledged as Community Action Awareness. This was demotivating for students, and seen as unfair. The issue had been raised repeatedly with management without success.

Some parents commented that they wanted to follow a plan of action that gave results. The comments showed the frustrations of parents concerning the matters discussed in the meetings. They realized that there were many issues, but wanted to focus on something concrete. However, it became evident that the sole agenda of one parent was to bring forward his own issue of the level of the fees for mother-tongue lessons. He suggested a petition. Other parents mentioned that such matters were 'difficult', and 'not in our hands'; this suggests a blind obedience to authority and an unwillingness to take on a matter that, whatever perceived obstacles may lie ahead, is reminiscent of Bourdieu's insight in *Distinction* (1984) that those in privileged classes are unwilling to challenge the authority of the dominant power. There was a distinct possibility that if parents had made a concerted effort they could have pressed the issues successfully. In the event one determined parent followed through with a petition about fees for mother-tongue classes, which got a negative response in a public forum later. It might have been more productive to set up a committee of parents to bring the matter up with the school management. Such procedures, however, are time-consuming and demanding, and professional parents chose not to take the initiative.

Change requires pressure on power structures

Ultimately it is about one factor. As Rusbridger writes,

> Real change can only follow from citizens informing themselves and applying pressure. To quote McKibben: 'This fight, as it took me too long to figure out, was never going to be settled on the grounds of justice or reason. We won the argument, but that didn't matter: like most fights it was, and is, about power.'
>
> (Rusbridger, 2015)

Jones (2015) goes further and quotes the nineteenth-century social reformer, African-American slave turned abolitionist, Frederick Douglass:

> 'Power concedes nothing without a demand .... It never did and it never will.' In saying this, he concisely summed up an eternal

truth of social progress. Change is not won through the goodwill and generosity of those above, but through the struggle and sacrifice of those below.

(Jones, 2015: 312–13)

Any amount of research may show the best model for second language students, but the complex factors of a privileged class not wishing to go public with their concerns, various degrees of ignorance on the part of school directors and boards of governors, and the surging globalization and marketing trend of the IB, present considerable obstacles. Parents are unequipped to take up the struggle by virtue of their privileged social status, and perhaps also by lack of knowledge or sufficient mastery of English. ESL teachers are likely to be treated as lightweight, given their status in the curriculum.

SLLs and their parents locked in a culture of silence

The enforced silence of ESL students and their second-language-speaking parents makes it all too easy for them to be sidelined by educationally irresponsible decision makers. Freire believed that the Third World is not a geographical concept but essentially sociopolitical in character (Freire, 1972: 16–17). He was led by a concern for the oppressed, who belong to 'a culture of silence'. In international schools the second language learners are in a very real sense those who may be locked into a culture of silence: they are not fluent in the school's language of instruction, English. This can lead to a situation similar to that of Freire's oppressed: 'a lack of awareness, absence of self-respect – even a fear of freedom' (Crotty, 1998: 155). As Wittgenstein wrote, '*The limits of my language* mean the limits of my world' (Wittgenstein, 2007: Proposition 5.6). Many parents of these children are themselves also not fluent in English, do not have the knowledge to engage in critical vigilance of the school's programmes, and are hampered by the socially imposed unseemliness of protesting, as they are members of the international community with its respectable modus operandi.

It is the aim of this book to clarify exactly what is at stake here – the waste of the potential of large numbers of ESL students – and to appeal to the consciences of all those with the power to remedy this situation by following the recommendations given throughout.

Chapter 3

ESL students and their requirements in international schools: The encroaching politicization of ESL and MT provision

International Schools are the scouting parties of educational globalisation. At a time when population mobility and cross-cultural contact are at an all-time high in human history, International Schools are in the vanguard of exploring uncharted territory.

(Cummins, 2008: xi)

In several ways, not *asking why-questions is part of ESL tradition.*
(Skutnabb-Kangas, 2000: xxii)

Overview

The epigraphs at the head of this chapter can be construed in different ways. The Cummins quote leads the reader to believe that international schools are somehow the trailblazers of a new era, holding out the hope that there will be positive results. The second quote, from the magisterial book on linguistic human rights by Skutnabb-Kangas, is in fact part of a section critiquing the trend in ESL and EFL to focus on the business aspects of English language teaching (ELT). In the present volume, however, because in many schools ESL barely exists as a powerful – or any kind of – educational force, our aim is to refocus on ESL as a positive and necessary programme in middle schools from an educational perspective, not a business one.

International schools vary widely in their structure and size but one issue links them: the large number of students who are not fluent and literate in English, the language of instruction. Schools have responded to this issue in various ways over the years, borrowing ideas from the many national educational systems of English-speaking countries. May, for example, wrote (1994: 1), 'The gap between theory and practice in education is a worrying one', and added that 'For many teachers, education is simply a matter of survival; teaching children as best they can, and with what limited time and resources they have at their disposal' (ibid.), and 'Recent developments internationally to deskill the teaching profession have further removed theory from the realms of educational practice' (ibid., quoting Apple, 1986). V. Edwards (2009: 7) writes that 'decisions about best practice are sometimes driven more by politics than the evidence of research'. May (1994: 1) comments that there has been a tendency to simply 'insert' minorities into the dominant culture, which leaves the long-standing hierarchies intact. May also emphasizes that along with cultural pluralism there has to be structural pluralism.

In England the situation that persists into the present is one in which 'few of the English language support teachers had any specialist language training and ... such a role "would not always seem the most effective use of a trained teacher's time" ([Bourne,] 1989: 108)' (Monaghan, 2010: 18). In the UK England and Wales have a separate education system from the rest of the country. In this book, in examples that refer to the British model, teachers, or school leaders, the implication will be that they are from the English education system. This is the model that new international school directors, coming straight from the English system, are imposing willy-nilly on schools with well-established ESL programmes, adding insult to injury by making ESL teachers subservient to SEN. As Creese notes (2005: 143, quoted in Monaghan, 2010: 21) 'support modes tend to limit EAL teachers' abilities to influence school policies and practices around the needs of linguistic minority pupils'. More recently, the National Association for Language Development in the Curriculum (NALDIC, 2014, 2015) has stated that what is called English as an additional language (EAL), an inclusive term which subsumes ESL, is not a subject specialism in teacher training in England. This has the implication that no one is trained in ESL (EAL), and, furthermore, that no one needs to be trained in ESL, that is, anyone can teach it.

This is not a model that is relevant or suitable for international schools, largely private and fee-paying, where all students can be considered as being on a level socio-economic playing field, their parents mostly on professional contracts. The OECD Programme for International Student Assessment 'has shown that language and socio-economic backgrounds are the two factors that determine school achievement most of all' (Conteh and Meier, 2014: 2). Therefore, the political machinations which have gone into decades of the evolution of programmes – or the lack of them – for ESL students in national systems render them obsolete for international schools, and instead we need to look at research, and also examples of good practice, to see how productive, positive models can be instituted.

In national systems ESL students are categorized across four dimensions: proficiency in English, race and ethnicity, national heritage and culture, and socio-economic status. All four of these will affect how the students are treated in school. In international schools the principal factor is language proficiency: the other three dimensions will be naturally subsumed into the accepted mix of international school students.

Examples of the negative effects of poor policy on ESL students in international schools around the world follow. They will highlight the tensions between school leaders and staff with specialist knowledge of the needs of ESL students. Every attempt has been made to disguise the origins of these vignettes, as teachers have contributed them on condition that they remain anonymous, for fear of reprisals – a very real and justifiable fear – but the stories are so commonplace that each incident could probably be attested to by ESL teachers in many international schools. The only recourse that professional ESL teachers have in the face of institutional poor practice is their own professionalism. The parents of these students also politely trust that the school leadership will be handling the language aspects of their children's education according to the latest research. The milieu in which the parents move makes it improper to be overly vociferous in criticism of schools' programmes for ESL.

Linguistically responsive models

As long ago as 2005, it was announced that 'The majority of students in international schools are non-native speakers of English. In the annual statistical survey, 297 schools with a total enrolment of 161,863 indicated that over half the student population (56%) spoke "English as an additional language". Of these, 198 schools (67%) had 50% or more such students while only 21 schools had fewer than 10 per cent EAL speakers. In 18 schools none of the students spoke English as a first language' (*ESL Gazette*, 2005). Since that time the numbers of ESL students have risen sharply.

In many international schools there are about 25 per cent native speakers of English, 25 per cent speakers of the host-country language, and 50 per cent speakers of other languages, some students being single speakers of their language. Forward-looking international schools are beginning to recognize that if ESL students are to gain maximum benefit from the curriculum it is important to institute, as described in detail by Carder (2007a),

- an English as a second language programme (L2 literacy);

- a CPD programme of linguistic and cultural awareness strategies for all staff and management; and
- a mother-tongue programme (L1 literacy).

The first element aims to provide students not fluent in English with the skills necessary to follow the entire curriculum with increasing success. It has been shown that this process can take five to seven years in a good programme (Crawford and Krashen, 2007; Thomas and Collier, 1997). The second element can be provided in the form of a professionally designed course such as TESMC (https://lexised.com, accessed 13 February 2018), through which school staff receive regular training. The third element comes in the form of arranging for every child to receive instruction in their mother tongue: research has given a clear message that maintaining and developing fluency in the mother tongue enhances fluency in English, and that students of middle-school age new to English transfer the subject knowledge they already have from their mother tongue (August and Shanahan, 2008; Cummins, 2001c; Rolstad *et al.*, 2005; Thomas and Collier, 2002). An overview of the most appropriate programmes is given in Carder (2007a), and strategies for content teachers can be found in Mertin (2013) and T. Chadwick (2012).

Scanlan and López state that

the goal of crafting effective and inclusive service delivery for CLD [culturally and linguistically diverse] students is widely espoused yet infrequently attained. Though work always will remain to strengthen the knowledge base for reaching this goal, school leaders cannot claim that empirical research is ambiguous about the means toward this end. The way is clear: Cultivate language proficiency, provide access to high-quality teaching and learning, and promote the sociocultural integration of all students.

(Scanlan and López, 2012: 615–16)

Unfortunately, some researchers can paint a confusing picture by stating at conferences and presentations that 'there is no one-size-fits-all programme for ESL students', a scenario that can be wilfully misinterpreted and misused by school leaders. Researchers provide invaluable facts about language learning, but when presenting their hard-won data to the public often do not foresee the reality of leadership response and how it impacts on students and teachers.

The aim of relating the incidents which follow is to show how the knowledge of school leaders about the needs and potential of ELLs has not kept pace with latest research and good practice, and is too often based on norms in national systems. Since 'racism and linguistic intolerance have often been closely linked' (Wiley and Wright, 2004: 145), school leaders need to ponder deeply their provision of language programmes for ESL students: racism is strongly rebutted and seen as shameful; linguistic intolerance or lack of equality of provision – linguicism – needs to be seen in the same light. In addition, the detrimental effects of rulings that impede bilingualism and biliteracy have been comprehensively documented (Y.G. Butler *et al.*, 2000; Rolstad *et al.*, 2005). The aim is not to disparage the hard work of dedicated school heads but rather to show that they are often unaware, because of the national backgrounds they come from, of the harm that can come to ESL students from misguided practices. (Ideally, of course, models of good practice for ESL students should be instituted in national systems as well, but that mammoth issue is not the subject of the present book. In the European Union (EU), 'Only in AT and DK [Austria and Denmark] does initial teacher education systematically prepare all prospective teachers for their role in facilitating the integration of students from migrant backgrounds' (European Commission, 2017: 94). Through such a realization, and subsequent implementation of good models, the remarkable potential of ESL students can be truly developed, and schools can only benefit.

ESL staff and programme structure affected by management
School directors' ignorance of SL issues impacts negatively on meaningful second language programmes and their staffing

The following events may appear routine to seasoned international school leaders, but this only highlights the complacency and ignorance concerning pedagogical programmes for ESL students which can arise from an uninformed approach. Training and qualifications in second language issues should be seen as essential for all those involved with international education, and *continuing* professional development should be the aim: a one-off six-week course will not suffice.

What follows are examples of what, unfortunately, has become accepted practice, submitted to me by SL teachers in international schools around the world on condition of anonymity.

A book was published for international school leaders which had a section on 'the particular problems of those of your students who are being educated in a language other than their mother tongue'. The nature of this wording immediately falls into the trap of defining certain students as a problem, and subscribes to a deficit model for these students. As long as ESL students are seen as a problem and not as potential successes they will be demotivated.

In one large international school, a new director from England was greatly surprised to discover that all the members of the ESL department had MAs in applied linguistics or ESL-related fields, as he was used to a scenario where ESL teachers were mostly unqualified assistants. In the same school a retiring head of the ESL department reported that she had really enjoyed the pedagogical aspects of her job, but 'simply could not face having to educate another director about the ESL issue'. These examples show the opposed poles of those involved with and responsible for ESL students, and those who have the power to shape provision for them.

> An ESL teacher at an ECIS recruiting fair was informed by a school leader that 'a qualified ESL teacher is not very high on the lists of many directors' priorities'. Many ESL department heads face a situation where ESL is seen as a safe area for teachers who cannot cope, and also as a suitable position for the unqualified wives of directors and teachers; in one school an ESL department was made to change its name to EAL as it was considered more modern although all the ESL teachers were against it.

International school leaders may bring in consultants who recommend the abolition of ESL departments. This appears on the surface to be educationally progressive and to aim for the second language aspect of ESL students' education to be undertaken by mainstream staff, and it often brings in the buzzword 'inclusion'. However, content staff frequently do not have the training to do this; such training is not often done (Crawford and Krashen, 2007: 45), and ESL departments are essential to provide the knowledge required for teaching beginning and intermediate ESL students, and spread their expertise throughout the teaching staff and management. An experienced ESL teacher's response to these factors was:

> It seems that in international schools anyone can become a manager and then make decisions which may have wide-ranging negative effects on second language programmes and staffing, and there is no recourse.

One recourse is for teachers to become more empowered by following the precepts of Goodson and Hargreaves (1996) for building their own professionalism, laid out in detail later in this book.

The need for ESL to be recognized as a distinct discipline

An apparently recurring event is this:

> An experienced and qualified ESL teacher was placed under the school's English department. In spite of lengthy discussions of how he could develop a better programme for ELLs by heading a separate department, the head of English, who was English (British), would not allow this and the school director deferred to her. The ESL teacher persevered for a year but then left the school, finding the conditions unworkable.

This is not a unique example. English departments often presume that they have the right to take care of all things to do with English. Unaware school principals may go along with this. In fact, English department teachers are rarely, if ever, trained in linguistics, bilingualism or ELT, and ESL teachers are the experts who should be deferred to. As Harper *et al.* note:

> the expertise and roles of EAL teachers cannot be subsumed by teachers of English language arts, reading, or other subjects. Rather, EAL teachers and other content area teachers must coordinate their distinct, complementary roles to provide a coherent curriculum and comprehensible instruction.
>
> (Harper *et al.*, 2010: 91)

Becher and Trowler point out: 'It often happens that adjoining disciplinary groups lay claim to the same pieces of intellectual territory' (Becher and Trowler, 2001: 60).

This example also reveals the amount of politics that often exists in international schools, and about which new school directors, fresh from less political settings in their home countries – or at least with a different type of politics – have scant understanding. As Pedalino Porter commented (1990: 121), 'political motives play a more decisive part than considerations of good education in the language field'.

There are several issues surrounding the matter of power in schools, and who controls it. English departments often believe they have the power to control a curricular area even though none of the teachers in such departments have any training or qualifications in second language acquisition or bilingualism. ESL department members may have MAs in these areas, but even so an ESL department is often perceived in a school as having low status, certainly lower than the English department.

Lack of experience of school directors, and ambition versus ability

A further factor is the increasing lack of experience of school directors. A letter written by Carl Gavin, from Bangkok, relates:

> My wife and I left UK in 1999 to embark upon a teaching career in international schools. Over the past 16 years the average age of headteachers has fallen with every school that we move to.
>
> These days teachers tend to join the profession in order to become a head in the shortest possible time and therefore earn more, more quickly. A modern career progression would be: degree, PGCE [Postgraduate Certificate in Education], masters degree in international education (online course, done while teaching). All of the above will normally be completed within five or six years. These teachers then spend a short amount of time as teachers, carrying out a pastoral role and an academic management role, and will then apply for senior management jobs. All of a sudden most managers are seemingly about 30 years old with little hands-on experience but with a CV that states that they have 'done it all'.
>
> (Gavin, 2015)

I can back up these developments from my own experience. For example, when I was acting as vice-chair of an accreditation visit to a school in Latin America, the head and assistant head of the school, apparently seeing me as an influential person in the world of international schools, bombarded me with enquiries about the best places to go to further their careers, and how I could help. This was at the very beginning of the visit. A Spanish writer sums up such go-getting zeal:

> His life seemed destined for the bitter, grey existence of mediocrities whom God, in his infinite cruelty, has endowed with delusions of grandeur and a boundless ambition far exceeding their talents.
>
> (Ruiz Zafón, 2013: 68–9)

How national systems permeate thinking on ESL

An international school requested advice on the following points:

- The best ways to structure EAL support;
- Advice on supporting EAL students with the language of their academic subjects (rather than teaching them the content);
- How to make the most of in-class support with EAL students;
- Advice on the best resources, apps and materials to use with CLIL/ subject support;
- Supporting students who are EAL and SEN, or EAL and low-ability, or EAL and AGT.

These points all show how the school has not only taken the vocabulary of second language delivery from England – 'EAL', 'support' – but is evidently under the impression that they have the only possible model. They ask for the best ways to structure support, not the best ways to provide successful and meaningful ESL instruction; they want to know 'how to make the most of in-class support with EAL students', with no suggestion that such a model may not be the most appropriate in an international school; and they ask how to 'support students who are both EAL and SEN/EAL'. On the website of the school in question the secondary school departments are listed, but the EAL teachers are listed under EAL support. Parents also have to pay extra for EAL classes; the potential consequences of such practice are pointed out below.

Fees at these schools are high, and there are usually large numbers of SL students. Parents are often ignorant of the many issues surrounding education for children who do not speak the language of instruction of the school, and will probably be confident that a British international school will have professional second language programmes in place. The request for advice from the above school and the wholesale importation of the British EAL model suggest that this may not be the case.

To counter the national support model that incoming school leaders may bring from England, below is a summary of Leung's comprehensive analysis and searching questions in order to show that it is unlikely that the questions he poses will, or perhaps even can, be answered in a satisfactory manner. The questions are addressed to the practices of schools and content teachers (named as mainstream teachers) in their treatment of SL students.

1. What is the variety of backgrounds of pupils in the school, and are teaching approaches, teacher expectation and task organization responsive to this variety?

2. Is the distinction between language development and cognitive/academic ability clearly understood at school policy level and translated into practice accordingly?
3. Does a school acknowledge and publicly display second language pupils' achievement in culturally and linguistically sensitive ways?
4. Do teachers in the mainstream (i.e. content) classroom provide
    a. content-based comprehensible input?
    b. opportunity to use language appropriately for the full range of naturally occurring purposes, such as recounting an experience, justifying a decision, describing a process and giving instructions?
    c. opportunities for the pupils to receive feedback on appropriate language use and to act on such feedback?
5. What proportion of class time is devoted to group work? Is group work organized with explicit reference to participant role, responsibility and task outcome in a way that is sensitive to pupil needs?
6. Is the language requirement of the mainstream (i.e. content) task clearly understood by the content teachers?
7. Does the content teacher consider ways of organizing tasks for both language and content goals, according to some common agenda?
8. Is there any evidence of a common (language-content) agenda in teachers' experiences of teacher training and professional development?
9. Is there any evidence of systematic task-based assessment being conducted in the mainstream context?
10. Is there a conscious recognition of what tasks are being used?
11. When the suitability of a task is being established,
    a. do the pupils have the necessary background content and language knowledge and skills to understand and engage with the task?
    b. are the learning activities involved familiar to the pupils? (Do they know what to do?)
    c. are the learning activities appropriately presented and organized to promote the desired understanding and sharing of thinking (in the case of a collaborative task)?
    d. does the language use required to perform the task contribute to the pupils' language development?

(adapted from Leung, 2001: 177–98)

This summary does not do justice to the seven pages of carefully argued educational practice that these eleven points are abstracted from, but it is hoped that it will serve to illustrate how much is expected of schools and content teachers when they cater for ESL students' needs. Clearly the answer to many, if not most, of the questions posed will be negative. These questions need to be asked in every international school, of every content teacher. Recruitment policies need to ensure that only suitably qualified and trained teachers are employed, who can honestly report that they follow the guidelines implied by Leung's evaluative questions. This of course implies that those recruiting new staff also understand the importance of such good practice for the educational success of ESL students.

More examples from international schools, showing the low status of ESL teachers
Both at recruitment level and within schools, ESL teachers are regularly downgraded

In one international school, an ESL teacher was told by the principal of a large international school that 'the last thing directors are looking for at recruitment fairs is qualified ESL teachers'. At a recent conference for international school teachers there was a steady stream of ESL teachers asking for advice, as their directors were reducing their status, relegating them to smaller rooms and even physically pushing them into mainstream classrooms, saying 'this is where you should be'. The ignorance surrounding the true needs of ESL students seems to be reaching new depths.

Another example: in a well-established international school the entire ESL department of ten teachers were told by their new director, a monolingual-English North American, that in future they would be seen as language support, and not as an academic department. They were relegated to a lower status, with a coordinator instead of a head of department, and correspondingly lower pay. Their teaching rooms were also downgraded. When they attempted to have a discussion with the director he told them, 'My decision is made, there will be no discussion'. This sort of behaviour will have unpredictable, lasting effects on SLLs as the position and status of the ESL teachers will reflect on the status of the students, allowing a perception throughout the school that ESL students are not important, which in turn will affect their learning potential (see Carder, 2014a, for more examples of such practice).

A group of teachers reported:

In a large international school with a well-established ESL programme the new, British director downgraded the status of the department to that of language support, thus undoing years of consistent effort to create a model which would demonstrate to ESL students that their teachers were responsible for a professional programme of instruction which would also provide a sense of equity for the students themselves, thereby empowering them. Previously with the status of a full secondary department they are now in a support programme, as if ESL students' needs are not academic but only emotional.

This follows the model in England, where ESL students and teachers have low status and academic standing. The influence from the English system is clear, as the word 'additional' has been added: the term EAL was first proposed in England by Rampton (1997), as various government edicts, produced as a result of fears of allegations of racism over separate ESL classes, had tainted the use of the term ESL. The school website now reads 'the programmes for students who have English as a second or additional language', a tautology, of course, as 'second' and 'additional' describe the same learning process: that required to learn a language for the entire curriculum. It is possible that the new status has been given in order to fit in with the IB's use of 'language support' on its website. The director of the school involved commented that the IB was 'moving forward' in its treatment of SL issues, showing his ignorance of the matters at stake and also the almost obsessive need of some school principals to be positive and uncritical about any initiative undertaken by a higher body. This is in spite of the IB's stated aim of encouraging students to develop critical thinking in all the subjects they study, while denying that power to staff.

The extent to which school leaders are ignorant of the circumstances relating to the status of ESL in their own countries can be seen from the following situation, from a well-established, prestigious international school in Europe, with a British leadership team. A parent wished to work as a substitute teacher in the ESL department: she had a master's in TESOL. The school insisted that she have a teaching qualification, which she did not possess. She was referred to the online facility for doing such a course in England. However, in England there is no requirement for ESL/EAL teachers to be qualified as teachers, and thus no component in the PGCE course that she could follow, the nearest equivalent being 'foreign languages'. Thus a British-run school was demanding a qualification from a well-qualified ESL professional that was not only not required in England, but was not available.

Negative impact of this downgrading on SL students' access to professional programmes

In one school a well-established ESL department was attempting to develop more content-focused classes in humanities subjects. This initiative was strongly supported by the humanities department, and is strongly supported by research on good practice (T. Chadwick, 2012; Schecter and Cummins, 2003; Wolff, 2003). However, it was rejected by the school management, who decided that the Humanities teachers were just trying to have smaller classes, off-loading students to the ESL department.

This reveals both the cynicism of management and their lack of knowledge of *sheltered instruction* (see Echevarría and Graves, 2014).

Many school leaders reject the model of ESL students in the middle school having separate classes, as this offends their basic educational principle of not allowing 'tracking' or 'streaming', that is to say providing separate classes for students of different ability. However, students with no knowledge of English learn very little in a class taught entirely in English to native speakers, especially when the teacher has little or no understanding of second language pedagogy. Models of good instruction for middle-school ESL students have been published by experts in the field (for example, Crawford and Krashen, 2007; Schecter and Cummins, 2003). In maths classes, grouping for different abilities is routine.

An ESL professional on the failure of valid recruitment policy

Here a dedicated ESL teacher, with a well-developed and conceptualized middle-school ESL programme, expresses his frustration, after many years of trying:

> The only thing missing [in the excellent ESL programme] is for the admin to have the gumption to tell new recruits that they must attend mandatory sessions in ESL pedagogy. I gave up that fight as hopeless a while ago – but it still distresses me how some teachers can be unsympathetic to or unknowledgeable about the needs of ESL students.

Incoming school director reduces ESL staffing because groups are smaller

This event shows a lack of awareness of the needs of students who are developing their language-learning skills:

> A new director (British) reduced the number of staff for ESL without any consultation with the head of the ESL department. His decision was entirely arbitrary, based on a cursory look at group sizes. ESL classes are necessarily smaller than content classes as individual students benefit from more individual focus. The director saw ESL as coming under the heading of 'support

services', the CIS and British term, and it was therefore an easy area to cut in order to balance the budget. No other subjects received any cuts. As a result of his decision, middle-school ESL beginners were sent to mainstream content classes where they understood next to nothing, and were frequently in tears.

Research evidence that smaller class sizes benefit SLLs comes from Özerk:

by creating rich possibilities for teacher–student verbal interaction and curriculum-oriented academic questioning, small classes can provide conditions for better academic performance in content area subjects ... for bilingual students in general and bilingual girls in particular than do large classes.

(Özerk, 2001: 353)

A similar example is this, from the head of an ESL department in an international school:

I hope your book [Carder, 2007a] might give us some ammunition to set up a proper ESL department again next year, with its own base and specialist ESL teachers. We have had this in the past, but each director has his own priorities and our present incumbent sees ESL as something which gets cut when you are short of teaching units.

SLLs affected by uninformed policies concerning pedagogical programmes for SL students
Linguicism in action

Two ESL teachers in an international school in the EU (European Union) reported that there was a large sign at the school entrance that stated, 'You are now entering an English-only zone'. Speaking any other language was discouraged, which discriminated against all speakers of other languages, gave students a sense of shame about their own language, and detracted from any efforts made by ESL staff to encourage development in students' mother tongues.

Cummins wrote (2000: 13), 'In the vacuum created by the absence of any proactive validation of their linguistic talents and accomplishments, bilingual students' identities become infested with shame'. If there was a sign saying 'Only white children may proceed beyond this point' there would be outrage, as racism is rightly condemned; 'linguicism', however, is allowed, as can be seen in this example:

In an international school a teacher gave two students detention for speaking in their mother tongue, the national language of the country, as it was against school policy.

NNESTs

Here is an example of teachers 'mobbing' colleagues:

In one international school, ESL teachers who themselves were speakers of English as a second language were intimidated by other staff, suggestions being made that they could not perform their job properly.

In fact, ESL teachers who have learned English as a second language often have greater insights and empathy in teaching SLLs than mother-tongue English teachers. They have been through the same process themselves, and now belong to the majority of speakers of English worldwide, those who speak it as a second language. They are also reported as speaking more clearly. As Shin surmises,

Despite a great deal of training, non-native speaker teachers may be viewed as inadequate language teachers because they often lack native speaker competence in the target language and culture. However, non-native speaker teachers possess distinct advantages over native speakers including a deeper understanding of learners' first languages and an ability to explain second language features in ways that students can understand.

(Shin, 2008: 57)

Cherng and Halpin carried out research on students' perceptions of minority versus white teachers in the USA. They found that students perceived minority teachers more favourably than white teachers, and concluded that their findings underscored the importance of minority teacher recruitment and retention. They point out that '[a]n overwhelmingly White teaching force is working with a majority non-White student population' (Cherng and Halpin, 2016: 407), that minority teachers 'are more multiculturally aware than their White peers and that higher levels of multicultural awareness are linked to better classroom environments' (ibid.: 416). They add:

It also may be the case that minority teachers are particularly well perceived by minority students because minority teachers may have personal experience navigating racial stereotypes about academic achievement and can equip students to combat these stereotypes. And this rapport, built on positive student perceptions of teachers, might contribute to academic success for students.

(ibid.)

They conclude that their findings attest to the importance of having a diverse teaching staff: research has shown that students' perceptions of teachers are associated with motivation and achievement. Ultimately, they suggest, minority teachers are often able to form strong ties with students, and can thus help to empower youth of all backgrounds. Though they do not specifically focus on language, the overall message is clear.

At the annual international IATEFL conference in Birmingham in April 2016, Silvana Richardson, the head of teacher development at the Bell Foundation, gave a plenary devoted entirely to the issue of NNESTs. As she mentions in her presentation:

> What quality am I emphasizing by saying that I am a NON-Native English Speaking Teacher?
>
> How is asserting what we are by negating what we are not a meaningful and constructive way of referring to ourselves?
>
> Why do we still refer to an aspect of the professional identity of over 80% of the teachers of English in the world as a 'NON'?
>
> How is it possible that it is still a legitimate term in our professional discourse in 2016?

(S.Richardson, 2016)

In the following slides and in her talk she goes into depth to respond to these questions, with the clear message that

> As a profession, we need to move beyond the unhelpful and pernicious dichotomy, and conceptually stop separating professionals into different camps. In many cases, this absolute division is artificial, given the global mobility of many ELT professionals, and how some of us live in other countries for long periods of time.

(ibid.)

International schools are ideally placed to recruit local *professional* ESL teachers, who are well qualified for the job.

The downside of charging extra for ESL

In one international school the management wanted to charge families for ESL 'support', thereby stigmatizing them.

Nineteen reasons why such a policy is counterproductive are listed in Carder (2007a):

- The term 'international' attached to a school may imply that a distinct proportion of the student population will be ESL speakers; it is thus possible to assume that a programme for their language development in English should be included in the school fees.
- The majority of students in International Schools are now L2 speakers of English (ESL Gazette, August 2004). Rather than charging extra for ESL classes, it is more important to have a Language Policy to ensure that all students are challenged appropriately in their various languages.
- Invariably Mother Tongue classes are paid for in addition to school fees. However, those in ESL classes are by definition those who have a Mother Tongue other than English. They would therefore be paying twice if ESL classes cost extra. This might lead to financial difficulties, a reluctance to take Mother Tongue classes, pressure to leave ESL, and a downward spiral to subtractive bilingualism.
- An extra charge may take advantage of a group already at a disadvantage, i.e. ESL parents who are often less vocal in arguing for a cause.
- ESL students do not have an educational problem; they are engaged in acquiring academic proficiency in another language, which generally takes many years to achieve.
- An extra charge would ignore the essentially long-term nature of second language acquisition, where academic proficiency is the goal and invariably takes a long time.
- The low self-esteem which some ESL learners are naturally subject to may be reinforced by an extra charge for ESL lessons.
- It can be argued that ESL students actually receive less instruction overall, as they 'miss time' in mainstream subjects while they attend ESL classes.
- Pressure on ESL students will increase. Parents are likely to be unhappy about the cost of instruction and pressure their children for unrealistic academic and linguistic progress.
- This in turn may lead to more English being spoken at home by parents who are not proficient in English at an academic level. This

may contribute to the detriment of students' progress in English and also to their cognitive development in general.

- Such pressure would also reduce the effectiveness of ESL instruction as students under strain generally learn less effectively, and they will leave the ESL programme more quickly than advisable due to parental pressure. Both these factors may well have a negative impact on long-term academic achievement, and hence the school's academic reputation.

- Where ESL fees are charged, ESL teachers are put in the difficult position in parent–teacher conferences of having to focus on what a student cannot do in order to provide a rationale for their remaining in ESL, rather than giving a positive slant on their progress.

- In international education, fees are relatively high compared with alternatives – state schools, etc. Adding to these costs is likely to reduce the client base of an International School, not increase it.

- Extra charges may be seen as a form of discrimination against speakers of other languages and reflect non-inclusivity or even language prejudice. The diversity of a school population which is multilingual, and thus consists predominantly of second language learners, brings linguistic and cultural richness.

- A negative image of ESL would be presented; ESL students would be seen as a group placing a burden on the school, which in return would put more pressure on those students and their parents.

- A school mission statement may say that it treats each learner as an individual and caters to each individual's needs. It would be seen as contradictory if ESL learners' needs require extra payment; they are needs which must be met before these students can have full access to the curriculum and are therefore routine in an International School.

(Carder, 2007a: 182–4)

An example of a school showing ignorance of good educational practice for developing bilinguals is as follows. In an international school new parents of young children had to sign a form stating that they would speak English at home (where the family previously all spoke Spanish, their mother tongue) and agreeing that if their children had not made sufficient progress in English within a year they would have to take their children out of the school.

Such policies show a distressing lack of understanding of SLA, and bring to mind right-wing demands in certain countries in Europe that immigrants should only speak the host-country language at home. It is perhaps an example of how members of the international community, largely well-off and educated, are subject to polices originating from a conservative milieu that they may well have been sympathetic to in their own countries, but which are now backfiring on them. This highlights a particularly bizarre paradox of international schools: all the parents are from a high socio-economic bracket, but the ones who do not have good English, or whose children do not, are subjected to the humiliation of being treated to policies devised over decades for immigrants.

Lack of effective scrutiny of language ability and its effects

In one international school an ESL teacher was doing reading records to pre-assess a group of grade-6 ESL students. A Korean boy was reading one of the *Lord of the Rings* books. He read fluently and with full comprehension and no Korean accent, so he was asked how he could read so well in English. He said Korean wasn't his first language and that neither he nor his parents spoke Korean. He had been put in ESL simply because of his nationality.

This may be seen as a simple mistake, but reveals that comprehensive language and literacy screening for all new students, essential in an international school, was not being carried out.

An Israeli girl with only conversational English was given a 35-page humanities hand-out to read and then answer questions on. When the ESL teacher found out about it the girl had already begun to try to read three pages on her own. Over the top of every other word was a translation written by her in Hebrew. When asked how long it had taken her to get that far she replied, 'About six hours'. The teacher went to the humanities head and pointed out what the student was having to cope with. However, that person ignored the issue.

This girl, a top student in Israel, was trying out the very good learning strategies that she had honed in an Israeli school, but she was failing and was completely confused as to why. This scenario encapsulates the handing out of 'one-size-fits-all' documents, which should no longer be acceptable but still takes place in many accredited international schools. It is similar to an incident in which a grade-6 teacher gave an ESL student a document about God being 'incorporeal'. When another teacher was shown the hand-out he said, 'Even I can't understand it'.

An extreme example of leadership ignorance

In an international school an ESL teacher, along with her entire class of ESL students, was physically pushed by the director into the mainstream classroom, and told 'this is what you will do:

you will not teach separately; you will support the mainstream teacher'.

This is an example of the type of activity that has led to many teachers in international schools leaving ESL and moving to other disciplines, as they feel unvalued in ESL.

The position and status of the ESL teachers will reflect on the status of the students, allowing a perception throughout the school that ESL students are not so important, this in turn affecting their self-esteem and their learning potential.

The education system's wariness of segregation along racial and language lines, crucial for the future development of second language provision, is apparent from this extract from the UK Ministry of Education:

> As far as the school is concerned, whenever it is desired to treat immigrant children in a rather different way from our own children, for example by putting them in a special class for intensive English teaching, the parents should be briefed as fully as possible about the school's purposes; otherwise it may be cited as an example of *racial* discrimination.
>
> (Ministry of Education, 1963: 9, quoted in Leung and Franson, 2001a: 158; emphasis added)

Support is the currently preferred model in England, and has evolved over many decades of *political* interference over fears of accusations of racism, by separating students. Issues concerned with ESL teaching had become political and ideological, focusing on race, not language-learning needs.

In schools in England language support teachers come under the umbrella of special educational needs departments. The negative effects of treating ESL students as SEN students have been documented throughout the literature (e.g. Cummins, 1984). Leung and Franson comment:

> As a curriculum area ESL has not been allowed a distinct discipline status; there are no ESL curriculum specifications and no national ESL scale for assessment. In the past few years the funding for ESL has been reduced repeatedly and the cuts have always been justified on financial grounds. These can be seen as indicators which point to ESL's loss of academic status and curriculum value in the official view, and with it the privilege to argue for its protection and development.
>
> (Leung and Franson, 2001a: 163–4)

This mirrors the view of Lo Bianco, who argued:

> ESL learning cannot be left entirely to incidental, indirect, inductive or implicit acquisitional processes. ... Whatever practices are favoured in any case they all derive from the trained expertise of the ESL specialist.
>
> (Lo Bianco, 1998: 1, quoted in Davison, 2001a: 28)

ESL professionals in Australia continued to resist any tendencies to cut staffing and programmes for ESL students, and argued that ESL programming is necessarily complex. It involves interrelated decisions about curriculum focus, first language input, modes of delivery, learner groupings, and teacher roles. It is also assumed that ESL learners will require regular and intensive small group work with qualified and experienced ESL specialists (Davison, 2001b: 31, 34).

The British model had consequences for international schools: in 2002 the CIS reallocated ESL and put it in the same section as SEN; in 2006 the IB devised a new post of second-language-learning specialist, placing the appointee in the SEN section; she eventually gained separate status. International schools in Europe are more affected by the proximity of the British experience and many ESL teachers in international schools in Europe are British, and bring with them the British experience. The result is often a docile acceptance that ESL will not be seen as a separate discipline, and will be subsumed under the SEN umbrella.

Insights into a SL student's perceptions

This subsection relates how one student felt about her language development, and how it affected her (from Carder, 2008b):

> Maria (not her real name) begins by saying that her mother tongue is Spanish, and she came to this large, international school in Grade 11, so is in her second and final year. Before that all her schooling had been in Spanish. She announced that this was her first year of being 'bilingual', which she understood as meaning 'I can communicate, I can say what I'm feeling, I can express myself completely, I can write, I can read, and if I feel angry I can say everything I feel'. Asked why she felt angry, she replied 'I am a very explosive person and if someone did something bad to me I feel that I have to tell people how I am feeling so they change what they have made wrong.' Asked if not being fluent in English made her feel lost, she said 'Yeah, I feel lost. At the beginning when I came I was really shy because I didn't know how to talk

so I was afraid of making mistakes and people make fun of me, but now with time I got more language and I can talk and say whatever I want.'

Her mother tongue is Spanish, and interestingly she says that she is now 'bilingual' and this may imply that she considers English has reached equivalence with Spanish as a language of function, though this is questionable. Expression is obviously important for her, as is self-esteem, shown by her declaration that she doesn't like others to make fun of her mistakes.

Maria had been an excellent student at her last school, so when asked 'how does that make you feel, from being a really good student and you come to a school where you suddenly realize that the language is going to be the barrier?', she answered 'That was terrible for me. I cried many days because of that, because in my country when I was there I was the fifth student in the entire school, I got scholarships, all the teachers loved me, I had friends, I could teach everyone if they need help, now maybe I know this already but I don't know the language, so it was really hard.' Asked if she had now overcome these factors, she answered 'Yes and no. Because when I need to read something for Physics or for Design Technology there're still words that I don't use every single day so I don't get the real meaning in my mind, so I kind of know what they mean but maybe I don't use it in the proper way. I am a really really good writer in my language, I can write poetry and I can do songs and all of that, but when I try in English it's so hard.'

(Carder, 2008b: 57–60)

Here she shows more of what it is like to be a new student in a new language. From being a high flyer she has had to adapt. She has literacy in Spanish to an advanced level, and has realized that gaining CALP skills and being able to write in a specific register require more time and work. She has also had to accept that her identity will have to be re-established. She had been used to being surrounded by friends and respected as one of the best students in the school. At this school she is a student with limited English skills among a student body of high flyers in English; this has affected her deeply.

Asked if she was keeping up her Spanish, she replied:

That's a problem, because I'm talking in English the whole day most of the time, I spend most of my day reading, talking or doing things in English and if I talk at home basically I say 'Hi mum, how are you, how was your day?'; I go to my room and start to do homeworks in English, then I go on-line, talk in English, I also talk in Spanish with some friends, but then I got the word in English but I don't get really quickly the word to express that in Spanish, so my mother is like 'you have been talking Spanish for all your life, what is wrong with you?' and I'm feel so bad about it. She added 'First of all, I find it really unfair the fact that the English-speaking students and the German-speaking students have four lessons per week of literature mother tongue, and then I got to pay more [for Spanish] than the school fee that's already high and then I got two lessons per week, and I'm doing IB Spanish A1 High.

(ibid.)

Many fundamental issues of students' learning identities are revealed in this long extract. There is again a plea for more time for mother tongue lessons. It lays bare the fundamental lack of equity across language provision in the school, even for a language as widely spoken as Spanish. Students studying English or German are taught within the curriculum; those doing other languages pay full fees but receive one less language in the curriculum, and pay extra for their own language. It also reveals the impact of a lack of understanding on the mother's part of what it means to be an emerging bilingual: the mother is only concerned about the failure to find the right word in Spanish, and her 'What is wrong with you?' can hardly be seen as supportive.

Asked how she saw English as a part of herself now, she answered:

I feel it's the best thing ever happened to me because now I can go wherever I want and if I get lost I can communicate, so I can go and explain what I want. That's really important for me because here I cannot make friends outside the school because they speak German and I can go to the shopping centre here, and I can express what I want. As long as English is the world language, I can make new friends in different countries that open opportunities for me, I can go to different countries to study.

(ibid.)

Asked why she was taking the school German course she responded:

Because it's really important for me to express myself, whatever someone outside of school make something bad to me, I want to listen and know what they are saying. Most people in school speak German and so I find really annoying, that they talk in German in front of people who doesn't understand so they could make fun of you. That's another wall when you came because if they're going out, in the city as friends and they will talk in German, but you cannot go with them because you cannot speak the language, so German is also really important because I live here.

(ibid.)

Maria values German because it enables her to express herself, and to be included in a conversation rather than be the object of gossip. She also values it because she is living in a German-speaking community and wishes to participate. The German course is not obligatory in grades 11 and 12, so Maria has made a real effort to learn the language for personal reasons.

There is much to comment on here. Maria is in a school with a well-developed ESL and mother-tongue programme, but her comments give valuable insights into the effects of not speaking the languages used for schooling and social life. Scheff (1988) said that shame was *the* social emotion. By 'shame' he meant the many emotions to do with feeling which make a person feel ridiculed, an outsider, inadequate or incompetent, and vulnerable or insecure. These are all issues that affect Maria, and probably all ESL students. As Wilkinson and Pickett comment

our sensitivity to shame continues to provide the basis for conformity throughout adult life. People often find even the smallest infringement of social norms in the presence of others causes so much embarrassment that they are left wishing they could just disappear, or that the ground would swallow them up.

(Wilkinson and Pickett, 2010: 15)

These are vital issues for schools to be aware of.

Managerialism in the international school context as relevant to second language issues

Managerial professionalism has had a significant impact on the work of teachers because of such factors as restructuring, and the emphasis on economic efficiency. In a review of *Education Management in Managerialist Times* (Thrupp and Willmott, 2003), Cambridge (2006) writes about the increasing dominance of various practices relating to control 'that have "precluded debates about the purposes of education beyond preparation for the economy" (Tomlinson, 2001: 2)' (Cambridge, 2006: 369). The practices include '"a language and practice of managerialism, of accountability, inspection, testing and targets"' (ibid.). These are coupled with a focus on outputs and performance rather than inputs, and, crucially, view organizations as low-trust relationships. He concludes, 'International schools and other institutions offering education in an international context have not been insulated from such developments' (Cambridge, 2006: 372). These insights neatly tie together the impact of managerialism on education, on international schools and on valid programmes for ESL students.

In the book under review, Thrupp and Willmott (2003: 182) wrote that current 'school change is fundamentally about extending and legitimating the neo-liberal managerialization of education, and not about change (for example, curricular) that promotes real learning and engenders creativity in pupils and students'. They trace the sources of this trend to the marketizing reforms of the Thatcher and Reagan era, and see texts on education management that arose from this mindset as legitimizing the marketization of education.

Clarke (1995) defines two terms which are the basis of the new managerialism: universalism and isomorphism. The former is defined as 'all organizations being basically the same and needing to pursue efficiency, irrespective of their specific functions'; the latter is defined as 'the assumption that commercial organizations are the most naturally occurring form of coordination, compared with which public sector organisations are deviant' (quoted in Whitty *et al.*, 1998: 52). Furthermore, Rees (1995) states that managerial discourses make two claims: 'that efficient management can solve any problem; and that practices which are appropriate for the conduct of private sector enterprises can also be applied to the public sector'.

Taking this argument to what might be seen as an extreme, Pollitt (1990) describes how the values of managerialism have been promoted as being universal; therefore, management is inherently good; managers are heroes; managers should be given the autonomy to manage and others should accept their authority. Moving on from this position, Clarke and Newman (1997: 92) believe that the new discourses of managerialism 'offer new subject positions and patterns of identification – those of management as opposed to professionalism'. This suggests, alarmingly, that managers are outside and above the professional sphere.

Teachers and democratic professionalism

It seems that the managerial discourse has won out over the democratic aspirations of teachers when it comes to appropriate curriculum, assessment and instruction for second language students in international schools. The power wielded by school leaders, frequently unknowing and biased by their national education backgrounds when it comes to ensuring professional programmes for ESL students, is backed up institutionally by the curriculum bodies and accreditation agencies that set standards. Against such apparent authority, there is a limit to what teachers can do. To paraphrase Wolin, teachers of today have been subsumed by the 'managerial revolution: they have become jobholders, salaried employees', hirelings with tenure. The real problem lies in the fact that for genuine second language pedagogy it has 'become a labour of Sisyphus to emancipate itself from the limitation of teaching as a job' (R. Wolin, 1992: 2).

ESL teachers are stuck in an endless Groundhog Day of fighting for the language rights of their students, but there are fewer qualified ESL teachers, directors are not looking for such teachers in any case, and the students have been second-language-washed into an amorphous programme of language learning and support that does not meet their needs.

It is worth noting that research shows that:

> Teachers who are given more support are shielded from teaching-related stress; they experience less burnout and are more likely to remain in the teaching field. The support the teachers receive also influences their performance; those with greater support are more motivated, display superior teaching efficacy and are more willing to adopt new teaching methods. Teachers who believed they were giving feedback to [ethnic-minority students] supplied more positive feedback than teachers who believed they were giving feedback to a white student.
>
> (Harber *et al.*, 2012: 1156)

ESL teachers are generally not given support – often quite the opposite – so the effects on their performance, and by extension their students', will be disabling, not empowering.

Conclusion

Shaw, himself a school principal, writes:

> Principals are often tempted to view themselves as experts, people who have all the answers. Principals who succumb to this

temptation tend to play the role of program implementers, where curriculum lies within policy documents and can be addressed through programs that exist in texts.

(Shaw, 2003: 105)

A better solution would be 'Rather than being the program implementer, the successful principal practices pedagogical leadership by investing in the capability development of colleagues and by bringing focus and adherence to the work of the school' (ibid.: 106); 'He [sic] also emphasizes the need for turning top-down mandates into bottom-up commitment in order to benefit all students' (ibid.: 99).

The benefits of bilingualism and biliteracy – improved metalinguistic awareness, and considerable cognitive advantages – have been attested (Adesope *et al.*, 2010; Bialystok, 2010), as has the building of a 'cognitive reserve' (Craik *et al.*, 2010). It is disturbingly paradoxical that the international community which international schools serve is being harmed by educational models and personnel, unsuited to international students, that come from national systems built on political agendas and machinations. The international community is influential in the world in many ways; if it cannot succeed in arranging appropriate, equitable educational provision for its own children one might be forgiven for asking what other world-shaping issues it is failing in. Equity on the basis of gender, race and sexual preference was only achieved after massive movements by those adversely affected by prejudice. For SL learners there is no possibility of fighting for their rights as they do not have the language to articulate them; their parents are usually in the same position, unknowing and not articulate in English. The entire responsibility of establishing equal language rights therefore falls on educators: we must ensure that there are comprehensive, successful, non-peripheral ESL programmes for second language students. Not to do this would be the educational equivalent of breaking a medical doctor's Hippocratic oath.

Part Two

Bilingualism and second
language acquisition:
Developments in theory
and research

Chapter 4

How the fields of bilingualism and SLA can guide good practice for viable SL models in international schools

Relevant research and other publications

The published research and other writings on bilingualism, SLA and mothertongue programmes in international schools, is limited, perhaps because of the mobility of the students, and teachers as potential researchers, and thus the difficulties involved in carrying out long-term studies. The 1991 edition of the *World Yearbook of Education* (Jonietz and Harris) was devoted to international schools. Contributions in this volume relevant to SL were by Tosi (1991) on language in international education, and Carder (1991) on ESL programmes. Carder (1995) contributed a chapter on language issues in international schools to Skutnabb-Kangas's *Multilingualism for All*.

The International Schools Journal Compendium, *ESL: Educating non-native speakers of English in an English-medium international school* (Murphy, 2003), contains all the articles relevant to SLLs for the 22 years during which Murphy edited the journal (1981–2002). There she writes:

> Articles that have appeared regularly in the *ISJ* through the years, however, show that in many international schools whose client base includes large numbers (in many, the majority) of students whose native language is other than English, such research has been slow to gain currency, and even slower to produce genuine change. Even today, many schools organize themselves and create their curricula as if all their students shared not only the same language, but the same culture as well.
>
> (ibid.: 9)

In the same Compendium, an article by Carder (1993) discusses the importance of having a language policy in schools, and of creating 'biliterate bilinguals'. In 1994 Jonietz proposed the term 'trans-language learners' to describe how international school students gain or lose proficiency in languages as they travel around the world (Jonietz, 2003).

The other journal which focuses on issues in international education is the *Journal of Research in International Education*. Allan, writing about a research project on cultural dissonance in an international school in the Netherlands, concludes: 'Schools must adopt a culturally democratic pedagogy where different learning styles are recognized in the classroom, and a non-culture-specific curriculum is delivered in a more pluralist style which makes it accessible to all pupils' (Allan, 2002: 82). Both these insights point towards the development of appropriate teaching styles by subject teachers.

Carder's (2007a) book presents the 'three-programme model' of ESL taught through content, alongside a mother-tongue programme and CPD for staff, as the most viable way of providing an enriching linguistic framework for multilingual students. Gallagher's (2008) book devotes a chapter to 'Hidden and overt power structures in international schools' (ibid. 1–34), distinguishing between the often encountered authoritarian mode of management, and the more desirable authoritative approach, in which school leaders provide equitable models of language programmes. De Mejía (2002), in a chapter headed 'World-wide elite bilingualism', traces the history and development of international schools, noting that while many of the students are in fact bilingual, the emphasis in curricula and school language provision is monolingual, and often monocultural.

In the *International Handbook of English Language Education* edited by Cummins and Davison, Carder (2007b) contributed a chapter on the 'Organization of English teaching in international schools'. Carder (2009a) edited the special issue of NALDIC on *International Schools*. The volume on *Bilingual and Multilingual Education* edited by Abello-Contesse *et al.* has a chapter by Carder (2013a) on 'International school students: Developing their bilingual potential', and the compendium edited by Pearce, *International Education and Schools: Moving beyond the first 40 years*, has a chapter by Carder (2013b) on 'English language teaching: The change in students' language from "English only" to "linguistically diverse"' and how school leaders can meet this challenge. In two articles in the *International Schools Journal* (Carder, 2014b, 2015), Carder traced the path of ESL provision in international schools over the previous four decades.

Sears's (2015) book, *Second Language Students in English-Medium Classrooms*, gives a good overview of the issues facing mainstream teachers of ESL students. It contains useful information on how to help ESL students adjust to their new school in the first days and weeks.

Mertin's *Breaking through the Language Barrier* (2013) contains a wealth of advice and useful strategies for teachers to use in the classroom in order to facilitate SL learners' understanding of subject matter, as well as chapters on teaching specific subjects. Mertin *et al.*'s *Translanguaging in the Secondary School* (2018) discusses how SLLs can build on previous knowledge and transfer it from their mother tongues.

Tosi's PhD thesis (1987) has a section on the language needs of SLLs in the IBDP. This research led to a working group and to the creation of language A2 in the IB Diploma Programme. Tosi (1991) pointed out:

> In the IB schools as in European Schools, there are three different language learning processes at work with their multilingual population:
>
> 1. Mother tongue learning for the native as well as the non-native speakers of the school language;
> 2. Foreign language learning for the native speakers of the school language;
> 3. Second language learning for the non-native speakers of the school language.
>
> (Tosi, 1991: 94)

Tosi also noted:

> The IB emphasis is still on assimilation rather than on diversity .... [The IB] must rid itself of its Anglocentric cultural and linguistic biases if schools wish to avoid the criticism of those governments which are seriously committed to bilingualism and language equality.
>
> (ibid.: 97–8)

As we have seen, some researchers have labelled linguistic discrimination (discrimination against students by not providing programmes of instruction for them in their language) a form of racism, terming it 'linguicism' (Fishman, 2009: 426; Skutnabb-Kangas, 2000). Fishman, after reflecting on the 'joys of one's own language and ethnicity', states:

> [D]emocracy guarantees the right to retain one's ethnicity, ... to enable one's children ... to develop creatively, and to reach their

full potential without becoming ethnically inauthentic, colorless, lifeless, worse than lifeless: nothingness.

(Fishman, 2009: 441)

It is to counter such a dire fate that this book has been written.

Bilingualism: Introductory comments

In 1945 bilingualism was viewed largely negatively. Since then, its study has become an autonomous discipline, and bilingualism itself has come to be seen as an asset, though complex: the teacher requires attention to detail, and sensitivity to each child's needs and language trajectories. Knowledge of this discipline, with an awareness of latest developments, is essential for those working in international schools, especially for those working in leadership and management positions. As will be outlined below, English no longer has specific cultural bases to which students can become integrated, but has an 'international posture' (Dörnyei and Ushioda, 2009: 145). Coetzee-Van Rooy writes:

English is an international auxiliary language. It is yours (no matter who you are) as much as it is mine (no matter who I am). ... No one needs to become more like Americans ... or any other English speaker to lay claim on the language. ... It isn't even necessary to appreciate the culture of a country whose principal language is English in order for one to use it effectively. This argument assumes a much more complex view of the identities of second language learners in world English contexts.

(Coetzee-Van Rooy, 2006: 442)

About the mother tongue, she writes:

The fascinating challenge for these groups [L2 speakers] however is to keep their own cultural and linguistic identity while mastering the second language. What has been most encouraging to us throughout these investigations is the fact that with the *proper attitudinal orientation* and motivation one can become bilingual without losing one's identity.

(Coetzee-Van Rooy, 2006: 441; emphasis original)

This sets out the position of international school students (although written in the context of South Africa): they learn English as a tool which will belong to them, and they will keep their own cultural and linguistic identity, their mother tongue. S. Wright (2004:14) observes, 'Currently globalisation is producing worldwide social diglossia and ever extending personal bilingualism.' This is the world we live in today. The often encountered alternative to bilingualism is described in the next section.

The status of English in the contemporary world
English language teaching in the world

From a research perspective, English language teaching has changed dramatically. Until recently, the concept of 'integrativeness', defined by Gardner and Lambert (1959: 271) as 'a willingness to be like valued members of the language community', was seen as the main motivation for students to learn English – or any language. Thus the model held out was that of native English speakers. This view has been challenged with the rise of English as an International Language (EIL) in a sea of speakers of World Englishes (SWE) (Sharifian, 2009: 3). The methodology currently accepted as most relevant to motivation is 'the "L2 Motivational Self System"', with its concepts of the *'ideal self'* and the *'ought-to self'* (Dörnyei and Ushioda, 2009: 3, 4). Coetzee-Van Rooy believes:

> The main foundations of the criticism of the notion of integrativeness are the 'simplex' views of the identity of second language learners and the incorrect assumptions made about the sociolinguistic contexts of many learners of English as a second language across the world.
>
> (Coetzee-Van Rooy, 2006: 442)

She explains:

> I use the term 'simplex' view of identity to refer to the underlying notion held by some researchers that learning a second language necessarily results in the loss of the first language, and the establishment of a new 'simple' identity as monolingual speaker of the target language.
>
> (ibid.: 440)

She also quotes Lamb, who comments:

> As English loses its association with particular Anglophone cultures and is instead identified with the powerful forces of globalization, the desire to 'integrate' loses its explanatory power in many EFL contexts. Individuals may aspire towards a 'bicultural' identity which incorporates an English-speaking

globally-involved version of themselves in addition to their local
L1-speaking self.

> (Lamb, 2004: 3, quoted in Coetzee-Van Rooy, 2006: 442)

These findings relate directly to international school students: they remove
the previously held focus on learning about the culture of the target language,
and emphasize that students will maintain their own language and culture.
It is fair to say that Western-based TESOL is still the model employed in
many schools: textbooks still contain British or American cultural models.
However, international school ESL teachers create their own materials for
language teaching, and their focus is on adapting other subject materials,
such as history, geography and biology. But not all international schools
recognize the language needs of SL learners.

Native English speakers as smug

A reason for getting beyond the English-only approach of the majority
of international schools is students' identities. Although Crystal (1997)
estimates that two-thirds of the world's children grow up in a bilingual
environment, the West is largely monolingual in outlook. Even bilingual
countries like Belgium, Finland and Switzerland have populations that
exist in a state of 'territorial unilingualism' (Romaine, 2004: 398). English
speakers especially, are prone to entrenched attitudes in the climate of the
current dominance of English. Ireland and the UK are now the only countries
in the EU where there is no requirement to study a foreign language. English
and American monolinguals are often characterized as having no aptitude
for foreign-language learning, this failing often being accompanied by
expressions of envy for multilingual Europeans,

> sometimes (more subtly) by a *linguistic smugness* reflecting a
> deeply held conviction that, after all, those clever 'others' who
> don't already know English will have to accommodate in a world
> made increasingly safe for anglophones. All such attitudes, of
> course, reveal more about social dominance and convention than
> they do about aptitude.
>
> (J. Edwards, 2004: 11; emphasis added)

Fishman uses the same word, 'smug', to describe the situation in the USA:

> Unfortunately, a country as rich and as powerful as our own,
> *smugly speaking* 'the language that rules the world,' can long
> afford to continue to disregard the problem.
>
> (Fishman, 2004: 418; emphasis added)

Factors which have a negative effect on students keeping up their mother tongue include: the perception of many parents that English is the solution (O. García *et al.*, 2006: 39–41; Krashen, 2006), the all-pervasive use of English in popular music and media, the spread of the internet, on which most sites consulted by students are in English (although other languages are increasingly being used) (Graddol, 2006), and the failure of the school's accrediting agency, the CIS, to acknowledge the situation of SLLs (Carder, 2005, 2009b).

Scant attention may be paid to what J. Edwards (2004: 22–3) calls 'linguistic axles and gears occasioned by bilingual competence', let alone to the relationship between language and identity, and how it may alter when more than one language is involved. Other reasons for the slow development of appropriate SL and MT programmes in international schools are now discussed.

Models of practice
Theory, practice and the reality in international schools

As mentioned above, there is a worrying gap between theory and practice in education. May (1994) believes that schools, in order to make a difference, have to show collective, coordinated resistance, which should be formalized in a critical practice.

It seems that many international schools still have the view laid out by Mullard 28 years ago:

> the assimilationist perspective was seen ... as one which embodied a set of beliefs about stability. The teaching of English along with a programme of cultural indoctrination and subordination ... would help in short to neutralize sub-cultural affinities and influences within the school.
>
> (Mullard, 1982: 123–4, quoted in May, 1994: 33)

International schools are nearly all private, and parents expect a quality English-language education. Directors are conscious of this and are anxious to have staff who do not disturb a smooth operation with ideas of structural change, even when this would be of benefit to the multilingual community. As Sennett points out,

> An organization in which the contents are constantly shifting requires the mobile capacity to solve problems; getting deeply involved in any one problem would be dysfunctional, since projects end as abruptly as they begin. ...The social skill required

by a flexible organization is the ability to work well with others in short-lived teams, others you won't have the time to know well. ... Your skill lies in cooperating, whatever the circumstances.

(Sennett, 2006: 126)

This describes the author's experience of attempting to institute systemic change in the treatment of SL learners. In order to enable change it is advisable to have good grounds for recommending it; since there was little research evidence from international schools it had to come from national systems, and this is addressed in the next section.

Bilingualism as the basis of good practice
The development of bilingual studies

An unwillingness to appreciate and acknowledge the burgeoning literature on SLA and bilingualism and to recognize them as disciplines in their own right has much to do with why there is not better provision for SL students. The study of bilingualism, and interpretations of its effect on young people, have developed immensely over the past century. Early studies generally associated bilingualism with lowered intelligence (J.V. Edwards, 2004: 15), and one well-known study concluded that 'the use of a foreign language in the home is one of the chief factors in producing mental retardation' (Goodenough, 1926: 393, quoted in J.V. Edwards, 2004: 16). However, in the early 1960s Peal and Lambert (1962) carried out studies which confirmed a positive relationship between intelligence and bilingualism. They controlled the relevant variables in an examination of ten-year-old bilingual and monolingual children, and the bilinguals were found to 'outperform their monolingual counterparts on both verbal and non-verbal intelligence tests'. The authors concluded that the bilingual child had 'mental flexibility, a superiority in concept formation, and a more diversified set of mental abilities', while noting that 'it is not possible to state from the present study whether the more intelligent child became bilingual or whether bilingualism aided his intellectual development' (Peal and Lambert, 1962: 277, quoted in J. Edwards, 2004: 16–17).

This produced a surge of publications on language acquisition by psychologists and linguists investigating bilingual children during the 1960s, and led to an increase of research activities from the 1970s on, which in turn contributed to 'the establishment of bilingual studies as an *autonomous discipline* with its own textbooks and journals' (emphasis added) (Meisel, 2004: 92). This is immensely important: there is now a separate discipline which has devoted vast amounts of research, investigation, conferences and literature to varied topics that come under the heading of bilingualism.

The advantages of bilingualism

Various authors have written on the earlier metalinguistic awareness of bilinguals compared to monolinguals (e.g. Ben-Zeev, 1977), their increased metacognitive abilities and metalinguistic awareness (e.g. De Avila and Duncan, 1979), and their greater separation of form and content (Leopold, 1939–49). Cognitive advantages attributed to plurilinguals by psychologists, such as advantages in conceptual development (e.g. Cummins and Gulustan, 1974; Peal and Lambert, 1962), higher verbal intelligence and greater psycholinguistic skills (e.g. Lambert and Tucker, 1972), and more divergent thinking (e.g. Landry, 1974), are all related to metalinguistic awareness about the practice of switching between languages (Dewaele *et al.*, 2003: 48).

Bialystok (1991), Cummins (1984, 1993b, 2000), Hakuta (1986) and Lambert (1974) also show that maintaining the mother tongue and adding English – in other words bilingualism – confers advantages. This academic base is vital for practitioners in international schools so that they can argue their case for appropriate programmes.

C. Baker (2006: 255) records eight potential advantages of bilingual education, namely, engagement in wider communication across generations and cultural groups, a sympathetic understanding of differences in creeds and cultures, biliteracy, increased classroom achievement, cognitive benefits, raised self-esteem, a more secure identity, and economic advantages.

Baker (ibid.: 252) summarizes the situation in international schools, saying they are '[m]ainly for the affluent, ... [o]ne language of the school is frequently English. International Schools that have English as the sole medium of transmitting the curriculum cannot be included under the heading of Bilingual Education in Majority Languages'. Skutnabb-Kangas also comments on international schools, noting that those who want to be included in the new globalized elites need to be multilingual, and

> [f]or them multilingualism means enhanced symbolic capital and, through a conversion process, economic and political capital. 'International Schools' have a similar goal even if they do not use several languages as media of instruction.
>
> (Skutnabb-Kangas, 2000: 624–5)

This suggests that international schools are perceived by elites as providing symbolic capital, while not using several languages as media of instruction.

The situation is not clear-cut, as many discussions with parents have revealed that they are grateful for *any* school which can accommodate their children with English as the language of instruction, since it is the global lingua franca. My perception is that such elites focus principally on their children becoming fluent in English, without considering what might happen to their children's own language and identity.

Bilinguals as more numerous, but more complex, than monolinguals

Bilingualism is considered to be more common than monolingualism in the world. Crystal (1997) estimates that some two-thirds of children in the world grow up in a bilingual environment. On the issue of 'who does better', monolinguals or bilinguals, commentators are increasingly pointing out that there is an inbuilt bias towards monolinguals, an attitude that:

> reflects a perspective strongly biased toward monolingualism in that it implicitly assumes that monolingual acquisition is the norm. Indirectly, at least, such an approach conveys the view that multilingualism deviates from what may be regarded as normal.
>
> (Meisel, 2004: 93)

It is equally important to understand, as Grosjean (1989) writes, the necessity of seeing that the 'bilingual is not two monolinguals in one person'. He argues that bilinguals rarely use their languages equally frequently in every domain of their social environment, but that they use each of them for different purposes, in different contexts, and in communicating with different partners (Meisel, 2004: 93, quoting Grosjean, 1989).

Bialystok takes the issue one step further by pointing an accusatory finger at researchers, who, she says, have:

> essentially developed their models from the simplifying assumption that children have one mind, one conceptual system, and one language. The limitations of this assumption are quickly apparent when one considers the inevitable and prolific interactions between language and thought in virtually every cognitive endeavor.
>
> (Bialystok, 2004: 577)

She then reviews the major researchers who have contributed to a more positive view of bilinguals' potential. First, Peal and Lambert, who 'saved' bilingualism by their study (1962, already mentioned); Vygotsky (1962, but written some thirty years earlier), who said that knowing two languages led to awareness of linguistic options; Clark (1978), who wrote that learning two languages might heighten awareness of linguistic devices in both languages; Leopold (1961), who discovered that understanding the nature of the relationship between words and meanings is superior in bilingual children; Cummins (1984), who found that bilinguals have greater flexibility in grasping concepts and solve problems faster than monolinguals, and who also developed the 'threshold hypothesis', which posited that a minimal level of bilingual competence is necessary to avoid deficits and enjoy the advantages of bilingualism: the context of each bilingual's community of practice is paramount here. Bialystok's conclusion is that bilingualism makes it easier for students to master skills, though she leaves open the matter of their overall achievement, in comparison to other researchers who point, for example, to metalinguistic advantages for bilinguals.

Each bilingual community is unique
Another tenet to bear in mind when discussing bilingualism is that 'any meaningful discussion must be attempted within a specific context, and for specific purposes' (J. Edwards, 2004: 8), a point elaborated on by Baker and Prys Jones, who conclude:

> there can be no preferred term that is capable of summing up all the complexity, dynamism and color of bilinguals existing in groups. Simple labels hide complex realities. What is needed is an awareness of the limitations of these simple terms [and] of the many dimensions underneath them.
>
> (Baker and Prys Jones, 1998: 99)

Or, as Sharp (1973: 11, quoted in Romaine, 2004: 387) has it, 'each bilingual community is unique'. This shows that bilingualism has come to be seen in a positive instead of a negative light, and that definitions of bilingualism will depend on each separate community. This has clear implications for international schools, which each have a unique bilingual community. Parents come from all around the world, their children are at school for differing lengths of time, and families have varying linguistic needs and repertoires. Many of them have developed some understanding of the situation they find themselves in, but some are entranced by promises of English in which it is seen as the language of success, and do not realize the hurdles their children may face.

A further comment on this important point is made by Auer, who concludes that the impasse of defining bilingualism can only be overcome if it is:

no longer regarded as 'something inside speakers' heads', that is, a mental ability, but as a displayed feature of participants' everyday linguistic behaviour. Bilingualism must be looked upon primarily as a set of complex linguistic activities, and only in a 'derived' sense as a cognitive ability. Consequently there is no one definition of bilingualism: bilingualism becomes an interactionally constructed predicate.

(Auer, 2009: 491)

The issue of a 'multilingual ethos', of considerable relevance in our setting, is discussed by various researchers, e.g. Crawford, 2000; Ferguson, 2006; Graddol, 2006; Shohamy, 2006; Skutnabb-Kangas, 2000. V. Edwards (2004) addresses broader issues of bilingualism and how it benefits the wider community. Edwards suggested that such policies 'create a disruption' and 'feelings of alienation and inadequacy' (ibid.: 163); these words were spoken by the judge at a hearing investigating policies of English-only in the workplace in the USA, and quoted by Susan Berk-Seligson, an expert witness at that hearing. Edwards also quotes former Canadian Prime Minister Pierre Trudeau, who commented: 'Of course, a bilingual state is more expensive than a unilingual one, but it is a richer state' (ibid.: 49), which leads to further important concepts concerning bilingualism, outlined below.

Those interested in the economic factors surrounding issues of bilingualism are referred to Hogan-Brun's 2017 book *Linguanomics: What is the market potential of multilingualism?* To give one example which shows the economic importance of multilingualism:

'One in four UK and one in six US businesses [is] losing out due to lack of language skills and cultural awareness in their workforce' [(*IDMP Europe*, 2015)]. Corporations with international ambitions need multilingual employees to sell their goods and services. Many other organizations also require among their workforce people skilled in at least one non-native language. This need is reflected in today's hiring strategies.

(Hogan-Brun, 2017: 1)

Factors involved in academic success: Additive and subtractive bilingualism

Maintaining literacy in the mother tongue, or first language (L1), has been shown to confer considerable benefits relating to the academic and social aspects of each student's life, including better performance in the second language (L2, usually English); this is *additive bilingualism*. In this situation, the second language and culture are unlikely to replace the first language and culture. Cummins stated:

> Educators who see their role as adding a second language and cultural affiliation to students' repertoire are likely to empower students more than those who see their role as replacing or subtracting students' primary language and culture.
>
> (Cummins, 2001f: 182)

There are other recognized benefits on a variety of cognitive and metacognitive tasks:

> Their performance on tasks such as counting the number of words in sentences and judging the grammaticality of anomalous sentences suggests that they have higher levels of metalinguistic awareness, allowing them to focus on the form rather than the meaning of language. There is also evidence of greater sensitivity to the social nature and communicative functions of language. Finally, psychologists point to the greater mental flexibility of bilinguals.
>
> (V. Edwards, 2009: 19–20)

Conversely, not maintaining literacy in the mother tongue has been shown to have negative effects, leading often to poor performance in the second language; this is *subtractive bilingualism*. Schools which ignore children's mother tongue and provide education only in the second language, usually English, are increasing the likelihood that children will become academically 'disabled' (Baker, 2006: 415). When literacy is attempted only through the second language, a child's oracy in English may be insufficiently developed for such literacy acquisition to occur (Baker, 2006: 332). These terms were proposed in the model devised by Lambert (1974). The model is valuable as it combines the individual and societal elements of bilingualism.

The European Schools offer a well-developed model of bilingual education. These schools were set up for the relatively elite workers of the European Community, are largely subsidized by the EU and have up to eleven different language sections. C. Baker (2006: 252–3) writes, 'Younger children use their native language as the medium of learning but also receive second language instruction (English, French, or German) in the primary school years.'

The vehicular language of instruction, one of the three in brackets, is used for giving classes to mixed language groups in history, geography and economics from the third year of secondary education. This second language – that used for instruction – is also taught as a subject before students begin studying through the language. The result is that students gain very good results in the European Baccalaureate.

The work of Cummins on bilingual issues
The threshold hypothesis and the developmental interdependence hypothesis

Cummins has had a great impact on the field of bilingual studies; a comprehensive collection of his writings is to be found in Cummins (2001a). In 1976 Cummins first postulated that 'there may be threshold levels of linguistic competence which bilingual children must attain both in order to avoid cognitive deficits and to allow the potentially beneficial aspects of becoming bilingual to influence their cognitive growth' (Cummins, 2001b: 71). He elaborated on this in 1979 (2001c) with his developmental interdependence hypothesis, in which he suggested that a child's second language competence is partly dependent on the level of competence already achieved in the first language, implying that the more developed the first language, the easier it could be to develop the second language:

> To the extent that instruction in L_x is effective in promoting cognitive/academic proficiency in L_x, transfer of this proficiency to L_y will occur provided there is adequate exposure to L_y (either in school or environment) and adequate motivation to learn L_y.
>
> (Cummins, 2001g: 122)

Thus if the first language is at a lower stage of development it will be more difficult to achieve proficiency in the second language. Cummins acknowledged (2001c: 75) that the basic idea had 'been previously expressed by Toukomaa and Skutnabb-Kangas (1977)'. He then reviewed research evidence by Toukomaa and Skutnabb-Kangas (1977: 76), who found that the extent to which the mother tongue had been developed by Finnish-speaking children before they had contact with Swedish was strongly related to how well they learned Swedish. Skutnabb-Kangas and Toukomaa also reported that mother-tongue development is especially important in school subjects that require abstract modes of thought:

> Subjects such as biology, chemistry and physics also require conceptual thinking, and in these subjects migrant children with a good mastery of their mother tongue succeeded significantly better than those who knew their mother tongue poorly.
>
> (Skutnabb-Kangas and Toukomaa, 1976: 69)

Cummins comments on studies by Hébert (1976) and A.G. Ramírez and Politzer (1976) that:

> The major educational implication of these hypotheses [on time spent learning L1 and L2] is that if *optimal* development of a minority language child's cognitive and academic potential is a goal, then the school program must aim to promote an additive form of bilingualism involving literacy in both L1 and L2.
>
> (Cummins, 2001b: 91)

Although developed for students in national systems, Cummins's research is directly relevant to the international school context.

BICS and CALP

Two concepts that have become well known to teachers involved with bilingual children are basic interpersonal communication skills (BICS) and cognitive and academic language proficiency (CALP). These terms, defined by Cummins (2001d: 112), refer to the types of language that children acquire, and require for school. He showed in his 'iceberg' representation of language proficiency how children acquire, 'above the water', basic interpersonal communication skills in their first language by natural processes of communicating with their family and peers. The literacy skills acquired in decontextualized academic situations are 'below the water', and are comprised in cognitive and academic language proficiency. This is a simplified description of a student's language ability, but it does point out the fundamental differences between the language most used for everyday discourse and that required for higher-level thinking skills. The BICS skills are acquired rapidly in the first five years, after which they develop more slowly. The CALP skills follow a steady curve similar to that of overall cognitive development, beginning to flatten out around mid-adolescence. Development in each area also depends on the context of each child's learning environment.

Cummins writes that he defined the terms BICS and CALP because he

> intended to draw educators' attention to these data and to warn against [the] premature exit of ELL students (in the United States) from bilingual to mainstream English-only programs on the basis of attainment of surface level fluency in English. In other words, the distinction highlighted the fact that educators' conflating of these aspects of proficiency was a major factor in the creation of academic difficulties for bilingual students.
>
> (Cummins, 2000: 58)

Along with this hypothesis, Cummins proposed a Common Underlying Proficiency hypothesis, by which:

> experience with either language can, theoretically, promote the development of the proficiency underlying both languages, given adequate motivation and exposure to both, either in school or wider environment.
>
> (Cummins, 2001d: 131)

This model thus rejects the Separate Underlying Proficiency model of bilingualism which 'involves the misconception that a bilingual's two ... sets of linguistic abilities are separate' (and was used as a pretext for moving children out of bilingual programmes into English-only programmes 'in order to learn English') (ibid.: 130).

Cummins further elaborated on the differences between the language proficiency required in face-to-face communication and that involved in most academic tasks by showing schematically (in Cummins, 2001e: 144) the relationship between them as two continua, consisting of two types of proficiency: context-embedded and context-reduced. The former refers to language embedded in meaningful contexts and supported by situational props, as happens for example in experiments in a science class, whereas in the latter a student has few or no such props, for example if a teacher is simply talking, with no overheads or other aid, or a student is reading a text or writing, again with no supporting material. Cummins points out that ESL students quickly develop context-embedded skills, whereas gaining proficiency in context-reduced aspects of English takes much longer.

Time needed for second language learners

Cummins refers to his own studies of immigrant students' learning of English in successful bilingual programmes, which substantiate that it takes 'from five to seven years, on the average, for minority language students to approach grade norms in academic (context-reduced) aspects of English proficiency' (2001e: 145). This finding was confirmed by the work of Thomas and Collier, discussed later in this chapter. Cummins makes a further point, reinforced by Thomas and Collier, namely the 'moving target' analogy: 'a major reason for this is that native English-speaking students are not standing still waiting for minority language students to catch up with them' (ibid.). ESL learners need two years to reach the same level in 'face-to-face' proficiency as native English speakers, whereas for more 'academic' work, which is typically required in schools and for which grades are given, it takes seven years for second language learners to 'catch up' with native English speakers.

In other words, ESL students are aiming at a moving target: as native English speakers make academic gains routinely every year, ESL students have to learn not only the academic content of the curriculum, but also the language needed to understand and use that language (Cummins, 1979).

These are facts which need to be continually reiterated to colleagues, parents and school management. Such communications also reinforce the fact that SL learners simply need time and appropriate programmes and should not be compared to learners with special educational needs.

Empowered versus disabled students

Cummins moved on to look at the situation within schools, and how the relationships between teachers and students affected the development of students; he believes there is a difference in how students develop that depends on the extent to which educators redefine their roles with respect to second language students. In his 1986 paper he states: 'Implementation of change is dependent upon the extent to which educators, both collectively and individually, redefine their roles with respect to minority students and communities' (Cummins, 2001f: 175).

He lays out three sets of power relations, the daily interactions between teachers and students, the overall relationship between the school and the local community, and the power relations between groups within society as a whole. There is no reason for these power relations to be any different in the international school context, as the same groups exist, though there is the added complication of having an extra community: the international community. Cummins reports that sociological and anthropological research, based on that of Fishman (1970) and Paulston (1980), suggests that status and power relations between groups make up an important part of the account of minority students' failure in school. The main tenet of his theory is that minority students are either 'empowered' or 'disabled' as a direct result of interactions with teachers in school, and that the degree of empowerment or disablement will depend on four characteristics of the institution of the school: how much the minority language and student are integrated into the school; how much each minority community is encouraged to join in the affairs of the school; how much the pedagogy encourages intrinsic motivation in students to use language to develop their own knowledge base; how much educators involved in assessment use it to encourage students rather than put them in a failing box. In most international schools second language students are not a minority, and the international community occupies a different type of space from local communities, being transient.

Research evidence for the effect that 'disablement' can have on students is presented by two World Bank economists, Hoff and Pandey (2004), who reported the results of a remarkable experiment:

> They took 321 high-caste and 321 low-caste 11- to 12-year-old boys from scattered rural villages in India, and set them the task of solving mazes. First, the boys did the puzzles without being aware of each other's caste. Under this condition the low-caste boys did just as well with the mazes as the high-caste boys, indeed slightly better. Then, the experiment was repeated, but this time each boy was asked to confirm an announcement of his name, and caste. After this public announcement of caste, the boys did more mazes, and this time there was a large caste gap in how well they did – the performance of the low-caste boys dropped significantly. This is striking evidence that performance and behaviour in an educational task can be profoundly affected by the way we feel we are seen and judged by others. When we expect to be viewed as inferior, our abilities seem to be diminished.
>
> (Hoff and Pandey, 2004, quoted in
> Wilkinson and Pickett, 2010: 94)

Cummins goes on to posit that, though theorists have shown that academic failure can be attributed to a lack of cultural identification (Cummins, 1984) or the disruption of intergenerational transmission processes (Feuerstein, 1979), school failure does not generally occur when minority groups are positively oriented towards both their own and the dominant culture. This is particularly relevant in international schools, where there are so many nations and languages. Clearly it will be necessary for each individual language community to recognize that it is a part of the 'international community' and, as such, is equal to, not above or below, any other one. An example of how much the attitude to a language and culture can affect a student is given by Troike (1978), who points out the academic failure of Finnish students in Sweden, where such students are 'low-status', and then compares this situation with their academic success in Australia, where they are seen as a 'high-status' group.

The cultural values of the predominant school nationalities, the culture of the school rules of discipline and expected behaviour, the cultural style and content of the lessons, and the teaching styles and attitude of the staff, all form a framework within which less dominant nationalities interact. All of these factors can impact negatively on the motivation of other national groups.

Cummins devised a framework to show how schools can provide a model which aims to provide equity across the curriculum. In this framework there is a cultural and linguistic pedagogical model in which ESL students are nurtured in an additive rather than a subtractive approach, community participation will be collaborative rather than exclusionary, pedagogy will be reciprocal and interaction-oriented rather than transmission-oriented, and assessment will be advocacy-oriented rather than legitimization-oriented. Cummins stresses the enhanced metalinguistic development found in association with additive bilingualism, which is also reported by Hakuta and Diaz (1985) and McLaughlin (1984). The more second-language students' parents are involved in their children's education, the more the parents will feel that they understand and can contribute, for example by encouraging reading in the mother tongue at home and providing a book-rich environment, with positive academic results. The pedagogical model is vital, and this is where CPD for all staff plays a key role. Informing and involving parents are important factors in the process of ensuring that children can benefit appropriately from their two or more languages. All new parents can be engaged in discussion of what is at stake, given information booklets about the importance of literacy in the mother tongue, referred to websites, and told about the possibility of having mother-tongue lessons. The crucial time of arrival at an international school can be seized on by those responsible for the MT programme in order to establish a firm foundation for each child in their mother tongue, which can be maintained and built on.

Cummins (2000) points to the model that is most unhelpful to ESL students, and terms it a 'banking' model; in it students are the passive receivers of knowledge, which is 'banked' in their brains by a transmission model of pedagogy. More successfully, a 'reciprocal/interactiove' model will encourage students to enter into discussion, dialogue and continual exchange with teacher and other students, which will encourage feedback in both content and form (Wong Fillmore, 1983). Haynes (2002: 2) comments: 'Critical thinking in schools is limited by the boundaries of a system where teachers not only teach but also control the behaviour of pupils through regimes of discipline.' However, developing a climate of self-discipline in which students can be involved in productive critical thinking is not only possible, in my experience, but vital to meaningful education.

Finally, assessment is a key factor in how ESL students are judged, and thus how they value themselves in the school environment. A grading system that sees only their insufficiencies in language will fail them and 'disable' them, resulting in many being classified as having special educational needs. Schools could develop alternative methods of assessing ESL students' true knowledge and abilities through suitable training of all staff, and also by offering portfolio assessment tasks, and modified grades in content-subject material. The latter involves each subject teacher making allowances for ESL students' developing proficiency in English and giving a grade based on the teacher's perception of the student's real proficiency in that subject rather than on that revealed by their knowledge of English, which, superficially, may look flawed. It will require a whole-school language policy (see the example in Carder, 2007a: 173–81).

It is the daily approach to SLLs by teachers that leads them to succeed or fail. Mainstream teachers and administrators who refer to 'the ESL students' are instantly classifying them, and this may, depending on a school ethos, disable them. ESL students do not need to be isolated as a group, any more than any other group of students: this is a sensitive issue, but one which could be included in teacher training. Having an SEN department, separate from the ESL and MT department, is a solution. To transcend 'disablement' Cummins proposes the solutions outlined in the next section.

Societal agendas

Convincing, in this section on the work of Cummins, is his suggestion in a paper published in 1993, and reinforced through his 2000 book *Language, Power and Pedagogy*, that in some countries at least, particularly in North America, there is an agenda of producing students who will follow the societal power structure, and not giving students enough critical literacy 'to deconstruct disinformation and challenge structures of control and social justice' (Cummins, 1993a: 270). The importance of critical literacy has also been discussed by Wallace (2003: 200), who makes the point that, in a world of globalization in which English is the language of power, '[a] critically nuanced, elaborated English offers learners a potentially powerful identity outside the classroom, as well as within it'. V. Edwards (2009: 2) writes: 'reading is not only about decoding the word from the page; it is also about the ways in which literacy can be used to empower and disempower people'.

It is therefore important for educators to select curricular topics that relate to societal power relations, and then give students the opportunity to analyse such topics from multiple perspectives. At international schools this is crucial as students come from so many different parts of the world, which may have different outlooks on any number of topics. Nieto (1992) also urges a focus on critical pedagogy. However, Hedges believes that:

> most elite schools ... do only a mediocre job of teaching students to question and think. They focus instead ... on creating hordes of competent systems managers. Responsibility for the collapse of the global economy runs in a direct line from the manicured quadrangles and academic halls ... to the financial and political centers of power.
>
> (Hedges, 2009: 89)

It is easy to see international schools, with their clientele of wealthy students and their spacious, well-equipped facilities, as a successful model of education, and many parents seem entranced by this superficial impression. However, my experience of visiting similar schools throughout the world has revealed that SLLs are often treated in just the ways that researchers have shown to be inadequate, with no MT programme, an approach to pedagogy that may not encourage critical, interactional teaching, and in which testing has become valued above all other projects, often to the disadvantage of SL students.

Another area of concern is attitudes towards bilingualism; Baetens Beardsmore (2003), for example, quotes comments on the politico-ideological fears of many people concerning bilingualism: 'Unease about language is almost always symptomatic of a larger unease. ... The issues in question, I would suggest, are much more likely to be such things as dominance, elitism, ethnicity, economic control, social status and group security' (McArthur, 1986: 87, 88, quoted in Baetens Beardsmore, 2003: 20). Calvet characterizes the situation: 'derrière cette guerre des langues, se profile une lutte pour le pouvoir' ['Behind this war of languages looms a struggle for power'] (Calvet, 1987: 181, quoted in Dewaele, Housen and Li, 2003: 21).

Edwards brings together the issues of racism hiding behind linguistic discrimination when she writes:

> While it is no longer politically acceptable to express deep-seated fear and mistrust of minorities in direct terms, the same restrictions do not apply to opinions about language. It has become increasingly clear, however, that debates which on the surface focus on language are actually about culture, identity, power and control.
>
> (V. Edwards, 2004: 216)

This makes it all the more important to make a determined effort to demystify bilingualism and consistently strive for the best models.

The work of Collier and Thomas on bilingual issues
Models of good practice

Two key researchers on second language learners are Collier and Thomas. They carried out various studies, published in Thomas and Collier (1995, 1997, 2002), and Collier and Thomas (1999a, 1999b, 1999c, 2007). Collier also wrote about many aspects of providing appropriate provision for ESL students in Collier (1989, 1992, 1995a, 1995b, 1995c). A comprehensive overview of their research is given in Collier and Thomas (2017).

They related, on the basis of their research,

- the amount of time needed by second language learners to reach the same level of proficiency as native speakers of English (Collier, 1989; Thomas and Collier, 1997), and
- the best models for achieving proficiency in English (Thomas and Collier, 1997; Collier and Thomas, 2007).

Their main conclusion is that maintaining and improving literacy in the mother tongue has been confirmed as a key variable in their studies on the 'how long?' question. Other researchers have reached a similar conclusion (e.g. Baker, 2006; Cummins, 1991, 1996; Genesee, 1987, 1994; Hakuta, 1986), and in a newspaper article de Lotbinière (2009) writes: 'Developing countries are unlikely to meet UN targets for improving education because of the widespread marginalisation of students' first languages, which results in teaching being delivered in languages that children struggle to understand or to use effectively.'

International school students are in many ways privileged, but some SL speakers are in the same situation as students in developing countries in this regard. Thomas and Collier devised a model for ensuring that SL learners could be treated equitably.

The Prism model

Thomas and Collier developed their Prism model to portray a holistic paradigm for the successful education of second language learners. It has four components that drive language acquisition: sociocultural, linguistic, academic and cognitive processes. The components are equally important, and the prism should be imagined as complex and multidimensional, like a triangular pyramid viewed from above, with the student in the centre, i.e. a 3-D image, so the point of the pyramid rises, and the sides are seen sloping down. The model can be seen diagrammatically at http://brittanychansen. weebly.com/uploads/2/5/2/8/25282281/prism_model.pdf.

SOCIOCULTURAL PROCESSES

This is the central area of the prism. Collier and Thomas state:

> Central to [the] student's acquisition of language are all of the surrounding social and cultural processes occurring in everyday life ... – home, school, community, and the broader society. For example, sociocultural processes at work in SLA may include individual students' emotional responses to school such as self-esteem or anxiety or other affective factors.
>
> (Collier and Thomas, 2007: 335)

LANGUAGE DEVELOPMENT

Emphasized under this heading, is: 'To assure cognitive and academic success in the L2, a student's L1 system, oral and written, must be developed to a high cognitive level at least throughout the elementary school years' (ibid.). The authors also clarify that 'Linguistic processes ... consist of the subconscious aspects of language development ..., as well as the metalinguistic, conscious, formal teaching of language in school' (ibid.).

There is a wealth of literature on ways of giving students the language skills they need. A good entry point to this area is scaffolding, written about by Gibbons (2002, 2006). She describes how to give students structures and frameworks around which they can develop their learning. Scaffolding is an instructional technique in which teachers model learning strategies and build up students' abilities to perform tasks themselves. One scaffolding strategy is for teachers to model working skills in the classroom which help children learn to operate in the school culture. When faced with an unfamiliar problem, they can construct a similar but simpler problem; in this way students manage their own gradual self-regulation and can carry out new tasks successfully.

ACADEMIC DEVELOPMENT

This includes all school work in all subjects, for each grade level. Since academic work transfers from the first to the second language, Collier and Thomas argue that it is best if academic work is developed in the first language, while the second language is taught through meaningful academic content. The authors state that 'research [their own] has shown that postponing or interrupting academic development while students work on acquiring the L2 is likely to lead to academic failure in the long-term' (Collier and Thomas, 2007: 335–6).

Collier and Thomas argue that this is a natural process, as when an infant builds thought processes through interacting with loved ones at home, which they then bring with them to school. They again emphasize the importance of this development continuing through a child's L1 at least through the elementary school years:

> Extensive research has demonstrated that children who reach full cognitive development in two languages ... enjoy cognitive advantages over monolinguals. ... Too often neglected was the crucial role of cognitive development in the L1. Now we know from the growing research base that educators must address linguistic, cognitive, and academic development equally through both first and second languages if they are to assure students' academic success in the L2. This is especially necessary if English language learners are ever to reach full parity in all curricular areas with L1 English speakers.
>
> (ibid.: 336)

Finally, it is again emphasized by Collier and Thomas that all four components are interdependent, and that it is crucial for educators to provide 'a socioculturally supportive school environment, allowing natural language, academic, and cognitive development to flourish in both L1 and L2' (ibid.).

Other research

More recently, the neuro-scientists Petitto and Dunbar (2009: 188) found that early bilingual exposure (before age three) had a positive effect, with language and reading comparable to those of monolinguals. The research also showed (from imaging studies of adults who had themselves been bilinguals at an early age) that their brains showed the same overlapping regions as those of monolinguals. In contrast, adults who had become bilingual at a later age had a more bilateral pattern. Petitto and Dunbar's research has demonstrated that early bilinguals appear to have cognitive advantages in terms of linguistic flexibility and multi-tasking. It is also clear that children nurtured at home in one or two languages will find it less challenging to embark on a further language in school, as they will be able to connect familiar words and concepts from one language to another.

Professional models of practice for ESL in international schools
Sheltered instruction

An effective professional pedagogical model is that of 'sheltered instruction':

> Sheltered subject-matter teaching is a form of communication-based ESL instruction in which the focus is on academic content – science, math, history, and so forth – taught in a way that is comprehensible for students with limited English. The goal in the minds of both the students and the teacher is mastering subject matter, not particular rules of grammar or vocabulary. In this way, students absorb academic English naturally and incidentally, while they are learning useful knowledge. If students are tested, they are tested on subject matter, not language.
>
> (Crawford and Krashen, 2007: 24)

It is included as part of the training for content teachers of ESL students in the USA in the Sheltered Instruction Observation Protocol (SIOP) teacher-training courses.

As Crawford and Krashen relate:

> At first, subjects such as science or math are chosen because they can be more easily contextualized, and thereby made comprehensible through the use of realia and pictures. Beginners in the second language are not included in sheltered classes, because the input will not be comprehensible for them. Fluent English speakers are not included either, because their interactions with the teacher and with each other may be incomprehensible to the other students. … Studies with intermediate, literate foreign-language students have consistently demonstrated the effectiveness of sheltered subject-matter teaching. Students in these classes acquire as much or more language as those in regular intermediate classes, and they learn impressive amounts of subject matter at the same time. Moreover, the kind of language they acquire is academic language, the cognitively challenging competencies needed for school success.
>
> (Crawford and Krashen, 2007: 25)

A further description is given by Collier and Crawford:

> At the secondary school level, students attend classes in subjects that they need to graduate from high school …. Sheltered

instruction refers to a content subject (science, math, or social studies) taught to ESL students by a teacher who has certification in the content area being taught.

(Collier and Crawford, 1998: 56)

The Sheltered Instruction Observation Protocol (SIOP) Model is a research-based and validated instructional model ... [for] addressing the academic needs of English learners throughout the United States. The SIOP Model consists of eight interrelated components: Lesson Preparation, Building Background, Comprehensible Input, Strategies, Interaction, Practice/Application, Lesson Delivery, Review and Assessment' (www.cal.org/siop/about, accessed 13 February 2018). 'The SIOP Model can be applied successfully in any context where English language learners are learning content and language simultaneously. It is most frequently implemented in content-based or thematic ESL classes, secondary content classes ..., [and] specifically designed sheltered content courses' (www.cal.org/siop/faqs/ (accessed 13 February 2018).

All evidence points to the need for ESL students to have content-related instruction in a paradigm of separate classes for ESL beginners, gradually segueing into a programme of partial separation and some integration, parallel classes of selected and adapted content (described in full in Carder, 2007a). Crawford and Krashen (2007: 44) state: 'For diverse schools, a program of communication-based ESL and sheltered subject-matter instruction, combined with native-language support by paraprofessionals, is often the best solution', and Janzen (2008: 1030, quoted in Scanlan and López, 2012: 601–2), writes, 'The academic uses of language as well as the meaning of individual words need to be explicitly taught for students to fulfill the genre or discourse requirements privileged in academic settings and to understand the material they encounter.'

CLIL: Content and language integrated learning

A comparable model is CLIL – Content and language integrated learning (Wolff, 2003; Nikula *et al.*, 2016; Bentley, 2010; Coyle *et al.*, 2012; Dale and Tanner, 2012) – in which the focus is on academic content – science, maths, social sciences – taught in ways adapted to the linguistic abilities of ESL students. Above all, different modes of assessment are required for ESL students.

An effective ESL programme in the middle-school years will have an ESL class for beginners in which, over the year, students may exit in controlled stages to sheltered instruction classes in maths and possibly science. Intermediate students will require sheltered instruction in maths, science, social studies/humanities and English (literature) for a longer period.

ESL students (beginners excepted) need to be assessed on 'sheltered content', i.e. the quality of the content, not the language. How long students remain in the sheltered ESL class is an important issue: many schools 'rush' the exit process in order to respond to parental demands, or those of administration. The weakness of many ESL programmes is that students are transferred to the mainstream before they have acquired enough 'second language instructional competence' (SLIC) to do well in content classes. Five to eight years is the time shown by research for ESL students to score at the 50th percentile level on tests of reading comprehension in English (Thomas and Collier, 1997). This is a high level of achievement, and a SLIC level may be acquired in a shorter time. Rolstad (2017: 497) has suggested that there there is a need for 'attention given to how SLIC, rather than the BICS/CALP dichotomy, might usefully guide effective teaching for second language learners'. Crawford and Krashen (2007: 22, 23) point out that it is a mistake to exit the SLIC class before the students have enough English to do well in the subject-content classroom. They add that there is often an urgency to exit which may be misplaced.

SLIC is the level of language proficiency required for ESL students to learn in English-language classrooms. Crawford and Krashen (ibid.) also write that it will vary according to students' background knowledge of subject-matter; for example, young children are quicker to develop SLIC in mathematics than in social sciences, namely geography and history. This is because maths is easier to contextualize using non-linguistic means, and the humanities involve abstract concepts that are harder to clarify.

Ovando elaborates further on this:

> Content ESL is based on two important linguistic concepts. The first one is Krashen's (1982) familiar concept that language acquisition occurs when students, in an interesting, low-anxiety context, are provided with comprehensible input which is slightly above the students' level of understanding. The second one is that second language proficiency entails control not only of social but also of academic language … [A]cademic language tends to be more abstract and complex, and thus more challenging for students. It takes more years to master than social language. This is the type of language that is present in math and science classrooms, and by integrating these subjects with linguistically

appropriate support in L2 development, the student has a better opportunity to develop academic language.

(Ovando, 1998: 185)

And:

> According to Crandall (1987: 7): 'Many content-based ESL programs have developed to provide students with an opportunity to learn CALP [academic language], as well as to provide a less abrupt transition from the ESL classroom to an all-English-medium academic program. Content-based ESL courses ... provide direct instruction in the special language of the subject matter, while focusing attention as much or more on the subject matter itself.'

(ibid.)

The following strategies are identified for use in sheltered classes:

- promoting collaboration between teachers and among students
- modifying language
- increasing the relevancy of [content] lessons to students' everyday lives
- adapting [content] materials; and
- using language teaching techniques in presenting [content] concepts.

(Fathman, Quinn and Kessler, 1992: 4,
quoted in Ovando, 1998: 185)

Conclusions

However, there are schools in which practitioners have built up programmes that recognize students' multilingual identities, and provide programmes for their cognitive, academic language growth. As Genesee writes (2004: 550–1), 'The success of bilingual education, like general education, depends on the day-to-day quality of instruction (including materials), continuity in program delivery, competence of instructional personnel, class size and composition, etc.' This may sound self-evident, but in fact it is these factors which will make or break a successful programme, and which are so difficult to institute and keep running.

Part Three

The human factor

The reality of teacher relationships, their implications for teachers and pedagogy, and the consequences of a deficit model for SLLs

Teacher relationships

The bland statement that 'all content teachers are also teachers of language' is one that resonates throughout schools today, without any rigour to ensure that content teachers know anything at all about teaching 'language'. A further requirement that is imposed by managerial diktat is for ESL teachers, in whatever capacity, to have successful interchanges of ideas with content teachers, without the management having any knowledge of the complexity of teacher–teacher relationships in schools, or providing any training or advice on the subject. In the absence of such knowledge or training this is like saying, 'The role I envision is one where the principal is not the expert with all the answers but the head learner and teacher who guides his or her colleagues through example' (Shaw, 2003: 110), without taking any steps to ensure that such practice ensues. As Shaw, himself a school principal, notes:

> Almost every study on successful schools acknowledges the important role of collegiality among teachers. Notwithstanding the rhetoric, in my own research I have found little evidence of teachers working collegially. Indeed, I have found that the traditions of professional privacy and teacher isolation are alive and well.
>
> (Shaw, 2003: 104–5)

This does not bode well for a supposed successful interaction between content teachers and ESL teachers.

Many academics have not worked in schools and are not in any way cognizant of the daily tensions in school life, especially in secondary schools. Block, for example, writes (2003: 11) that there is 'a sneaking tendency in the field [of research] to disengage from practical teaching matters'. Fortunately, some researchers have looked into the issue of relations between ESL and content teachers, and their results are revealing.

Contrived collegiality

Arkoudis and Creese write about 'Teacher–teacher talk' exposing the potential pitfalls of ESL teacher/subject teacher collaboration. They note that:

> Central to teacher collaboration is the relationship between the ESL and content teacher. Within policy documents this has been represented as a simple relationship, where ideas are shared in planning for the ESL students within mainstream classes (Arkoudis, 2003; Creese, 2002; Leung, 2004). Yet within the same policy documents we have a framing of ESL curriculum as adjunct to the mainstream curriculum. The ESL curriculum is offered as a strategy-based methodology. It is used to supplement the mainstream curriculum, but is not considered to have a content area of its own (Arkoudis, 2003). ... The subjects do not have equal status, and ESL is in effect an adjunct to the mainstream curriculum.
>
> (Arkoudis and Creese, 2006: 411)

Furthermore, Davison writes:

> Teacher collaboration is promoted as a panacea for many ills, from breaking down the professional isolation of the classroom to compensating for inadequate professional development to salving the wounds wrought by overly ambitious curriculum reform (Corrie, 1995; Hargreaves, 1994; Hargreaves and McMillan, 1994; Little, 1990). To some critics teacher collaboration is yet another poorly conceived but increasingly popular imposition on teachers from above, a contrived collegiality (Hargreaves, 1994: 208):
>
> > In contrived collegiality, collaboration amongst teachers was compulsory, not voluntary; bounded and fixed in space and time; implementation- rather than development-orientated; and meant to be predictable rather than unpredictable in its outcomes.

89

The literature suggests, however, that effective collaboration between teachers is not only rare, but extremely difficult to sustain. As Little (1990: 180) comments:

> The closer one gets to the classroom and to the central questions of curriculum and instruction, the fewer are the recorded instances of meaningful, rigorous collaboration.
>
> (Davison, 2006: 458)

This robust description of the reality in schools is a pre-eminent justification for having experts in their field – qualified SL teachers – be responsible for 'all things ESL' in international schools.

Implications for relationships

Arkoudis and Creese (2006) go on to point out that many researchers have indicated that discourse between content teachers and ESL teachers is a key element in developing appropriate 'linguistically responsive' teaching for ESL students. However, anyone who has worked in an international school knows that more time for discussion of important pedagogical matters is frequently at the top of teachers' priority lists and is just as frequently rejected by directors.

As Arkoudis writes (2006: 417), 'Educational policy on collaboration between ESL and mainstream teachers has assumed that the professional relationship is unproblematic and uncomplicated.' She continues:

> ESL as pedagogy has claims to content such as knowledge about the English language, knowledge about first- and second-language development, and knowledge of relevant language-teaching methodologies (Hammond, 1999: 33 [untraced]). These are substantial areas of expertise, yet within the institutional context of secondary school education, ESL is positioned as strategy-driven and does not have the same authority as subjects such as mathematics and science within the secondary curriculum. Therefore ESL is perceived as being lower in the subject hierarchy of the school. This institutionalised positioning of the subject has an impact on developing collaborative practices between ESL and mainstream teachers.
>
> (Arkoudis, 2006: 417)

This sums up precisely the status of ESL in schools and the effect it has on ESL staff, and is why it has to be completely turned on its head in international schools with the same type of positive discrimination that has been seen in the fight for race, gender and sexual equality. Davison (2006: 472) summarizes: 'Among the many conclusions that can be drawn from this study is that partnership between ESL and classroom teachers is neither easy nor unproblematic.'

Arkoudis (2006: 429) goes on to write about her research in schools, and to document the relationship between an ESL teacher and a science teacher. The ESL teacher, she explains, does not have the epistemological authority in the school to force the science teacher to reposition the science curriculum in ways more appropriate for ESL students, whereas the science teacher has a high-status subject. Arkoudis then writes that after many conversations the ESL teacher makes some headway. However, in international schools there is a constant flux of staff, and for every ESL teacher to devote much time and energy to persuading individual content teachers might be beyond their powers, and in any case possibly wasted as either teacher might soon leave the school.

Creese exemplifies the lower status of the ESL teacher in relation to the subject teacher in the lived reality of the classroom in this conversation between a student (S1) and a subject teacher (T):

S1: Miss, what have you got that for [referring to the tape recorder]?

T: Because she [the researcher] wants to record what I am saying and what Miss Smith [the language specialist] is saying and then she can play it back and she can see if there is a difference between the two of us.

S1: There is.

…

T: Why?

S1: Miss, you're the better teacher, aren't you?

…

But you're the proper teacher, aren't you?

T: Well, no. We are both proper teachers.

S1: She's like a help.

(Creese, 2002: 605, quoted in Monaghan, 2010: 20)

We know from Cummins's work (2000) that ESL students' perception of their teachers' status reflects on their own status, then on their self-esteem and ultimately on their potential.

Arkoudis's comments about the science teacher leaving the school are all too true for international schools. ESL teachers spend much time developing worksheets on content-area materials for ESL students and for specific teachers, then the teachers leave, the curriculum changes, the new head of school does not understand the process, or the number of ESL teachers is reduced as they are 'support', therefore peripheral, therefore the first to be subject to budget cuts.

Davison also writes:

> There are a number of essential elements for effective collaboration between language and content-area teachers, which have been discussed elsewhere (see, for example, Davison, 1992; Hurst and Davison, 2005), including the need to establish a clear conceptualisation of the task, the incorporation of explicit goals for ESL development into curriculum and assessment planning processes, the negotiation of a shared understanding of ESL and mainstream teachers' roles/responsibilities, the adoption of common curriculum planning proformas and processes, experimentation with diversity as a resource to promote effective learning for all students, the development of articulated and flexible pathways for ESL learning support, and the establishment of systematic mechanisms for monitoring, evaluation and feedback.
>
> (Davison, 2006: 456)

This is a wealth of advice for school leaders to take on board.

Implications for pedagogy

The long-term degrading of ESL as a subject has profound implications for pedagogy, as the entire subject area – one of extreme complexity – has been sidelined to the status of support, taught by non-professionals. In England it is:

> no longer regarded as a distinct subject area, and ESL and the needs of ESL students are subsumed in the mainstream curriculum. ESL teachers and the mainstream class teacher 'should work together'. ESL has no distinct discipline status; there are no ESL curriculum specifications and no national ESL scales for assessment. Funding

for ESL has been reduced repeatedly, giving the impression that ESL has no academic status or curriculum value. Mainstream teachers now have some awareness of the specific needs of second language learners, but ESL may well disappear as a distinct professional practice.

(Leung and Franson, 2001a: 163)

This paints a bleak picture for ESL students in England (where many teachers and international school leaders come from); they no longer have any informed professionals to receive instruction from, or to turn to for advice.

Franson comments on the realities of what has happened to SLLs in the wake of mainstreaming in England:

[O]ne might argue that the National Curriculum programmes of study and assessment, which are continually being advocated as applicable to *all* learners, have absolved the teacher from taking responsibility for the distinct and separate learning needs of EAL pupils. And perhaps one result of this continued reliance on the EAL teacher to take responsibility for EAL learning is that the issues are not articulated or debated within the professional remit of the class teacher, nor are they present in initial teacher training.

(Franson, 1999: 68)

It must be emphasized that the 'EAL' teacher referred to is probably an assistant and may have no training or qualification.

In another extract, Franson comments on interviews that have taken place with class teachers:

One interesting aspect of the three interviews could be simply described as a perception of 'resentment' or 'resistance' about the responsibility placed upon the class teacher of an EAL pupil. One teacher spoke at length about the parents' responsibilities for their children's language learning. 'I wonder sometimes whether they know exactly what it is we're trying to teach them or whether they actually think that they're going to come here and just learn English ... and if I had children and suddenly wanted to take them to another country and send them to school there I don't think I'd just suddenly put them into a school with no ... language and expect them to get on with it ...'.

(Franson, 1999: 69)

This is an issue which is more complicated for international school parents. In my discussions with them about why they choose a particular school, the response is always the same: 'We had no choice. We arrived in this country and this is the school which our [embassy, organization, agency] recommended.' This puts the responsibility entirely on the school to provide a professional ESL and mother-tongue programme, which it should now be in a position to do after so much experience of the international school network over the last four decades.

Here Franson understates the effects of 'mainstreaming' on teachers and students:

> Teaching EAL learners continues to be a daunting responsibility for teachers who, in the past decade, have been subject to significant and demanding innovations in the education system. Asked how they felt about this responsibility, one teacher commented, 'apprehension and fear that one won't be able to … that it will be an overwhelming task'. Another spoke of her colleagues feeling 'very frustrated and de-skilled in a way …'. And the new pupils? 'Overwhelming for them … it's quite hard, it's quite hard'.

> The teacher takes a predominant role in ensuring the inclusion of EAL pupils in shared classroom practices. However, in light of these interviews with class teachers, and despite their expressed good intentions, one might suggest that mainstreaming EAL pupils may have granted EAL pupils equality of presence, but has not necessarily secured equality of participation and achievement.
>
> (Franson, 1999: 69–70)

'Not necessarily' can probably be taken as meaning that most 'EAL pupils' are not receiving an instructional programme appropriate to their linguistic needs.

The grim reality for ESL students in England is that:

> Unfortunately, in England at the moment, there is no consensus on an appropriate EAL pedagogical framework, although there are often advice and materials produced at a local level, nor are there programmes of work that a class teacher can access, nor is there an agreed framework of EAL development that will help teachers to monitor and evaluate the progress of their EAL learners. … [I]t would seem that one of the key issues vital to effective practice, that of teachers' personal and professional

beliefs (Richards and Lockhart, 1994; Day, 1987; Diamond, 1991), has not been sufficiently addressed.

(Franson, 1999: 68, 69)

As far as it has been possible to ascertain, teachers doing a year's training for a PGCE in England spend just half a day of that year on second language issues. As Leung and Franson state (2001b: 169), 'Sometimes this lack of recognised and recognisable training has led to difficulties in establishing the credibility of the ESL teacher among school staff.' This also seems like a considerable understatement.

Most poignant, and extraordinarily negative as regards the approach of the government, is this statement:

> In England language support teachers may end up mediating between the class teacher and the pupils often in hushed voices at the back of the classroom. Even in well-managed classes the ESL support teacher role, under such circumstances, is reduced to a teaching assistant. In lessons where the teaching and learning activities and the work materials are disorganized, the contribution of the ESL support teacher may be reduced further.
>
> (Leung and Franson, 2001b: 170)

This is the pedagogical framework that ESL teachers and, of more concern, school leaders and decision makers come from before embarking on a career in international schools. The implications for pedagogy are clear: international schools should take note.

Teachers' professional lives

Goodson and Hargreaves point out that:

> The aspiration for teachers to have professional lives is not a given phenomenon but a contested one. It marks a struggle to redefine the work of teaching by governments, administrators, business and teachers themselves. Achieving the actuality of professional lives in teaching is not easy. Nor is it totally clear what this aspiration for professional lives might mean, or entail, even if it could be realized.
>
> (Goodson and Hargreaves, 1996: 4)

They then give descriptions of various types of professionalism, summarized below:

- *Classical professionalism* defines the practices of law and medicine as the traditional professions which fulfilled basic criteria for having specialized knowledge, professional ethics and internal regulation.
- *Flexible professionalism* describes our present world, characterized by manufactured uncertainty and where postmodern chaos, complexity and uncertainty are not merely contingent or unintended, but also to some extent the results of wilful acts by governmental, corporate and financial powers which seek to maximize their own interests by keeping everything flexible, interest groups fragmented and everyone off-balance.
- *Practical professionalism* is an attempt to give dignity and status to teachers' lives and work. It shows how teachers' personal practical knowledge allows us to talk about teachers as knowledgeable and knowing people. It gives them status as practitioners but not the power to influence the system of values that education is based on.
- In *extended professionalism* teachers look beyond the classroom to visualize the wider social context of education. All pedagogical practices – work in the classroom, methodology – are seen as rational rather than intuitive. This may lead to *distended professionalism*, in which teachers overstretch themselves as they attempt to manage other workers, write new curricula and plan staff development, and thus short-change their students.
- *Complex professionalism* describes the situation in a world of accelerating changes in global economics, where teachers have more administration to do and are often overloaded. Schoolwork is highly complex and becoming more so, and teachers are expected to be knowledgeable, experienced, thoughtful, committed and energetic. This expectation may lead to long-term damage to their health, lives and staying power.

(ibid.: 4–19)

Goodson and Hargreaves go on to recommend that in the current atmosphere of increasing demands for technical competency and subject knowledge, professionalism should be defined under a new heading, *postmodern professionalism*, with seven areas:

1. Increased opportunity and responsibility to exercise discretionary judgement over the issues of teaching, curriculum and care that affect one's students.

2. Opportunities and expectations to engage with the moral and social purposes and value of what teachers teach, along with major curriculum and assessment matters in which these purposes are embedded.

3. Commitment to working with colleagues in collaborative cultures of help and support as a way of using shared expertise to solve the ongoing problems of professional practice, rather than engaging in joint work as a motivational device to implement the external mandates of others.

4. Occupational heteronomy rather than self-protective autonomy, in which teachers work authoritatively yet openly and collaboratively with partners in the wider community (especially parents and the students themselves), who have a significant stake in the students' learning.

5. A commitment to active care and not just anodyne service for students. Professionalism must in this sense acknowledge and embrace the emotional as well as the cognitive dimensions of teaching, and recognize the skills and dispositions that are essential to committed and effective caring.

6. A self-directed search and struggle for continuous learning related to one's own expertise and standards of practice, rather than compliance with the enervating obligations of endless change demanded by others (often under the guise of continuous learning or improvement).

7. The creation and recognition of high task complexity, with levels of status and reward appropriate to such complexity.

(ibid.: 20–1)

Leung (2013) also discusses two kinds of professionalism, which he labels 'sponsored professionalism' and 'independent professionalism'. By sponsored professionalism he means the qualified status that any teacher needs to obtain in order to practise in a national system. He notes elsewhere:

> By independent professionalism is meant a commitment to reflexive and critical examination of the educational values, pedagogic assumptions, knowledge bases and curriculum practices built into sponsored professionalism, and to take initiative and action to open up debates and to effect change where appropriate.

(Leung and Creese, 2010: 126)

In the current book this is our aim: to effect change. For teachers in schools it is not so easy: in the private sector of international education criticism of established ways can be unwelcome and lead to non-renewal of contract. The authors are continually receiving emails from distressed ESL teachers about how their programmes are being downgraded, merged with SEN departments, forced to accept teaching assistants, and how they are told not to contact outside experts on ESL: they add that they are worried about losing their jobs.

The consequences for teachers of decisions taken by school leaders or educational agencies without consultation may be severe, as recounted by Stringer:

> People sometimes tell lies deliberately to misinform others. The issue of 'truth' is much broader than this, however. Truth is brought to question when information is distorted or misrepresented in attempts to persuade or deceive. Inflated estimates of costs and unwarranted promises of the benefits of particular projects are but two ways in which practitioners can distort truth and damage communicative action. ...
>
> Manipulation through the use of distorted information or failure to make covert agendas explicit is so common that it is often accepted as an unfortunate but necessary part of social, organizational, and political life. Damage to communicative action through untruthfulness, however, often leads to more general problems. When people have been tricked or duped, they are frequently unable to continue to work harmoniously with those they feel have cheated them, and the chances of productive and effective work taking place are diminished accordingly.
>
> (Stringer, 1999: 33)

He continues:

> A feature of modern life is the concentration of power in the hands of small groups of people. ... [M]anagers are given decision-making power over large groups to enable them to control and organize activities. ... Management is greatly affected by the needs to play off the agendas of the various client groups and to deal with political machinations that often arise. ... All too often, superficial solutions provide the semblance of immediate action but in effect can actually exacerbate the situation.
>
> (Stringer, 1999: 39–40)

Barnett discusses the complexities of managing universities in a 'super-complex age'. He notes the advantage of forming a distinction between *leadership* and *management*:

It would take the general form of the following: the *task* of leadership is that of bringing into view new frameworks; the *challenge* of management is that of producing an environment in which such frameworks can be given a fair hearing; and the *achievement* of leadership/management lies in developing institutional processes such that new frameworks are spontaneously sought. In other words, the concepts of leadership and management *both* do worthwhile work (Middlehurst, 1993) but, in an age of super-complexity, they overlap each other. Effective leadership requires effective management (we might speak of *leadership-in-action*) and effective management requires effective leadership (having the intellectual generosity to envisage new frameworks of understanding).

(Barnett, 2001: 31)

This framework provides definitions of management that involve more responsibility towards the teacher as professional. International school providers need to wake up to the need for a re-professionalization of ESL programmes and skilled and qualified ESL teachers in international schools, where ESL teachers are seen as the key to success for the SL learners who are now a majority in international schools. In middle schools ESL departments will be seen as centres of expertise, serving to spread awareness of second language issues throughout the school for content teachers and management.

The consequences of a deficit model for students

Harper and de Jong write:

If ESL teachers' specialized knowledge and skills are not recognized in their schools it is unlikely that they will be called upon to represent or advocate for ELLs' curricular or assessment needs, provide professional development for teacher colleagues or assume roles as equal partners in collaborative team settings (Davison, 1992, 2006; Hurst and Davison, 2005). As a result, ESL students will continue to find themselves in classrooms with teachers who are unprepared to meet their linguistic and cultural needs or who are not willing or motivated to alter their instruction significantly because they believe that good teaching for fluent English speakers is good teaching for all students.

(Harper and de Jong, 2009: 144)

This reflects the conclusion reached by Leung, who explains how a phenomenon of inclusion (mainstreaming) of ESL students was justified in education policy in England following the 1985 Swann Report: 'In other words, mainstreaming ESL students takes priority over the adapting and extending the mainstream curriculum for ESL students' (Leung, 2007: 258). Everything these researchers have written is borne out by the present author's own experience. The well-intentioned research of academics has been watered down and politicized by school authorities, school heads, middle management, curriculum agencies and accreditation bodies to provide a bland 'ESL students should be integrated into the mainstream: deal with it', without any serious reckoning with the implications or consequences. As Fukuyama explains:

> [E]lite groups have a stake in existing institutional arrangements and will defend the status quo as long as they continue to remain cohesive. Even when the society as a whole would benefit from an institutional change ... well-organized groups will be able to veto change because for them the net gain is negative.
>
> (Fukuyama, 2011: 454)

In summary, various factors in the fields of research have led to new ways of looking at the potential of ESL students: different models are recommended for various situations. Bilingual models are seen as the most successful, but these are only possible where two languages are involved. It is necessary to search in depth to find references to appropriate provision for ESL students in places where there is the wide diversity of mother tongues found in international schools, and such references are often dismissive and rarely come up with viable solutions.

Part Four

The role of external
curriculum and
accreditation bodies:
Pitfalls and alternatives

The role of external bodies, such as the Council of International Schools and the International Baccalaureate, in international schools: The erosion of the acknowledgement of SLL needs and potential

Among a people without fellow-feeling, especially if they read and speak different languages, the united public opinion necessary to the working of representative government cannot exist.

(John Stuart Mill, 1861, chapter 7)

'Expediency,' Izzie said ..., 'generally trumps ethics, I've noticed.'
(Atkinson, 2013: 157)

Accreditation

International schools can choose their route to being accredited, and which curriculum they follow. Carder and Mertin have had extensive experience with the CIS for accreditation, and with the IB for curriculum and assessment; these will be reviewed in depth in this chapter. The world of international education has been described as a small one. Once on the circuit, teachers and administrators become known to each other to a degree that may appear surprising to those not involved. The intricate workings of the IB curriculum, and accreditation processes, are quite familiar to those working with these frameworks. Readers not familiar with these matters are advised to peruse the websites www.cois.org, www.ecis.org and www.ibo.org (all accessed 13 February 2018).

Each organization will be reviewed to evaluate its provision for ESL students, as will other agencies involved with international education.

The ECIS and the CIS began as one (i.e. ECIS) and remained so until June 2003, when the CIS split off from the ECIS. The ECIS was formerly known as the European Council of International Schools. The CIS is now the body responsible for accreditation, teacher and executive recruitment, and higher education recruitment, all offered worldwide, whereas the ECIS continues to devote itself to services such as professional development in Europe, awards, fellowships, advice on student and programme assessment, and curriculum development. The CIS has 700 affiliated schools, 320 of them accredited. It is based in Leiden. The ECIS website (www.ecis.org), with its new name, 'The Educational Collaborative for International Schools', states: 'ECIS ... is a non-profit global membership organisation that provides professional learning, research, advocacy, and grants and awards for the benefit of its members.' It is currently based in London.

ESL and mother tongues in the CIS and the ECIS

In 1983 at the ECIS autumn conference in Rome a group of teachers, including myself, saw the need for a committee to address the needs of SLLs, and the ECIS ESL committee was born. The first subject-specific conference took place at the Vienna International School in 1987, with keynote speaker Professor Jim Cummins, who has done so much to highlight the potential of ESL students, and the need for recognition of their pedagogical needs.

In the 1980s and 1990s the committee staged conferences every two years from 1987 to 1993, with keynote speaker Dr Virginia Collier, and again in 1995, 2000 and 2002. Committee members were active in working with the ECIS and giving valued input to the ESL section of the accreditation guidelines. Conferences were subsequently scheduled every three years, with increasing numbers of participants – 500 at the 2005 venue in Rome, the 2008 venue in Geneva, in Düsseldorf in 2011 on the theme 'Promoting linguistic human rights in internationals schools: From theory to the classroom', then in Amsterdam in 2014, and in Copenhagen in 2017.

When the CIS split off from the ECIS in June 2003, the CIS published a new 'Guide to Accreditation' in which ESL was placed at the end of the guide under 'Learning Support Services', and ESL was grouped together with SEN as a non-curriculum subject. The committee, which by this time had renamed itself the 'ECIS ESL and Mother Tongue Committee' in order to reflect the importance of the maintenance of students' mother tongues, protested vigorously about the new placement of ESL in the Guide and had meetings with the head of CIS accreditation services at that time, but to no avail. (In March 2017 the 'ESL and Mother Tongue Committee' renamed itself the 'Multilingual Learning in International Education Committee'

(MLIE).) In future there would be no input from subject committees. Thus a comprehensive listing of best possible practice for ESL students was no longer written by ESL educators, and the section for ESL was relabelled as learning support, placed under student support services, and was relegated to the back section of the Accreditation document: twenty years of consistent professional input on ESL matters was swept away by managerial edict (Carder, 2014a). The CIS has rewritten the relevant wording in the 8th edition of the guide as 'Effective language support programmes shall assist learners to access the school's formal curriculum and other activities', which is now in 'Section E: Access to teaching and learning'. This shows the continued use of the term 'support', which puts such programmes in the peripheral box and first in the line of fire to cut spending on.

An experienced accrediting teacher commented:

> The accreditation process is simply too bland. Schools can have minimum ESL programmes, taught peripherally, and such schools can be re-accredited, accreditation team members saying 'they can only make suggestions'. CIS accreditation has no teeth, and schools can do what they like. In any case probably only a small percentage of international schools are accredited, leaving many schools free to ignore professional ESL provision.

The New England Association of Schools and Colleges (NEASC), which frequently co-accredits schools with the CIS, actually states, 'NEASC Accreditation does not guarantee the quality of specific programs' (www.neasc.org/overview/faq, accessed 13 August 2018).

Since then the status of ESL has progressively declined, and incoming leadership, new to international education, simply takes it as a given that ESL, which is labelled 'Language Support', is in its rightful place, as can be seen from the following sections of the CIS accreditation guide:

PART TWO – SECTION E

ACCESS TO TEACHING & LEARNING

INTRODUCTION

Students' opportunities to access teaching and learning are influenced by the quality of school support programmes. These incorporate provisions for addressing learner needs including identified learning challenges or special talents, *language support* and counselling, guidance and health services. The nature and level of services should be determined by the school's Guiding

Statements, the learning and well being needs of the student body, and the age range of those enrolled.

(CIS/NEASC, 2014: 31; emphasis added)

A glossary in the guide defines support staff thus:

Support Staff: this term is used in the broad sense of school employees who contribute to school life by means other than the directly academic. These include classroom assistants, office staff, and employees involved in auxiliary services (canteen, cleaning, transport, security, etc.).

(ibid.: 5)

The status of those who support SLLs is made quite clear here, and the students themselves will no doubt be aware of their own status, which will impact on their self-esteem, and thus their potential.

The fact that the 'language support' standard comes immediately after the standard (E2) for 'Children with learning differences or specific needs' gives a green light for school heads to justify their decision to place the two areas in the same box, to the detriment of ESL students who need their own curriculum and programme of instruction. School heads from Britain will immediately place ESL under the supervision of a SEN head of department as this is the standard procedure in England, where ESL has no professional status. Evidence of this is constantly presenting itself as ESL teachers contact me (through my website) to ask for advice.

It is evident that the CIS and the NEASC urgently need to produce an entirely separate protocol for international schools.

Mother tongues in accreditation documents

For mother-tongue learning the accreditation document has only a bland 'Standard E3d: The school encourages parents to continue development of the student's home language(s)'.

The vital role of mother tongues in contributing to success in a second language has been confirmed by research studies:

The key finding ... is the crucial role that ... L1 plays in schooling English learners. Along with fellow researchers across the world, we continue to find in each study that we conduct that the most powerful predictor of LM [language minority] student achievement in second language is nonstop development of students' L1 through the school curriculum (including schooling through the second language, usually the dominant language of the host country).

(Collier and Thomas, 2017: 2)

They then give an extensive list of references that back up their findings:

Research syntheses from other countries on the importance of bilingual schooling for LM groups include, for example: [C.] Baker, 2011; [C.] Baker & Prys Jones, 1998; Christian & Genesee, 2001; Cummins, 2000; Cummins & Hornberger, 2008; Dutcher, 2001; [O.] García, Skutnabb-Kangas & Torres-Guzmán, 2006; Hélot & de Mejía, 2008; May & Hill, 2005; Skutnabb-Kangas, Phillipson, Mohanty & Panda, 2009; and Tucker, 1999. Meta-analyses and research syntheses of U.S. studies examining long-term English learner achievement in bilingual schooling and the importance of L1 development for success in L2 are summarized and/or analyzed in Collier, [1992]; Dolson, 1985; Greene, 1998; Krashen and Biber, 1988; Lindholm-Leary, 2001; Lindholm-Leary & Borsato, 2006; Lindholm-Leary & Genesee, 2010; Lindholm-Leary & Howard, 2008; [J.D.] Ramírez, 1992; Rolstad, Mahoney and Glass, 2005; Thomas, 1992; Troike, 1978; and Willig, 1985.

(Collier and Thomas, 2017: 2)

Further evidence comes from Umansky and Reardon:

Our findings support theory and research on second language acquisition and bilingual instruction. Transfer theory and underlying proficiency theory both suggest that acquiring a solid foundation in one's native language supports one's ability to acquire proficiency in a second language (Cummins, 1991; Goldenberg & Coleman, 2010). Studies have found a transfer effect of home language to English in areas including phonological awareness (López & Greenfield, 2004), vocabulary (Ordóñez, Carlo, Snow, & McLaughlin, 2002), and reading (Páez & Rinaldi, 2006).

(Umansky and Reardon, 2014: 904–5)

However, this major contributory factor to students' learning potential gets a mere footnote in the accreditation process.

The elephant in the room

I have been on many school accreditation visits as a team member and co-chair, taken part in three accreditation processes at my former school, and attended CIS workshops for accreditation team leaders. The emphasis in CIS accreditations is on openness, transparency, the space for teachers to raise concerns, and the chance to engage in debate for improvement in many spheres. But the elephant is still in the room. As long as ESL is not given a massive boost in its status and standing in international schools, and that central status is not enshrined in the accreditation process, ESL issues will continue to be peripheral and linked to SEN under support services.

As an example, at one large international school the leadership decided to put SEN and ESL in one department under a new position called Head of Learning Support, as this is the scheme laid down by the CIS accreditation process. This was against the wishes of the ESL staff, who proposed a head of IBPYP ESL and a head of IBMYP/DP ESL. The leadership response to the concerns of these ESL teachers was:

> The Head of Learning Support Services' role will be to identify the curriculum philosophy and principles together with any systems and structures for a more coordinated provision of learning and language support to students who require the means to successfully access teaching and learning at our school.

This implies that the person selected will have professional training and qualifications in both SEN and ESL. However, it is extremely unlikely that any head of department would have expertise in and experience of both fields. This argument also overlooks the fundamental importance of both the mother tongue and CPD to issues related to bilingualism and second language development for *all* members of staff.

It has become clear that the accreditation agencies – the CIS and the NEASC – are determined that ESL shall remain under 'support'. This will have the deleterious effects on both ESL students and their teachers already documented. It is vital that these two institutions go back to the drawing board and put the ESL programme where it belongs: at the centre of the curriculum. It should be situated under Section B, Teaching and Learning, at the beginning, with clear instructions as to its crucial role in international schools, which increasingly have 75 per cent or more ESL students. Fukuyama notes that 'Human beings can rarely plan for unintended consequences and missing information, but the fact that they can plan means that the variance in institutional forms they create is more likely to produce adaptive solutions than simple randomness' (Fukuyama, 2011: 446–7). Also, 'An adaptable organization can evaluate a changing external environment and modify its own internal procedures in response. Adaptable institutions are the ones that survive, since environments always change' (Fukuyama, 2011: 450). It is time for an adaptive solution.

Other international agencies that provide alternatives to EAL, and their impact on ESL programmes in international schools

Two agencies that offer short courses to equip principals and teachers to manage the teaching of SLLs in international schools are the International Schools Services – World Language Initiative (ISS WLI; www.iss.edu/Professional-Learning/World-Language-Initiative/Courses/Course3, accessed 13 February 2018), and the Principals' Training Center (PTC; www.theptc.org/, accessed 13 February 2018). The ISS is a 'private, non-profit organization serving American international schools overseas' (www.iss.edu/, accessed 13 February 2018).

A long-time ESL teacher wrote:

> Just heard today that one of our new incredibly competent EAL colleagues has been told to do all push-in (i.e. in-class support) or move on, by the school head who has done a WLI course. This online certificate course is constructed to train teachers and administrators to adopt wholly push-in teaching as a one-size-fits-all solution to addressing ELL needs. Any deviation from the narrow party line is frowned upon.

Reports have come to me over many years of entire, successful ESL departments being wiped out after an in-service visit by the programme designer.

The incident referred to earlier, in which 'in an international school an ESL teacher, along with her entire class of ESL students, was physically pushed by the director into the mainstream classroom' came about as a result of that principal recently having completed a WLI course.

As recommended later in this book, valid in-service training for ESL must be '[c]onsistent, long-term training in ESL pedagogy and methodology. … Quick and dirty 1-day, or 1-hour, in-service sessions simply cannot provide enough preparation and training for teachers expected to help ELLs succeed in their mainstream content classes in a new language' (Hansen-Thomas and Cavagnetto, 2010: 263).

There have been many extremely effective ESL departments in international schools throughout the world, often struggling for staffing and higher levels of professionalism in the face of cuts brought about specifically by school leaders unaware of the different histories of second language provision in national and international systems. An experienced, long-serving ESL department head has written:

> I'm convinced that it's simply the fact that administrators want to economize as much as possible and this model of push-in as opposed to offering legitimate English-language instruction is simply easier and cheaper, and ultimately they aren't concerned that it does not meet the needs of the students.

It needs repeating: in no other subject would a four- or five-day course qualify a teacher or a principal to make far-reaching decisions about a highly complex and sensitive subject area, or give the trainee the confidence to return to their school and threaten a dedicated teacher with dismissal for not submitting to the principal's injunction.

A further organization providing educational services for international schools, specifically in East Asia, is the East Asia Regional Council of Schools (EARCOS; www.earcos.org/, accessed 13 February 2018).

A working ESL model in the IBPYP

What follows is a description of the ESL programme at a large primary division in an international school which runs the IBPYP. It shows how a balance can be achieved by dedicated ESL teachers:

- For ESL Intermediate we have a flexible approach re: in-class support and out-of-class instruction (push-in and pull-out). This works partly because we are one ESL teacher per Grade Level (GL) and can really belong to the team, thus taking part in the weekly planning meetings (which are 3–4 periods of 40 min/week), planning days for Units of Inquiry (UoI), trips, etc. We help modify material for ESL students and so on.
- ESL Intensive (Beginners) teachers liaise with the ESL Intermediate teacher of the Grade Levels they work with and perhaps occasionally attend the meetings. So, I will liaise with X and Y for information re: Maths, UoI concepts/vocab, special items like outings and such.
- The ESL Intensive program is of course separate and 'pull-out'. What we *do* in the ESL Intensive lessons depends on the level of the kids year-to-year. This is the first time that there aren't combined ESL

Intensive groups. With the Grade 4 group, four kids have BICS so with them I've started doing UoI work on a healthy lifestyle, choices, balance, etc. The two who are complete beginners from Russia are joining in for the more basic parts of UoI and, otherwise, engaged in learning about food, expressing their likes/dislikes, number, etc.

• Doing all push-in is definitely a false approach! I believe our former principal wanted that and he managed to get the visiting expert to focus on co-teaching during her 3rd and last consultancy visit. He wanted everything to turn into co-teaching between class T[eacher] and ESL T[eacher]. I feared too that with our Language Policy expressing strong statements like those below that the Director would eventually justify getting rid of ESL specialists. What's mentioned below is the ideal world we should be striving towards but that this school and I'm sure every int'l school is far from:
  • 'All teachers are teachers of language'
  • 'The curriculum enables students to be multilingual and to develop multiliteracies'.

This brief summary gives a clear picture of how ESL professionals should be working, but also of the attempts of the administration to get rid of them, often by bringing in a well-paid expert. Again there is the 'All teachers are teachers of language' jingle, which is meaningless without a programme of CPD for all staff and leadership over extended periods. 'The curriculum enables students to be multilingual and to develop multiliteracies' says nothing meaningful. 'The curriculum' cannot enable students to be multilingual and multiliterate: rather the qualifications, training and experience of the staff will enable such a development if the right conditions are available, chief among these being the attitude and support of the school head. Shaw emphasizes the need to 'turn top-down mandates into bottom-up commitment in order to benefit all students' (Shaw, 2003: 99).

ESL in the IB, especially the MYP, in international schools

The IB has become a franchised commodity, and thus is very much part of the hypercapitalist transition of society. ... The IB has an image, evident in articles in the popular press, of being a curriculum for 'high flyers'. This entrenched perception now looks difficult to reverse, and is a moot point for many international educators. ... The education of the global elite ... [contrasts] strikingly with the inclusive notion of global citizenship.

(Bunnell, 2008: 158)

The IB curriculum is a common feature in international schools and is well known to educators working in such schools, for whom it is an integral part of their daily lives. The middle years of schooling, grades 6–10, are crucial for second language students as they develop the language skills necessary for success in the various content areas. A large number of international schools follow the IBMYP, and its failure to provide a credible programme for SL students, or valid in-service training for SL teachers, is documented below. It is suggested that those who are not familiar with this programme visit the IB website, www.ibo.org (accessed 13 February 2018), in order to become acquainted with this component of international education.

IB structure for languages

The IB began as a two-year course for the final years of the upper school. Two of the six subjects studied were languages, defined as language A and language B. Language A was 'mother tongue'; language B was 'foreign language'. The IB set up a working group in the late 1980s to revise the Diploma Programme language A/language B model; its efforts came to fruition in 1996 with the introduction of language A2, which gave more choice to bilingual students, and the new system was taught successfully by many enlightened teachers.

The basis of the argument for the change is given in the following declaration:

> For the purpose of assessing language competence in international schools, a fundamental distinction needs to be enforced between the notion of second language academic proficiency and that of knowledge of a foreign language. The first notion relates specifically to the academic use of a non-native language which is practised through the study of curriculum subjects. The second notion refers to an ability to function in communication with speakers of another language outside the school. The emphases are different. In the case of a second language proficiency, the emphasis is on the high levels of competence required for academic use. In the case of the knowledge of a foreign language, the linguistic competence is expected to be confined to basic communicative tasks rather than sophisticated cognitive operations.
>
> (Tosi, 1991: 93)

This is a lucid statement on the fundamental distinction between foreign and second language. Thus the new scheme was language A1 for native speakers, language A2 for proficient bilinguals, and language B as a foreign language.

In the 1990s the IB expanded its curriculum downwards, introducing the MYP in 1994 and the PYP in 1997. In the MYP, which produced guides for language A and language B, there was also an initiative and working group to devise a guide for 'Second Language Acquisition and Mother Tongue Development' (SLA and MTD), of which I was a member. By this means, the MYP would mirror the DP; the SLA and MTD component would be the approximate equivalent of language A2. It appeared in 2004; professional development materials were developed to go with it and teachers, including myself, were trained to pass these on at workshops.

However, a change of structure, with a more corporate image, was to envelop the IB. In 2005 the IB board of governors decided to restructure the entire IB. For the first time a businessman (American), not an educationalist, was appointed as director general, and three new IB centres were established in the wealthiest or most influential parts of the globe (Bethesda, MD in the USA, Singapore in Asia, in Europe The Hague), superseding the old ones. Language A2 was phased out in the Diploma Programme, with a reversion to language A and language B. In the MYP the 'SLA and MTD Guide' was not updated in line with other subject guides and was apparently intentionally sidelined, along with the training materials: they are no longer available. At workshops, ESL teachers were directed to language B (reclassified in 2014 as 'language acquisition'; see below), which was meaningless to them as it was for 'foreign language', and the IB resolutely stated that 'there would never be separate provision for SL students' (Carder, 2013b).

Second language students in the MYP: Reviewing the path of the IB

The SLA and MTD Guide is little known, no longer appears on IB websites alongside the language A and language B guides, and has not been revised since 2004. It is an extremely useful guide, and the IB's 'disappearance' of it speaks volumes about the IB agenda on SL students. An email enquiry to the IB in March 2017 regarding the status of the SLA and MTD Guide received the reply that 'the email would be forwarded to a colleague for a response', but no more was heard.

As one of the contributors to the guide I can affirm that the working group intended to develop and expand the guide as the SL programme progressed in MYP schools. It was an excellent curriculum document, and formed a basis for sound, constructive practice for SL learners and teachers, including advice and examples for content teachers on how to adapt materials in each subject for SLLs. (I am in possession of the pdf.)

At workshops for MYP language B teachers (now language acquisition), to which teachers of ESL students are now directed, workshop leaders are continually reported by participants to have little knowledge of the needs of ESL students, and ESL teachers leave wondering where they should turn for appropriate IB training. Those developing the SLA and MTD guide started work on producing a whole package of materials for training, and teachers were trained to pass these on at workshops. However, these materials have never been used and were intentionally 'disappeared'. Nevertheless, they show conclusively that the IB was and is well aware of the separate role of a second language, and the need for a dedicated programme of instruction with its own materials, assessment and in-service training, because in the Introduction to the materials the following appeared:

> For a group of beginners (i.e. teachers), it is recommended to focus on the importance of providing second language and mother tongue programmes within the school and the reasons behind the IBO's advice to do this. It needs to be emphasized that MYP schools should be following the guidance provided by the IBO in *Second language Acquisition and Mother Tongue Development: a guide for schools* that was published in 2004. Activities could also be designed to give participants a basic awareness of what they can do within their classrooms and schools to complement second language and mother tongue programmes.

Various slides were prepared, and slide 13 states: 'For the purposes of the MYP, "second language" describes the language learned by students, for whom the LoI (Language of Instruction) is not their mother tongue, in order to follow the curriculum of the school.' Slide 21 states: 'Needs of second language learners: Second language learners need a well-planned and well-delivered curriculum enabling them to access, take part, and achieve success in the academic, social, and cultural life of the school.' Slide 25 states: 'An effective second language programme includes: Admissions policy; Provision for SL programme entry/exit and transition assistance; Integration of MYP objectives; Provision for varying proficiency levels; Inclusion of SL teachers in planning; Programme of communicative language learning (core and generic language skills); Reporting processes.'

Thus a comprehensive SL programme and documentation were all prepared, but never launched. No information was given to those who had participated in the scheme about its demise.

I wrote an article in which two and a half pages are devoted to the SLA and MTD Guide. The article points out:

> [The Guide] contains a statement on page 7 which says the Guide is 'a document reflective of the educational beliefs and values of the IBO and the principles of the MYP'. There follows: 'The IBO bases its guidance and recommendations on current academic research related to the particular issue of students acquiring the language of instruction in schools, and the importance of mother tongue maintenance and development'.
>
> (Carder, 2006: 117)

Then follows:

> Most importantly, there is a statement in bold type which reads that 'without such a second language programme, these students cannot participate fully in the social and cultural aspects of school life nor will they be able to reach their potential in the academic use of language in the curriculum.'
>
> (ibid.: 118)

This is a statement of confirmation by the IB that there should be a dedicated SL programme in the IBMYP, a policy that was dropped and denied without any official announcement.

As regards certification, it is emphasized that:

> Students must take both a language A and a language B to gain full MYP certification. The result could be that ESL students will not gain full certification. It is important that the IBO take a robust line on this matter, ensuring when accrediting MYP schools that progress is being made as regards the situation of ESL students, and that they are being given the opportunity to take their mother tongue as language A.
>
> (ibid.: 119)

Under 'Recommendations' (ibid.: 120) is written, 'Ensure that the Second Language Acquisition and Mother Tongue Development Guide is an integral part of the MYP programme.' None of these recommendations was carried out: instead, the SLA and MTD Guide was shunted into obscurity, along with the very recognition of SLLs as a body of learners who had specific, separate curriculum requirements.

Foreign language and second language: Essential pedagogical differences

It appears that there has been a misunderstanding on the part of the IB and others as regards how researchers approach the labelling of languages for research purposes, and how appropriate designs for pedagogical programmes provide a clear distinction between 'second' and 'foreign' language. Happily, the distinctions have been elucidated by Ortega (2013: 5), who writes that 'the term "L2" or "second/additional language" may mean the third, fourth, tenth and so on language learned later in life', but adds (ibid.: 6), 'it is important to realize that in SLA the term "second" (or "L2") is often used to mean "either a second or a foreign language" and often "both"'. Then, crucially, Ortega writes, 'distinguishing among specific contexts for L2 learning is in fact important. In such cases, SLA researchers make three (rather than only two) key contextual distinctions: foreign, second and heritage language learning contexts' (ibid.). Thus in 2013 an American researcher is reiterating the conclusion of Tosi in 1991, namely that there is a clear distinction between foreign and second language.

At present, SLLs – largely ESL students in international schools, as English is the language of instruction in some 90 per cent of these schools – are not given any special status or programme in the MYP as regards curriculum or assessment, the two prime areas that the IB delivers for its clientele. They are referred to the language B – now Language Acquisition – programme, one of the eight curriculum areas on the MYP octagon.

Language B students are those who are studying a foreign language. Typically they begin the language in Year 1 of the MYP (grade 6) and progress to Year 5 (grade 10), where they gain certification. MYP students are required to take a language B – now language acquisition – and follow the designated programme. Language B foreign-language students usually have three or four lessons a week throughout their five years, and the assessment criteria focus on their language competence as foreign-language speakers. Language B students do not require the language for use in school. They learn the language as one subject of many. The MYP provides a Guide for language B which is obligatory. When language B students leave the classroom they will often not use the language again until the next language lesson.

Second language students, on the other hand, come to a school with varying degrees of competence in the language, usually English, which will be required for *academic use in all school subjects*, in social use, and in almost every aspect of their lives, and will thus involve their emotional and cognitive selves. It may eventually become their best language and be used for academic advancement, leading to career choice and general usage. They can be described as 'developing language A students'. They need the language all day, every day for learning. Their goal is to develop native speaker-level, academic competence for success in the IBDP. Three or four lessons a week are totally inadequate. In addition, the rubrics used for grading language B in the MYP are totally unsuitable for students learning through the language of study.

The following comments by Cruickshank about schools in New Zealand reflect the stance adopted by the IB:

> [S]chools ... seem to have found it much easier to deal with 'multiculturalism' in broad brushstroke terms rather than the complexity and challenges of 'multilingualism' and the changes happening in communities. It still seems the case that if an Anglo-background student has access to travel and study overseas and has access to gaining language practices in other languages this would be construed as of benefit to school learning; for young people of bilingual/bicultural backgrounds these skills and experiences are constructed problematically or ignored.
>
> (Cruickshank, 2014: 60)

This could have been written for so many international schools, where proud parents focus on their children learning French as a foreign language, but allow their mother tongue(s) to wither, and are unaware of the many factors that would contribute to their children improving their academic knowledge of English in a professional ESL programme.

Ortega points out that over a period of five years, students learning a foreign language experience 540 hours of exposure to the FL, SL learners experience 7,000 hours of exposure to the SL, and native speakers experience 14,000 hours of exposure to their L1 (Ortega, 2013: 17).

Simply stating that 'all schools are expected to cater for SL/MT and all teachers are expected to implement SL teaching strategies' is naive. We know very well that many school leaders come from national systems in which SLLs are marginalized and 'supported' by untrained and unqualified teachers, and these leaders are often ignorant of the huge potential of ESL students in a well-planned programme.

To say that creating an entirely separate programme (a parallel MYP) would be an enormous undertaking, as a former IB source insinuated, makes it appear that ESL students would be totally segregated, whereas it is rather a question of communicating to schools that ESL students are in a different category from language B students as they have different and more urgent linguistic needs. They need above all recognition that they are in a separate category from foreign language students, and to be given an appropriate programme, which was, in fact, provided by the SLA and MTD guide.

International schools and national systems in the IB

In the IB Programme Standards and Practices (International Baccalaureate Organization, 2014), Standard C3:7 states: 'Teaching and learning addresses the diversity of student language needs, including those for students learning in a language(s) other than mother tongue'; this statement constitutes the entire IBMYP ESL programme – which can simply be ignored with little fear of IB sanctions. The IB appears to have bent to the demands of a national system, that of the US, and placed the international schools network low on its list of priorities. Cambridge (2013: 174) notes that 'about 300 IB schools were international schools in 2004. This figure has fallen dramatically as a proportion from ... 58% in 1979 ... and is expected to be just 5% by 2020.' He goes on more forcefully to question:

> To what extent does an organization such as the IB, as it is currently constituted, continue to serve the needs of international schools and their students? As the IB continues to penetrate national systems, and adapts its distributive, recontextualizing and evaluative practices in order to accommodate the demands of local, national, official, pedagogic recontextualization fields, a critical question needs to be asked: Will the programmes of the IB continue to be fit for the purpose of international education, as practised in international schools?
>
> (Cambridge, 2013: 201)

The answer for the ESL community of students and teachers is a resounding 'no'.

The need for a dedicated ESL programme of instruction in the MYP

All evidence points to the need for ESL students to have content-related instruction. Crawford and Krashen (2007: 44) state: 'For diverse schools, a program of communication-based ESL and sheltered subject-matter instruction, combined with native-language support by paraprofessionals, is often the best solution'. Janzen (2008: 1030, quoted in Scanlan and López, 2012: 601–2) writes, 'The academic uses of language as well as the meaning of individual words need to be *explicitly taught* for students to fulfil the genre or discourse requirements privileged in academic settings and to understand the material they encounter' (emphasis added). This is a strong statement of the need for professional ESL instruction. Above all, a different mode of assessment is required for ESL students in the MYP, and ESL teachers need separate training workshops from those for language B/Acquisition.

Another issue is that, to qualify for full certification at the end of MYP Year 5, students must have completed study in language A. For ESL students this means their mother tongue. Most international schools (regrettably) do not offer such courses. This means that ESL students would not qualify for full certification – after working diligently at their English language skills. This once again peripheralizes, stigmatizes and demotivates ESL students – the very students who are at the core of international schools – by making them the only ones not to qualify for full MYP certification.

International schools, though they provided the original inspiration for the IB, made up only 12 per cent of the IB clientele in 2009 (Matthews, 2009), and this is falling. However, it has been suggested (V. Edwards, 2009) that we live in an age of 'superdiversity', implying that ESL students are on the increase in national systems as much as in international schools. Crawford and Krashen (2007: 13) estimate that 33 per cent of students in the USA will be ELLs by 2043. Therefore it may be thought to be in the interests of the IB to devise a specific response to the curriculum and assessment needs of ESL students – but it should be borne in mind that ESL students in national systems may not be in the same socioeconomic bracket.

The IB and critical thinking

One much-vaunted educational aim of the IB is to encourage critical thinking in students: 'The IB has always championed a stance of critical engagement with challenging ideas' (International Baccalaureate Organization, 2015: 1). This is a commendable and valid aim, but for those who do not have the language of instruction, usually English, at an advanced level, it will remain an often unachievable one. Monaghan writes:

> [S]chooling is fundamentally a linguistic process with students needing to be able (and to be enabled) to deploy linguistic resources that grow ever more complex alongside the increasing cognitive demands of ever-expanding specialized subject knowledge. In fact, a case can be made that it is the linguistic complexity of how ideas are expressed within subject disciplines rather than the nature of those ideas themselves that presents the greater

source of difficulty for students. As Schleppergrell (2004: 2) argues: 'Students' difficulties in "reasoning", for example, may be due to their lack of familiarity with the linguistic properties of the language through which the reasoning is expected to be presented, rather than to the inherent difficulty of the cognitive processes involved.'

> This is especially true of bilingual students, who may already be familiar with the concepts in their first language.
>
> (Monaghan, 2010: 24)

The IB has produced some interesting papers that make it clear that IB students in all their diversity are multilingual and that multilingualism is a resource for the IB vision (International Baccalaureate Organization, 2006, 2008a, 2008b, 2011, 2014, 2015). However, it is the daily routine and specific programmes that are the lifeblood of teachers' and students' lives in schools, and, comprehensive as stance papers may be, the reality in schools is not driven by distant rhetoric. A distinct curriculum and assessment are needed for ESL students in the MYP. Any policy will depend on its detail, its relevance, and above all its obligatory implementation in a school as a programme: otherwise it is simply one more piece of paper to add to the administrator's file and ticked during the ten-yearly authorization visit.

A review of journal articles about the IB provides useful insights into why such a separate area may not be being instituted. Doherty writes:

> I do not want to diminish what the IB may offer its students, but I do want to highlight how its current appeal stems not so much from its internal design as from its opportunistic fulfilment of a number of current political agendas. ... Parents will be buying the gift-wrapped promise constructed in the media before sampling the actual product, and having invested in that choice will carefully protect and promote their chosen brand and their high-stakes investment in its forms of distinction.
>
> (Doherty, 2009: 85–6)

Bunnell (2011) also notes, with reference to the huge, rapid expansion of the IB, that since late 2008, a new phenomenon has appeared – a willingness by IB insiders (mainly head teachers in international schools, such as Toze and Matthews) to openly voice concern about the growth, and their perception of quality being compromised.

It is possible to conclude from these insights that, since the IB is focusing more on a particular type of clientele, the majority of whom are now middle-class and in North America, having a set curriculum and programme for ESL students would diminish the marketing potential of the IB in the USA context, where ESL students are seen as immigrants.

The reality of ESL in practice in the MYP

An ESL teacher in a large international school in Asia summarizes the reality of working with ESL students in the MYP context, in answer to questions submitted by me:

> *Why does the IB not provide separate programmes for second language students in the MYP?*
>
> Having worked now in the IB in three different international schools, I believe the IB does not distinguish language differences of ESL and Language Acquisition/B students because although there is a clearly defined difference in pedagogy, there is not one acknowledged in the IB that would create an existence for ESL. It does not fit the octagon (the MYP scheme of subjects) and with the mantra 'all teachers are language teachers' the IB also allows for disjointed flexibility because the job does not fall on one subject, but on all. This is an ideology I agree with, but along with an ESL department and ESL teachers to engage in dialog with subject teachers to enhance the learning of ESL students.
>
> The change of name in 2014 reinforced this trend. To take the title Language B and change it to Language Acquisition (LA) ticks off the box in terms of ESL support in the program. The course is now seen as 'having aligned goals' like that of any ESL/EAL program because the definition of LA is 'one acquiring a language'. No longer is there a focus on which language is studied and for what purpose, so again the IB allows for individual schools to set up ESL support/programs that are using language acquisition as the framework with which to guide the curriculum.
>
> Oddly, semantics plays a bigger part now in the argument of whether ESL should stand alone as a separate group within the IB: they use it to argue that it does not interfere with the policy that all teachers teach language, the terminology – Language Acquisition – and the fact that most schools do not dispute the use of Language Acquisition along with Foreign Language as two opposing subjects with differing objectives in their schools.

The creation of 'Language Acquisition' by the IB as a stand-alone term is interesting. It echoes 'Second Language Acquisition', but since the IB does not want to recognize the separate status of ESL students it has manufactured its own terminology, which sounds credible. There is a field of First Language Acquisition, which researches children's mother tongues, and one of Second Language Acquisition, already discussed. In most cases, 'Language acquisition' is a general term which covers all aspects of learning a language. However, Krashen (1982) makes a distinction between 'language learning' and 'language acquisition', declaring that acquisition is a subconscious process, while learning is conscious. He believes that acquisition is more important, as the competence developed through it is responsible for generating language and thereby accounts for language fluency. He proposes that language acquisition develops exclusively through 'comprehensible input', by which he implies that SLLs acquire language competence by exposure to language that is at the same time understandable and meaningful. How this takes place is summarized in Krashen's formula of $i + 1$, where i is the student's current level of competence. 'Language acquisition' therefore can be understood in two senses, either as a general term to cover language learning, or in the specific sense of Krashen's terminology. The IB avoids the issue in order not to have to recognize the fundamental differences in pedagogy and student needs between second and foreign language. Using 'Language Acquisition' sounds progressive and non-divisive: who could argue against not discriminating about how one is learning a new language? But the reality is that it is a contested term, and SL learners are meanwhile left in a morass of specialized language for the various content subjects which they cannot surmount effectively.

The same teacher continues:

> My question would be: are they using titles like Language Acquisition – Language and Literature – and the fact that all teachers are language teachers in the IB to justify an inferred support of ESL students within the programmes?

> We use the Language Acquisition rubrics for both English (ESL) and Foreign Language, and in all discussions admin sees the two as the same as far as subjects are concerned: in Grading and Accreditation especially. They are all in one subject group and evaluated together. This is not disputed by anyone anymore.

> With all of the vague terminologies floating around the responsibility then becomes that of the individual schools and how

they interpret and initiate their ESL programmes based on the IB framework and philosophy. As long as it looks complimentary to the IBMYP/DP, it is a go for schools and they can create anything they want, or not.

Teachers make it work because they have to get on with the job of educating these students and arguing that ESL and FL are not the same gets you nowhere. ESL teachers may create ESL programmes in spite of the numerous hurdles set in front of them. If the IB cannot see the value in a separate ESL programme in the IB, then the teachers must create the value and curriculum from the MYP framework and make it work.

Any created programme, of course, will not be an approved IB programme so it once again puts ESL students and their teachers in the peripheral box; and many ESL teachers will not 'create ESL programmes in spite of the numerous hurdles set in front of them', as their directors may not allow them to. The teacher continues:

Also, the IB does not look at ESL as a subject group – primarily because it seems they feel these students are 'on the journey to Language and Literature' [the terminology of language A in the Diploma Programme] – and again the distinction of A and B no longer applies as the new title suggests the continuation of Language Learning within a classroom setting. It could be argued that this then is a program for second language students – *but in reality it is a foreign language program adjusted to meet the expectations of the ESL students.*

For example, my school has done the following:

–   Foreign Languages uses Phases 1–3
–   EAL Phases 3–4
–   Language Acquisition Phases 4–6;

'4' being the transition for EAL students to enter into Lang Acquisition [the IBMYP has given six levels of achievement or 'phases' within 'Language Acquisition', 1–6, beginners to fluent]; the oddity about this set-up is that the students who have achieved Phase 4 status are then taken out of EAL and are Language Acquisition students of the MYP, thus they receive no EAL support at this point. The students do not have an identity as ESL students once they hit Phase 4. They are seen as mainstream students and are expected to do the same work. If you take a look at the expected MYP skills of a phase 4 student one has to ask if the level of proficiency corresponds with the programme's academic expectations? Is this all the students need in English to succeed as a fully enrolled MYP student? For me, the evidence is in the writing as our students are across the board weak academic writers and the EAL students who float year to year are not really prepared for the expectations of the MYP by the time they reach Phase 4, or the DP as they enter 11th grade, but they are assessed as if they were. No modifications; no altered assessments: they are MYP students and sit in classes with this understanding.

This is where the failure of the MYP to provide a *second* language programme is shown to have profoundly negative consequences for ESL students, affecting their potential in the entire school curriculum, and perhaps their entire lives.

Why is there no separate assessment for second language students?

Having been in three international schools now with all three programmes: it is not about separate assessments, but differentiation and modification and whether this is applicable in the classroom environment. If provided, ESL students can work to achieve grades that sustain motivation; if not, they are demotivated by low marks.

The interesting challenge with this is that differentiation seems to mean various things to teachers and admin. We spent a good amount of time one semester in P[rofessional] D[evelopment] meetings trying to define the following terms: differentiation, inclusion, and modification. It was enlightening to see the various definitions and the various ways with which teachers used the terms in their classrooms, if at all.

Another issue that arises is the use of modification or better yet, the lack of it in assessments. In recent years, the mere mention of the word gets an awkward reaction. If teachers were to work with a framework that excludes separate assessment would it not be beneficial to modify assessments to meet the needs of the ESL students? And why is this a scary concept when discussed? What does modification mean to teachers/administration and students?

Why has the IB downplayed the SLA and MTD Guide mentioned above? Why is there no separate in-service training for ESL teachers?

This also addresses the question with regard to the IBMYP 'Second Language Acquisition and Mother Tongue Development Guide'. This guide supports and promotes modification in all subjects and even gives examples as to how to do this. No workshop in the last four years that I have attended has mentioned this guide or its use in the MYP or DP. [These comments were made in 2015.]

Again, every IBMYP international school should have a curriculum that follows the MYP framework, but also is intertwined with a scope and sequence that may not have ESL students in mind. For teachers, this is a challenge as they must adhere to the MYP framework, and the scope and sequence (whatever it may be), as well as differentiate for ESL and SEN, usually in the same classroom. At times, it gets blurry. It can be argued that this allows for better differentiation, but this depends on the development of the MYP planners and the intricacy of the ESL/differentiation section of the MYP planner.

What is the response of the IB to those criticisms of poor certification for ESL students with regard to both ESL and MT?

These are my impressions of the IB in MYP: I do not believe the IB even addresses this issue – do they even feel it deserves discussion? Most schools today just manipulate the framework to make it work as best it can for the sake of the ESL students in their school. So why would the IB acknowledge it as an issue? Everyone teaches with it, and without viable data from ESL communities how does one go about proving the framework excludes students who are at this very moment in programs in the MYP in ESL?

These comments are from a highly qualified and experienced ESL teacher, and give a true insight into the reality of provision (mostly lack of) for ESL students in the MYP in international schools in every aspect: pedagogy, programme provision, assessment, and in-service training for teachers. Some contributors to these vignettes have complained that ESL colleagues 'back down at the slightest hint of confrontation'. While one appreciates the frustration that goes into such a statement, so many ESL teachers seem to have been threatened that it is understandable why they would back down.

The language competences of students confused with appropriate pedagogical instruction

At a conference for ESL teachers in 2014 an IB spokesperson said that the IB was not in a position to differentiate between foreign language and second language as 'the IB was a global organization and such differentiation was not appropriate'. However, the IB finds it appropriate to distinguish between language A and language B in the Diploma Programme so the somewhat bizarre argument is flawed; globalization now has a new trend, apparently, namely deciding how to define languages. The IB seems to be confused about the difference between the *repertoires* of students, and the *types of pedagogy* they are best served by. Of course, seen as a whole, a cohort of students in any international school will have a range of language competencies from almost no knowledge of English to a high level of literacy. But this does not reduce the need to provide appropriate *programmes of instruction* for the various types of learners. It is one thing for students to have different levels of *competence* in a language; it is quite another thing for them to receive *appropriate pedagogical instruction* in each language according to their needs. The most important factor in any school is the structure of the programme students are taught in. This needs to be clearly identified. The IB has failed in the MYP to provide any programme structure at all for *second language* learners, who need it more urgently than any other students.

It should by now be common knowledge that 'Teachers must provide ESL students with content-specific academic language instruction to support their performance on content area assessments' (Kieffer *et al.*, 2009, quoted in Scanlan and López, 2012: 597). However, the MYP proffers the model noted by Cummins:

> The typical picture is that assessment regimens are initially mandated by the central authority with vague directions regarding the criteria for exemption of certain students or for accommodations of various kinds for students who might be unable to participate in the assessment without support, for example some ELL students.
>
> (Cummins, 2000: 145)

This statement is echoed by V. Edwards, who writes, 'policy-makers have repeatedly failed to predict the resources and the strategies required to deal with new demands, responding in piecemeal fashion with bolt-on "solutions"', which may 'pathologize language learners' (Edwards, 2010: xiii).

SLLs and the IBMYP: Examples of how the programme impacts on them

In the MYP all students have to reflect on all tasks and in all subject areas, and even for maths assignments grades are given for their depth of reflection. Thus ESL students with good maths skills but as yet undeveloped English language skills get dragged down by the 'reflection' grade. ESL students have difficulties even understanding the language of the criteria descriptions.

Teachers at one school commented:

> The problem with MYP for ESL students, really, is the fact that they need to write reflections in every single subject, even PE, IT, and cooking. With all the different criteria the amount of assessments has increased a lot, and ESL students are adversely affected. They also have to write a reflection for everything.

And:

> My 10th grade Japanese ESL students are seriously good at math but get lower grades because they can't write a reflection. I tried to modify the criteria for the math reflection, and then sat down with the head of math to talk it through. It soon became clear that I had not understood what was required; my simplification had lost the original meaning (which it took quite a while for the head of math to get me to understand). I went off to re-write the simplified criteria and now cannot remember what the thing really means. I did 'A' level math, I am a native speaker – and *I* don't get it.

A teacher at another school observed:

> The language of MYP 'ideas' is a major source of difficulty for ESL students. One quick look at the language makes it clear that for an ESL student the IT Design Cycle presents a linguistic challenge. The cycle revolves around the four key ideas: 'Investigate – plan – create – evaluate'. The command words alone are a challenge: 'identify, develop, formulate, design, create and evaluate' are all words which need careful, simplified explanations, together with the corresponding mother tongue translations.

Another teacher at the same school remarked:

> A good example of how only supplying a dictionary definition
> can confuse ESL students is this: the definition of access is 'being
> able to get into something'. The MYP visual supplied for the ESL
> students was a key to open a door, but the topic being studied
> was 'Access to Water', so that not only the definition but also the
> visual was misleading.

Another commented:

> A great number of subject teachers, for instance maths teachers,
> don't realize that students are being bombarded with lots of new
> words every day, not just in their subject. The solution is for ESL
> Beginners not to get grades in their mainstream subjects. They
> should not be punished by getting lower grades for not knowing
> vocabulary or for not being able to deal with the reflections.

An MYP ESL teacher commented: 'I saw all the IT jargon in my students'
booklets and even I had problems understanding what the design brief and
the specifications were. How do you explain this to a beginner?' Another
reported: 'In PE students have to write hockey tests, so if a student doesn't
have good language skills, especially beginners, they get low grades in PE, a
subject where ESL beginners could easily get good grades and feel proud of
themselves.' Her conclusion was:

> I think that more schools should give the MYP critical feedback.
> Our school is trying to deal with the problems but not with the
> source of them. We're expected to incorporate into our teaching
> whatever the MYP expects from us, but this is not in the best
> interests of the ESL students.

Meier (2014: 135) notes that 'Clearly, curricula need to be evaluated,
reviewed and adjusted.'

IB terminology on language as a contributor to misdirected programmes

Terminology in the field of language learning and linguistics is vast and
complex (a prime reason, it has to be emphasized again, for having people
who are qualified in this area teach ESL students). The IB has chosen one
term, 'language acquisition', as the umbrella term for all matters concerning
the learning of languages, foreign or second, and as the replacement term
for language B in the MYP, as shown here:

Language acquisition

The study of additional languages in the Middle Years Programme (MYP) provides students with the opportunity to develop insights into the features, processes and craft of language and the concept of culture, and to realize that there are diverse ways of living, viewing and behaving in the world.

MYP language acquisition is a compulsory component of the MYP in every year of the programme. Schools must provide sustained language learning in at least two languages for each year of the MYP.

(http://ibo.org/en/programmes/middle-years-programme/curriculum/
language-acquisition/, accessed 13 February 2018)

There is no distinction between foreign and second language learning, while the wording of the first paragraph above is clearly geared to foreign-language learning. SL learners need more precisely determined goals or curriculum objectives, not insights.

Thus, by using the umbrella term 'language acquisition', and ignoring the vast literature which has laid down separate paths for first language acquisition (MT), second language acquisition, and foreign-language learning, the IB not only shows its lack of understanding of what the term implies, i.e. picking up a language through usage rather than learning it through instruction, but has also failed to provide an appropriate programme for SL students, or provide assessment geared to their needs.

Correspondence continues to flood in from distressed ESL teachers in MYP schools around the world. For example: 'I cannot manage to make people understand that EAL is not English B. In my opinion, it is a different subject.'

The following information was sent from a large international school:

Mother Tongues

We have established ten home languages (MTs) under the MYP Language Literature programme. All languages taught in MYP5 go through the moderation process and the students have IB Approved on their certificate.

However, *The Next Chapter*, an IB communication which is now working towards the e-assessment/portfolio arrangement for MYP5, has now dictated that only specific languages can be assessed. We are now in a position that we have to inform parents, who have committed to our home language programme, that the language doesn't count and they have to reconsider their child's package. The students must have an A and B language and some students just don't have both because they are SL Learners. In a nutshell we now have five out of nine languages that are impacted by this decision so this completely contradicts any IB statements about promoting the maintenance of home languages.

This is a crystal-clear description of how ESL students are disadvantaged – the very students who need more encouragement because of the huge task that faces them of learning an entire curriculum in a second language. It reveals the complete lack of understanding that the curriculum providers have of the context of international schools, where most students have English as a second language and are actively maintaining literacy in their mother tongue.

The MYP Language Acquisition Guide can be seen at www.csdecou. qc.ca/ecolesecondairerochebelle/files/2014/05/Language-acquisition-guide-For-use-from-September-2014.pdf (accessed 13 February 2018). It gives detailed instructions on the six phases that can be followed in language acquisition. The language that describes the progression through these levels is carefully modulated to present a continuous flow, as if students naturally swim majestically from phase 1 in MYP Language Acquisition to language A in the Diploma. There is no indication of the need for carefully structured courses, or of the difference between learning a foreign language a few times a week and learning a second language for every content area. In addition it is acceptable to differentiate between A and B at Diploma level, but not at MYP level. On page 4 this Guide states again that language is central to critical thinking. This needs to be emphasized to the writers of the Guide: how can second language learners achieve a level of language in English that will enable them to be critical thinkers when they do not have an instructional programme that is geared to their linguistic needs?

Another teacher writes:

Throughout the year the MYP has been the thorn in our side when it comes to meeting the language needs of our students. The MYP Language Acquisition phases are geared towards the holy grail of literature and seem to neglect the real journey of language learning with its many variables and need for time.

It is safe to say we have endured the MYP and fulfilled tasks such as unit planning and MYP5 moderation as a mere administrative exercise. Behind the scenes we have dug our heels in and stayed true to the real needs of the ELL students. I cannot believe that we are having to fight for the needs of our students because our programme provider has no understanding of the complexities and nature of acquiring the language of instruction at an international school.

The above extract best sums up the failure of the MYP to either understand or provide appropriate programmes for ESL students in international schools. Conteh and Meier comment (2014: 3), citing Trowler (2003: 96), 'There is often a conflict between those who make policy and those who put it into practice.'

Many more such communications have been received, but the senders have requested that their comments are not published as they fear reprisals.

By sowing the seeds of doubt about SL issues, educational organizations can claim that 'there is no consensus on the best method', thereby laying the ground for whatever suits their needs best; in the case of the CIS and the NEASC, accreditation services for international schools, this means putting ESL students under 'support services', and in the case of the IBMYP they are included under the catch-all of 'language acquisition'.

Concluding statement

Until about 2004 the input of ESL professionals was welcomed by both the CIS and the IB. How could the advice of these experts, nurtured and respected to a fault up to that time, have then been so comprehensively ignored and emphatically discarded? The answers seem to come from the nature of neoliberal economics and its bedfellow managerialism, which have dominated institutions since the 1970s and have been embraced and promoted by the corporations. It shifted the right to make many decisions about the world away from the people who were involved with the fundamental knowledge of each profession and towards unelected bodies.

The market orientation of the IB can be demonstrated easily enough simply by looking at its establishment of the three global IB centres: Bethesda, MD, Singapore, and The Hague. The absorption of the IB by American leadership has allowed it to distort debate on educational matters by narrowing the discussion of issues to the technical problem-solving level, thereby denying the possibility of major conflicts in problem definition and pedagogical values. Thus the way the IB has established methods of communication undermines the very preconditions for communicatively rational queries. There is simply no way in which implicit validity claims pertaining to the truth, appropriateness or sincerity of statements made by the IB can be challenged, as communication goes almost entirely in one direction, from the IB website to school directors, to leaders, to teachers; students bear the consequences – though of course there is always the opportunity to chat on the websites.

The IB encourages critical thinking for its students: 'The IB has always championed a stance of critical engagement with challenging ideas' (International Baccalaureate Organization, 2015: 1). Iain McGilchrist has written interestingly about this area from the point of view of a humanist scholar and psychiatrist (McGilchrist, 2009). He traces the history of philosophy and relates it to the left and right hemispheres of the brain. He concludes that the right hemisphere, which governs how we see the world and feel empathy, and was originally the basis of humanity, is being taken over by the left hemisphere, which seeks control and power – and systems.

The world of education is already rubbing shoulders with the people who, in the words of Noam Chomsky, 'manufacture consent' (Herman and Chomsky, 2002). Children in schools are already working from multinational media companies' digital worksheets disguised as 'innovative learning', and education has ever less need for qualified teachers as students will need no more than a minder to check that the student in question is glued to a tablet. The IB claims to be something better, encouraging a critical approach to what is learned. John Stuart Mill (1869: 94) pointed out that truths that were not subject to continual challenge eventually '[cease] to have the effect of truth, by being exaggerated into falsehood'.

As will be related in the following chapter, a viable alternative for SLLs and their teachers can be found in the ESL examinations offered by Cambridge International.

Part Five

The current situation in an
international school

Chapter 7

How one international school is implementing the model proposed in this book

Sarah Porter

Bringing the issues alive

When I arrived at my present school in August 2013, I was not a likely candidate to implement change in an EAL department. I had trained as a Secondary MFL (Modern Foreign Languages) teacher, not in EAL, and the only experience I had of ESL learners at that time was a year and a half spent teaching English in a school in Russia. However, when I joined this school there was no room for me in the MFL department and I was offered a job teaching secondary EAL. 'As long as you think I can do it' was my nervous response. This turned out to be one of the best career choices I have ever made, as I fell in love with EAL teaching as soon as I started it.

As much as I was inspired by EAL, though, I sometimes felt that what I was teaching, and how I was teaching it, was not enough. From the perspective of teaching English grammar and vocabulary, things seemed OK and the students were progressing. However, I was often asked by subject teachers to give an EAL student 'help with her science/history/geography' and so on. I assumed that the student would turn up to my room with her textbook, and that I could read through the information with her and try to clarify the parts that she found tricky. This did help, to an extent, but having had no experience of ESL content support, though I knew that I could do more, I was not sure what that 'more' was. The other issue that I faced was one that is experienced by EAL teachers worldwide: because of timetabling issues I often had lessons with a group of Year 7 students, a Year 9 student and two Year 11s, all at different levels, all studying different topics and all in the same forty-minute lesson. Trying to teach anybody anything in lessons like these was a real challenge and was immensely frustrating for all concerned.

I was then fortunate enough to attend the ECIS ESL and Mother Tongue Conference in Amsterdam in 2014. I gained a wealth of information about content language teaching and was determined to take as much of it as possible back to my school. In a highly informative session, Patricia Mertin advised that I try to teach just one year group per lesson in order to focus on content support. Fortunately, back at school an EAL teaching assistant was allocated some EAL lessons on her timetable, and this enabled us to mostly split lessons into separate year groups.

The ECIS conference also helped me realize that when it came to content language teaching, what our EAL students really needed, and were not getting, was proper, structured and targeted content language teaching. Such lessons involve, among other things: strategies for memorizing and practising key words, phrases and definitions; learning general academic language; deconstructing exam-style questions; and learning to structure sentences and paragraphs in a logical way in order to answer written questions fully and effectively. In this way, our school has transformed 'a bit of help with history' into structured content language teaching, which is a key responsibility for us as EAL teachers.

The benefits of having NNESTs

As a native English speaker myself, I attended secondary school in the 1980s when English grammar was not taught explicitly. Like many other native speakers of my generation, I therefore had no idea how to explain tense use, adverb phrases or comparatives – I used them correctly automatically, but could never have taught them to a non-native English speaker. In international schools where many EAL teachers do not have a specific ESL qualification, teachers like myself are often consigned to learning English grammar and vocabulary rules 'on the job'. Is this how our ESL students should be taught?

In his presentation to the Council of British International Schools (COBIS) EAL Conference in February 2017, Maurice Carder discussed 'the myth of the native speaker' (Carder, 2017a). For me, this raised two important points: first, the perceived 'necessity' for international schools to employ native English speakers as ESL/EAL teachers; second, the fact that some international schools boast 'native-speaker teachers' in order to market the school. 'There is a monolingual bias in research and practice on language learning and teaching which has deeply negative consequences' (Ortega, 2014: 32, quoted in Carder, 2017a: 32). As a result, parents and students alike become convinced that ESL teachers especially must be native speakers, thus perpetuating the 'myth'.

My present school is fortunate enough not to be propagating the native-speaker myth, as we recognize that there is a wealth of superb EAL teachers whose first language is not English. In my time at the school alone, I have worked closely with three non-native teachers, all of whom are fluent English speakers and all of whom are excellent EAL classroom practitioners.

So what are the benefits of having NNESTs teaching ESL? It has become clear at this school that they are abundant. First, having studied English to such a high level, our teachers have a clear grasp of the structure of English grammar and vocabulary, far clearer than the average native speaker's. In addition, many hold a specialized ESL teaching qualification such as the Certificate in English Language Teaching to Adults (CELTA) – as is the case at this school – which ensures clear and effective teaching of English grammar and vocabulary rules. Moreover, being already bilingual, our NNESTs have first-hand knowledge of second language acquisition and are therefore well equipped to understand our students' learning journey, being able to foresee and empathize with any pitfalls they may come across.

In today's global society, the number of people in the world who speak English as a second language is far greater than the number of native English speakers, and I believe that our non-native-speaker EAL teachers serve as excellent examples for our students, demonstrating that bi- and multilingualism are not only possible, but also beneficial and indeed necessary. Furthermore, they show students that you do not necessarily need to aspire to being a quasi-'native'; you can achieve an exceptional standard of English as a *second* language while still preserving the mother tongue, culture and identity.

This is, of course, not to say that native English speakers have no place in ESL teaching. But it is a dangerous fallacy to assume that a native speaker has a knowledge of English superior to a non-native speaker's, or indeed has the necessary skills to teach it. For me, whether they are native speakers or not, *all* ESL teachers should hold a specialist qualification and ideally have experience of learning another language to a high level. There are too many teachers in international schools who have taught 'a bit of EAL' at some point, in addition to their completely different specialist subject: the schools rely purely on the fact that they are native English speakers and fill gaps in the EAL timetable with inexperienced, unqualified (but native-speaker!) staff. If EAL departments are to become centres of excellence in international schools, as they should be, the native-speaker myth needs to stop now, and schools must focus on establishing specialist ESL departments filled with specialist ESL teachers.

Building up content materials for the upper school, and sharing them worldwide with other international schools

One of the key issues facing secondary EAL content teachers is a real dearth of published resources. In a webinar I delivered for COBIS in September 2017, I stated that it can sometimes be difficult for EAL teachers not to cross over from content language support into actually trying to teach the content itself. It has certainly happened to me when, in the middle of an EAL science lesson, I have suddenly found myself trying to explain a scientific concept to the students (badly!). We are not content teachers, we are language teachers, but there is a distinct lack of available resources to help us to deliver effective content support lessons.

This school has responded to the above challenge by developing a range of content language resources, covering the different secondary year groups, academic subjects and subtopics. Of course, syllabuses change, teaching materials change, and students' needs change, but having a central bank of resources as a starting point is extremely useful – and we are adding to it year by year. However, the next issue that needs addressing is that there are EAL teachers in international schools all over the world 'reinventing the wheel', all creating similar resources which only their school will use. I recently created a resource to support students with key words for the topic of 'Roman life' in Year 7 history, and it can be guaranteed that EAL teachers in other schools have done exactly the same. There is a wealth of expertly produced resources out there, and EAL teachers need to be able to share and access them.

As a partial solution to this, the COBIS EAL Facebook group was established in the autumn of 2017. The group is intended to be a place where EAL teachers in COBIS schools can connect with each other, offer advice and suggestions, and upload and download resources. The group is very much in its infancy at the time of writing, but my hope is that this little community will attract more members and become a hub of EAL advice and teaching resources. That said, however, the ideal solution would be for ESL to be recognized as a valid, routine part of the curriculum, which would open the door to a properly structured syllabus with readily available resources.

The benefits of the Cambridge IGCSE: The importance of equal status for ESL students

In my third year at this school, I was offered a new challenge: teaching an ESL IGCSE class (www.cambridgeinternational.org/programmes-and-qualifications/cambridge-secondary-2/cambridge-igcse/, accessed

13 February 2018). Although I jumped at the chance, I did not have much to go on except a brief scheme of work and possibly the most tedious textbook I had ever seen. As this course had previously been taught solely by our school's English department, I had never seen an ESL examination paper before and so had to brush up quickly on the skills I was expected to teach.

We rejected the textbook and used other resources to teach the necessary vocabulary, grammar and skills, and the students seemed to both enjoy and benefit from the course. What was surprising were the similarities between the skills taught in the IGCSE course and the techniques that students need to learn when preparing for the International English Language Testing System (IELTS) test (www.ielts.org, accessed 13 February 2018). Granted, the IGCSE is broader than and not as specialized or advanced as IELTS, but the foundations are there: developing students' awareness of synonyms and paraphrases to help identify a missing word in a text or a multiple-choice answer; teaching formal, academic language to write a discursive article or essay, and so on. It became clear to me that the skills taught in this course were of key importance to our ESL students as they moved on to Key Stage 5 (the final stage of the English secondary school system), the IELTS test and higher education.

Having now taught this course for the last three years, I have become convinced that the ESL IGCSE should come permanently under an ESL department's teaching remit. What are the reasons for this? First, as stated above, there are numerous parallels between the skills needed for IGCSE and for the IELTS test, which many ESL students are nowadays required to take for university entrance purposes in the UK. Since IELTS is usually taught by an ESL teacher, it makes complete sense to bring the IGCSE under the same umbrella rather than allocating the course to an English 'first-language' teacher who may well never have taught the course before and may never have to teach it again. ESL teachers can, by building up year after year of experience, training and resources, turn the ESL department into a specialized 'centre of expertise' for delivering both the IGCSE and IELTS courses.

Second, it would appear that many first-language English teachers view the IGCSE Second Language as a less desirable option and would rather not teach it, preferring to focus on literature. After all, English teachers' specialism is English as a first language and English literature; they generally do not receive training in ESL and they are expected to teach the IGCSE Second Language solely because of the word 'English' in the title. ESL teachers, however, are generally much more used to teaching the skills required, can identify particular vocabulary or grammar areas which may come up or cause problems, and have a range of tried and tested strategies for targeted vocabulary and grammar practice. Above all, we *want* to teach it!

Finally, moving the IGCSE Second Language away from the English department into ESL may help prevent it from becoming a 'sink group'. In my experience, rather than being put in a lower-ability First Language set, lower-ability students are placed in the English as a Second Language group, regardless of their actual level of English. By doing this, are we not short-changing both our lower-ability students and our ESL learners? Surely students of lower academic ability should have access to a differentiated English as a first language course which focuses on both language and literature, while ESL students should benefit from a course that is specifically aimed at non-native speaker students of all abilities, including A* candidates?

The overriding necessity of CALP and academic language acquisition, and the need for *all* teachers to have CPD in these

A key tenet of Mertin's (2013) book *Breaking through the Language Barrier* is the need for subject teachers to simplify the language rather than the content when teaching EAL students. It is imperative for teachers to simplify CALP-level words so that EAL students can understand their meaning and therefore access the lesson more easily, without dumbing down the content.

Both EAL and content teachers then need to take this one step further. What we try to do at my school is to simplify the word, but once a student has understood the meaning, they are asked to learn the original word and encouraged to use it actively in their writing, whether this be a piece of homework from the subject that the word first appeared in, or something completely different, such as a piece of creative writing in English. The key point here is that practice makes perfect, and if our EAL students use new academic vocabulary in as many ways as they can, these words will be established in their long-term memory. In this way, we are bridging the gap between BICS and CALP right from the start, and this will, hopefully, pave the way to greater success later. After all, our EAL students will sit the same IGCSE examinations as their native-speaker friends, and have to understand the same CALP-level vocabulary. Gradually building on our students' academic vocabulary from as early as possible is, I believe, one way to ensure a solid transition from BICS to CALP.

A story to illustrate the above point comes from the head of humanities. He realized the importance of reinforcing the 'proper' word when he was reading a story to his young daughter. He saw the word 'enchantress', decided against saying it and instead used the simpler word 'witch'. However, he then turned the page, and there was the word 'enchanted'! His daughter didn't understand it, and my colleague wished that he had said the correct word in the first place and explained that it meant 'witch', so that his little girl could have made the connection between 'enchanted' and 'enchantress'.

My colleague did say at the time of telling me this, 'It's not really such a big deal – after all, she's only four!' But the point is that our 11-year-old secondary EAL students do not have this luxury of time. This is why, as EAL teachers, we need to know how to turn enchantresses into witches, but to then quickly turn them back into enchantresses.

The need to make an EAL department a centre of expertise

In a recent speech to the CIS (Carder, 2017b), Carder called for ESL departments to be 'centres of expertise', a theme that the authors return to in this book. I have heard stories of international schools with EAL departments that are anything but centres of expertise. This is partly because there are no PGCE courses for EAL teachers, and trainee teachers can spend as little as half a day out of a one-year course focusing on EAL; as Carder states, 'To gain QTS (Qualified Teacher Status) a knowledge of bilingualism and applied linguistics are totally missing from the standards, and no national standards and qualifications are required for EAL teachers.'

It is, in my view, crucial for an ESL department to be a 'centre of expertise', arguably even more important than for other academic departments because of its overarching role in an international school. It is the job of ESL departments and international school leaders to make this happen.

But what does being 'a centre of expertise' actually involve? At my school we still have a long way to go, but one major step forwards has been the establishment of a largely content-based secondary EAL programme, and most importantly the widespread acceptance and enthusiasm for the programme from our content-teacher colleagues. Such support has paved the way for effective liaison between the EAL teachers and academic departments, and with the content teachers regularly providing us with the resources, vocabulary and exam-style tasks that they will be working on our department has been able to create a large bank of EAL resources divided into topics, subjects and year groups. Content teachers have commented that they can see their EAL students progressing more quickly with this approach, and additionally the acquisition of this academic-level language enables the students themselves to reach CALP level earlier.

As Janzen writes, 'The academic uses of language as well as the meaning of individual words need to be explicitly taught for students to fulfill the genre or discourse requirements privileged in academic settings and to understand the material they encounter' (Janzen, 2008: 1030, quoted in Scanlan and López, 2012: 601).

A further step that must be taken on the road towards becoming a 'centre of expertise' is the realization by international schools that EAL teachers must have, or obtain, an appropriate qualification. A school would never employ a maths teacher without a maths degree, but somehow ESL is viewed as a subject that anyone can 'do a bit of' as long as they are a native English speaker. As Carder has asserted in the past, 'To be a Maths teacher, a Science teacher, a Geography teacher, it is necessary to follow a professional course of study, do teaching practice in the subject, and if successful, gain a qualification. ... [I]t is enough just to be in an international school to be an EAL teacher, which is qualification by osmosis.' Such an approach devalues the ESL department and relegates what it provides to 'support' rather than properly structured, properly functioning academic teaching.

Immediate and long-term benefits of the model

As stated already, this school is still very much on the way to fully rolling out the ESL programme proposed in this book, but even in its early stages the benefits have been evident. With the change from 'EFL' to a more content-based programme, students have reported feeling more confident when they arrive at content lessons, having previously worked on key language and structures in EAL lessons. It was most rewarding recently when a Year 7 student bounced into his EAL lesson saying, 'We just did the types of energy in science but I knew all the words already'. Just seeing the happy confidence in his face, coupled with his own awareness that he was making progress, summed up clearly for me why a content-based ESL programme is the way forward.

The assimilation of the IGCSE ESL course into the EAL department has, in my view, provided our students with a clearer sense of progression through ESL now that they can see the obvious links between the IGCSE and IELTS, as both courses are taught by the same department. Both our secondary EAL teachers will attend training courses for the IGCSE this year, which will pave the way for this course to become truly one of the EAL department's areas of expertise.

The immediate strengths of the ESL programme have also been recognized by the school's academic content teachers. It is true, as Carder states in chapter 5, that there is often an expectation 'for ESL teachers, in whatever capacity, to have successful interchanges of ideas with content teachers, without the management having any knowledge of the complexity of teacher–teacher relationships in schools', and for ESL teachers to find keeping such interchanges going fairly difficult. Fortunately, at this school our teachers have seen the benefits of a content-based ESL programme with their own eyes and are extremely helpful and forthcoming when asked to collaborate, be it by sending key vocabulary, pointing the ESL teachers towards resources, or simply providing feedback. It is my hope that this level of interaction will become second nature to all EAL and subject-content staff, however high or low the staff turnover.

What of the longer-term advantages? When our ESL programme has been firmly in place for some years, it is envisaged that there will be a fully resourced ESL scheme of work for every year group, specially created to practise language from the syllabuses taught at the school. With many of these resources already in place, it will, hopefully, not seem so daunting for new EAL teachers to continue what has been started. Although, of course, a worldwide ESL scheme of work for use among all international schools would be the ideal.

In the second place, all being well, it will become clear to school leaders that in order for content-based courses to be taught, coupled with the teaching of IGCSE and IELTS by the EAL department, it is absolutely crucial for teachers trained in ESL to be leading and delivering these courses. It is my hope, at this school anyway, that future EAL teachers will all be qualified ESL teachers, and the phrase 'I do a bit of EAL' will become obsolete.

The need for ongoing training in subject content support

As Patricia Mertin states in chapter 9 of this book, 'The days when it was sufficient to train as a teacher and then continue on the same path until retirement are long gone'. Although this, of course, applies to all areas of education, her statement rings particularly true for ESL. There is currently no ESL scheme of work that is taught in international schools worldwide, and it is therefore very easy for an ESL department to change tack completely when one member of staff leaves and a new teacher arrives. All too often, because there is no approved syllabus, new teachers are unsure what to do, feel apprehensive and out of their comfort zone when faced with delivering a content-based programme, and so revert to an area in which they feel more confident: 'TEFL'-style, stand-alone lessons.

Similarly, for academic content teachers, who may never have been made aware of the potential issues when teaching ESL students, it is easy to slip back into a rut, using tried-and-tested lessons which may have achieved success with native-speaker students, but not necessarily with ESL students, who in so many international schools nowadays make up the majority. At my school this came about recently when a new Year 7 student arrived, partway through the year, and with only basic English skills. The resulting flurry of worried emails that we received from the academic content staff prompted me to re-examine how much training the EAL department are giving our academic content teachers and just how regularly this needs to be done.

In the absence of an internationally accepted ESL syllabus, it is vital, therefore, both for ESL teachers to receive ongoing training in content teaching and for academic subject staff to be well versed in teaching methods which will help EAL students to achieve their full potential in their classrooms.

Compared with the wealth of teaching materials dealing with grammar and vocabulary, there are startlingly few materials focusing on content support. Mertin's 2013 book *Breaking through the Language Barrier* has served as valuable reference material for our EAL department, as it examines the typical language and structures which tend to come up in the different academic subjects, enabling the EAL department to anticipate such language and to incorporate it into our planning. Moreover, we have used many of the strategies in the book as a basis for the INSET (in-service training) days that the department has provided to academic content staff. When one reads Mertin's suggestions on how to make content lessons more understandable to ESL students, it may seem obvious: speaking clearly with your face towards the students, writing the homework in the same place every time, limiting teacher talk time to 'meaningful chunks' followed by paired or group discussions in any language and then feeding back in English, and so on. However, teachers are often so passionate about the subject matter they are teaching that the need to do all this often flies out of the window: I know that I have been guilty of this at times when trying to fit everything I have planned into a forty-minute lesson. Consequently, the above guidance needs to be reiterated regularly at this school to ensure that this happens more often.

A further key resource for every Secondary ESL department should be the Cambridge English *TKT Course: CLIL Module* book (Bentley, 2010), which makes up part of the Cambridge 'Teaching Knowledge Course' but can be taken as a stand-alone module. As well as providing information on key 'academic content language' subject by subject, the book deals with different types of writing (how to recount, discuss, persuade, etc.), the use of classroom language with non-native-speaker students, advice on scaffolding lessons, and so on. All ESL teachers could take a test in this module and then train academic content staff, or, ideally, every academic content teacher could work through the course themselves, thus gaining a deeper knowledge of the language issues that our ESL students are facing every day.

Tips for school leaders on putting the model into practice

My final section focuses on tips for school leaders. We are fortunate in my school to have had the support of our school leaders for a content-based secondary EAL programme, and their recognition of the need for content teachers to be trained in ESL; we now need to think about the next steps. So much advice can be given to schools on setting up an effective ESL programme, but if asked to provide another leadership team with the most important tips, I would offer the following.

Keep students in ESL lessons for long enough

By recognizing that it can take between five and seven years to get to CALP level, schools will ensure that their ESL students are not just able to 'speak English' with their friends, but also to use it successfully in an academic context. As students move into Key Stages 4 and 5, they are required to understand and use increasingly abstract language and concepts which demand a high level of critical thinking. Exiting ESL lessons too early, for many ESL students, means finding it difficult to progress further with their academic language and being left in a situation in which, as Kusuma-Powell writes, their mastery of language 'is not sufficiently robust in any language to support highly conceptualised academic learning …. [T]heir actual thinking remains "stuck" at a concrete level' (Kusuma-Powell, 2004: 160, quoted in Hayden, 2006: 62). ESL students who are at a more advanced level may appear completely fluent when they speak, but the gap between BICS and CALP demonstrates that they need much more time learning English in academic contexts, and if this means recruiting more ESL teachers, so be it!

Educating the parents of ESL students is of prime importance

Murphy (2003) writes that many parents of ESL students 'hope that such an education will equip their child with some knowledge of how the world works, so that a measure of success may be ensured in the future. All the child has to do is learn English' (Murphy, 2003: 26, quoted in Hayden, 2006: 61) – as if 'learning English' were something that will happen magically within the first few months. While acting with the best of intentions, parents are generally unaware of the level of academic English that is necessary for a student to even begin to access the curriculum. Thus, students with low levels of English who enter an international school from Year 7 upwards will most likely need to attend ESL lessons for a significant amount of their school career. As some parents believe that their child is somehow 'losing out' by attending ESL lessons, it is the job of the school leaders to educate parents about the benefits, and indeed the necessity, of keeping students in ESL lessons for as long as necessary. The good news, though, is that with the right amount of ESL, such students will be empowered to fulfil as much of their potential as they possibly can. Therefore, getting parents informed and on side is of great importance in an international school.

Acknowledge the importance of an effective language policy

Having a language policy which clearly promotes both ESL and mother-tongue maintenance is a categorical necessity for any school wishing to get all staff on board and also to enlist parental support. An effective policy will document the difference between BICS and CALP and the benefits of a mother-tongue programme, as well as clearly setting out the ESL programme aims and structure. In this way, a school's ESL programme will automatically become more concrete and long-term.

Recognize the need for ongoing training for both ESL and subject content teachers

Kusuma-Powell writes that all international school teachers, not just ESL specialists, must 'see it as part of their role to become knowledgeable about expected progression of language development' (Kusuma-Powell, 2004, quoted in Hayden, 2006: 63); that is, 'All teachers are ESL teachers.' But it is impossible for all teachers to be ESL teachers simply by working in an international school. In these schools, where staff turnover is often high, keeping teachers informed and trained in ESL issues is paramount. With regular guidance, either from an external body such as Lexis Education (https://lexised.com, accessed 13 February 2018) or by the ESL teachers themselves, subject content staff will feel increased confidence in employing strategies with their ESL students, and the ESL department will gain confidence in delivering the training: after all, not many teachers relish the prospect of delivering INSET to their colleagues! At the end of the day, though, all teachers have a lot to learn from each other, and establishing a mutual culture of staff–staff training in a range of specialist areas

(ESL, differentiation, SEN, effective marking, stretching the most able ... the list goes on) can only be a good thing.

Ensure that ESL staff are appropriately qualified, or willing to be

In writing my pieces for this book I have felt ambivalent at times when stating that all ESL teachers must be suitably qualified. I am a qualified MFL teacher and consequently have a sound understanding of how language 'works'; however, I have no ESL qualifications, and have therefore been extremely lucky to have been given the chance to teach EAL at my present school without one. However, I believe that had I not fallen in love with EAL teaching and chosen to develop my skills in this area, I would eventually have moved to a job in MFL once a space came up, and would have been replaced with a similarly inexperienced EAL teacher, thus perpetuating the 'I do a bit of EAL' approach. As it is, I have recognized the significant gaps in my knowledge and am embarking on a master's in applied linguistics and TESOL shortly, something which I believe is necessary to lead an ESL department. A deep understanding of second-language acquisition, grammar and phonology, as well as specialist knowledge of the methodology behind ESL teaching, are all vital, in my view, for an ESL department to provide its students with the top-quality level of education that they deserve. In order for the 'bit of EAL' practice to stop, school leaders must advertise for qualified heads of ESL, as well as ensuring that ESL staff are encouraged to further their professional development where necessary. Having qualified ESL teachers teaching and leading in every international school will make it easier for an internationally accepted programme to take shape, as well as enabling the IGCSE ESL to be brought permanently under the umbrella of ESL; the path to ESL departments becoming 'centres of expertise' will consequently be smoother.

I believe that by putting the above advice into place, school leaders will be well on their way to establishing successful ESL departments. It is also true that, little by little, ESL is moving nearer to the fore of agencies such as COBIS as its importance is recognized, and this can only be a positive step on the path to a worldwide ESL programme. As Carder writes, 'ESL students need to have an institutional backer for their cause, and this department will be strongly "empowered" by accreditation agencies, and curriculum bodies such as the IB .... School heads will be re-educated to promote this model throughout the world of international education, with the realization that the majority of international students are "emerging bilinguals" and that there is a new paradigm in this increasingly globalised world' (Carder, 2017c: 39).

It is my view that ESL is gaining in prominence in the world of international schools, but there is still some way to go; this becomes clear from reading Murphy's 1990 publication *ESL: A handbook for teachers and administrators in international schools*, which calls for steps to be taken similar to the ones Carder and Mertin are calling for now, but which was published thirty years ago. It is of prime importance, therefore, that the current generation of ESL teachers take up the baton and continue to push for ESL departments to become the 'centres of expertise' that they deserve to be – and fast. An internationally recognized, content-based ESL programme for international schools *is* possible, and today's internet-based society, where resources can be downloaded from a 'cloud' with the click of a mouse, makes the prospect yet more achievable. We need to be the ones to make it happen.

Part Six

Constructive solutions
that build consistently on
international students'
language trajectories:
Empowering ESL and MT
teachers as specialists

Establishing a department in the secondary school as a 'centre of expertise' for all matters ESL and mother tongue

Learning a language is a much deeper process than learning a somehow 'neutral' linguistic phenomenon enriched by some anecdotal cultural knowledge. It is something that involves the whole person: 'Nobody acquires a language as he/she would do for any other subject: language guides and filters our relationships, deeply questions what we have achieved but also our affective, symbolic and imaginary references, as well as our values'.

(Coïaniz, 2001: 248, quoted and translated in
Piccardo and Aden, 2014: 219)

Students are given approximately three years before they are encouraged to be completely mainstreamed. This time limit implicitly indicates that students are ready for non-sheltered English, both to the mainstream teacher and the students themselves. As researchers and ESL teachers, we know that [Cognitive and Academic Language Proficiency] usually takes anywhere from 5–7 years. Yet, are we making this distinction clear to ESL students, mainstream teachers and parents? It is quite possible that ESL students are leaving the ESL classroom with false expectations of their own abilities, and when they cannot live up to these expectations, anxieties increase, resulting in withdrawal from interactions with others.

(Pappamihiel, 2001: 36–7)

Theoretical background

It should by now be clear that SL teachers' input can easily be ignored. The inspiring chapter above, written by Sarah Porter, is at the same time, for me, shocking, as I encountered exactly the same situation in 1981, almost 40 years ago, when I commenced my career in ESL in international schools. It serves as a rock-solid argument for following the proposals presented in this book. The solution is to ensure that ESL and mother tongue departments are seen as 'centres of expertise' in international schools and are securely established throughout the global network, with appropriately defined curricular objectives, assessment and accreditation. In an age of the establishment of equal rights for women, for all races and for the LGBT community, equity for languages is long overdue. Many schools have in their mission statements clauses proclaiming their intention to have no prejudice on the grounds of race, gender or sexual preference, but do not mention equal access to languages, or the means to achieving such equality. It seems to be a bridge too far even for international schools. In fact the Independent Press Standards Organization, which covers discrimination, does not include language in its code of practice. Clause 12, part one of the editors' code of practice states: 'The press must avoid prejudicial or pejorative reference to an individual's race, colour, religion, sex, gender identity, sexual orientation or to any physical or mental illness or disability' (www.ipso.co.uk/editors-code-of-practice, accessed 13 February 2018). Once again, 'language' falls outside the spectrum of equality or protection.

May (2014a) discusses the inability of certain disciplines to broaden their scope. He writes about TESOL and SLA as being unwilling to extend their remit to include aspects of bilingualism. He argues that the theories of two prominent educational theorists, Bourdieu and Bernstein, are useful in providing theoretical justification for the establishment of new academic disciplines. 'Bernstein was particularly interested in exploring both the social organization and status hierarchies of academic subjects or disciplines, as well as their participants (see, e.g., Bernstein 1990, 2000)' (May, 2014a: 14). Bernstein used two terms: 'classification', which describes the boundaries established within and between academic disciplines or subjects, and 'framing', which refers to the locus of control over pedagogic communication and its context (Bernstein, 2000: 6, quoted in May, 2014a: 14). Bernstein uses these conceptual tools to analyse how distinct academic disciplines have been established from the nineteenth century until today, and how they became organized into 'singulars', a term he defined as 'bodies characterized by strong boundary maintenance (classification), which are supported culturally (via professional associations, networks, and writing) and psychologically (in students, teachers, and researchers). As a result, "singulars develop strong autonomous self-sealing and narcissistic identities" (Bernstein, 2000: p. 54)' (May, 2014: 14). They have certain 'rules' that determine which research is acceptable, how teachers enact the accepted research via textbooks, syllabuses and examinations, and what count as legitimate texts, such as journal articles, books and theses. These all reinforce the rubric of accepted and acceptable disciplinary knowledge (ibid.: 14–15).

Such 'singulars' describe the departments commonly encountered in the middle and high levels of international schools: maths, science, English, foreign languages, humanities/social sciences, art, music, drama, PE, IT, and so on. Occasionally there are attempts to merge some disciplines: art, music and drama may be brought together under the umbrella of 'creative arts', for example. As the majority of international schools now host over 50 per cent of students who do not have English as their mother tongue it is obvious which 'singulars' are singularly absent from the list: English as a second language and mother tongues – bilingual studies.

The reason for their absence may be their relatively late arrival on the scene: the disciplines listed above arose largely from subjects studied in the nineteenth century, whereas the overturning of negative approaches towards bilingualism began in the 1950s and 1960s, and an understanding of the immense amount of time needed to become proficient in academic English in the 1980s and 1990s.

However, this is not true for IT – information technology – which began its meteoric rise in the mid-1980s. IT can also be seen as a discipline which crosses into other subject areas, but it usually has its own 'singular' in schools. Moreover, in IT too there has been a spectacular rise in the number of students being educated in a language which is not their own because of globalization, migration and the ever-growing acceptance of English as the world's lingua franca.

As teachers who have worked in international secondary schools, we can report that the 'territorial' elements of subject departments are very much alive. Departments, each of which has its own specialist 'language', jealously guard their boundaries, and indeed one department head compared the situation to the rivalries between European countries in the nineteenth century. There is a clear pecking order, and ESL and MT are low down in it, unless there is on the one hand a separate department, and on the other a head of department with the confidence and integrity to assert herself, and skilful enough to avoid being dismissed in the process. Therefore only by establishing a 'singular' for the subject area of second language teaching, with its partner mother-tongue teaching, will a school have any chance of meeting the ESL students' pedagogical needs. This is particularly true because of the parlous state of the subject area in most national systems. Moreover, this subject area department will not only have to have equal status with other departments, but be continually boosted and given prominence by all levels of school leadership.

Because of the years of ignorance and neglect that have surrounded the subject, there will have to be extended periods of focus on the teachers in the department, on their central role in the school, on their expertise in ESL students' many needs when learning social English, reading and writing in each subject area, on the need to cooperate with subject teachers, and on their invaluable role as sources of expertise in all matters related to second language learning. The latter is a massive field, with a huge literature, and is immensely complex. It includes second language acquisition, theoretical linguistics, first language acquisition, language teaching, applied linguistics, child language acquisition, bilingualism, psycholinguistics, anthropology, sociolinguistics, ELT, sociocultural theory (which includes the role of the learner's culture in SLA), morphology, second language phonology, L2 semantics, pragmatics in second language acquisition, second language reading skills, the acquisition of second language writing, second language speech production, speaking and writing tasks and their effects on second language performance, systemic functional linguistics, age effects in second language learning, the role of educational level, literacy and orality in L2 learning, mother tongues and L2 learning, fossilization and SLA research, to name but a few!

Second language learning also encompasses scholarly outlets such as refereed journals, book series issued by international publishers, specialized conferences, professional associations, and university-based postgraduate programmes, at both master's and doctoral levels. There is a specialized vocabulary to discuss 'language matters' which acts as a shorthand for experts in the field. Critics snipe at this as 'jargon', but maths, science, economics and IT all have their own specialized language. It is often those who feel they have a right to own ESL students, typically English departments, who weigh in most heavily with the 'all that bilingualism stuff' comments. This is a fundamental reason why teachers in the department will need to be carefully selected as regards training, qualifications and experience: directors cannot afford to have any weak links in this area. Unqualified 'assistants' in a 'support' role will certainly be unsatisfactory.

Only through the adoption of this model can the subtractive paradigm, whereby students' mother tongues are largely unnurtured and their English language needs are relegated to support, be effectively challenged. It is thought in many circles that international schools are leading the way: perhaps they should be, given the clientele and the fee level, but such aspirations leave a lot to be desired as regards second language matters.

At present the survival model for ESL students is paramount. It has been labelled 'support', and this term has made the survival mode acceptable, and even promoted as the best solution. See, for example, the following extracts:

In today's classrooms, academic and social success often hinges on a child's language abilities. Children who need extra support in second language acquisition have been mainstreamed into classrooms where the teachers do not necessarily have the resources or the support to meet their needs. Without this support, the children who are struggling to acquire even basic skills in their second language begin to fall behind academically, creating an achievement gap that only widens over time (Harris, 2003). Providing teachers with adequate tools and techniques to support these learners is essential. ...

Teachers must research the way ELLs acquire their second language and choose the appropriate strategies to support each child as an individual. Research on this subject is constantly emerging and changing. ...

Any teacher working with ELL students should do research on their own to find out how all children acquire language.

(Facella *et al.*, 2005: 209, 220)

These extracts advise teachers to 'do their own research'; this is a tacit acceptance that professional ESL teachers, or CPD for content teachers, do not exist. We accept that content teachers do not have the resources to meet their needs. It could be argued equally that they do not have the knowledge or training. Teachers are advised to research the way that ELLs acquire their second language: why was this not a basic part of their teacher training? Then they have to choose the appropriate strategies to 'support' each child as an individual. Many middle/high school teachers are sufficiently challenged by fluent speakers of English, the demands of the curriculum, the paperwork related to assessment, meetings with parents, staff meetings and so forth not to have the time, energy or resources to follow this advice, with the result that ESL students are left to struggle and survive as best they can, which will create conditions in which they will indeed need support, but perhaps not that intended by the authors.

Every good ESL teacher knows that a fundamental strategy in every ESL class is to lower the affective barrier, that is, to create conditions for learning in which the students can feel at home and not threatened. This can bring remarkable results as ESL students learn to trust their teacher and take more risks than they would in a large class of fluent speakers who already have the tools to forge ahead. However, the class teacher cannot lower the affective barrier in a content class, as the native speakers will lose interest. Lowering the affective barrier involves creating a class atmosphere in which those who do not have a good knowledge of English, or have cultural factors that inhibit them from contributing, can feel comfortable making any sort of oral contribution, even if their level of English is low and they fear feeling mortified if they make mistakes in front of fluent speakers. This simple fact is wilfully ignored by policy makers and politicians, who of course are not in the classroom.

The final comment, that teachers should do research on their own to find out how all children acquire language, reveals the depth to which educational institutions have gone in abnegating responsibility for ESL students. We live in an era of globalization, of the mass movement of peoples around the globe, in which English has become a hyper-language, the language of power (see Ostler, 2005, on the chequered history of what languages that have power have gained from their relationship to empires), and almost a necessity for the whole world. (There is a theory that there is a language hierarchy in which languages range from peripheral or local, like Flemish, to central languages, like English in India, to super-central, like French, which is used in several countries for a limited range of subjects, to hyper-central, like English, which is used globally for all purposes. English is thus a hyper-language.) In this context the following facts stand out: there is a need for all teachers to be trained in the factors surrounding the education of ESL students, and a need for a radical reappraisal of disciplines and departmental structure, as presented below.

The reason May explores Bernstein's concept of singulars is to analyse the somewhat frozen status of academic disciplines, and explain why these, and

> particular sub-disciplines such as SLA and TESOL, are so often defined (and confined) by a narrowly derived set of research assumptions, approaches, and related models of teaching and learning. Such analyses also explain why such disciplines are equally resistant to change. After all, fundamental changes in the classification and framing of knowledge also necessarily involve significant shifts in the structure and distribution of power and in principles of control – that is, in who controls, and what counts as, disciplinary knowledge.
>
> (May, 2014a: 15)

May's argument, taken up by other researchers, for example Ortega (2013), is for a broader base for SLA to include the bilingual repertoires of English learners. Bernstein's term for interdisciplinary fields is 'regions', which are 'created by a recontextualizing of singulars' (Bernstein, 2000: 9). Regions allow a much broader understanding of the origins and research principles which form the basis of academic disciplines. This is exactly what the establishment of 'ESL and mother tongue departments' can accomplish. The professional teachers in these departments will have been trained not only in the complex theories and practices of SLA and TESOL, but also in what is involved for the students in this process. Teachers need to help students to maintain and develop their mother tongue, and transfer academic knowledge from the first to the second language so that they can build on their funds of knowledge. They also need to develop content language syllabuses in liaison with other departments and enable ESL students to become biliterate bilinguals. By also taking responsibility for the CPD of the remainder of the staff *and* the school leadership, they will demonstrate their complete dedication to their professional lives and pedagogical involvement.

Cummins (2000) has shown how important it is for ESL students to be empowered in order to have a sense of self-esteem, which will provide them with the drive to accomplish the momentous task of developing their second language abilities to a high academic level, which involves an effort far greater than that required of native English speakers. Leung *et al.* (1997: 544) point out that ESL students 'actively construct their own patterns of language use, ethnicity, and social identity', which can sometimes be in 'strong contradiction to the fixed patterns and reified ethnicities attributed' to the students. The situation of bilinguals can even reach the stage where '[n]umerous bilinguals do not feel fully accepted by either of the cultures in question. There again, the cause is often not bilingualism/biculturalism so much as "monolingualist" and "monoculturalist" ideologies dominant in one or both of the communities' (Lüdi and Py, 2009: 160).

ESL students need to have an institutional backer for their cause, and this will be the region of the ESL and mother tongue department, strongly empowered by international schools, accreditation agencies, and curriculum bodies such as the IB. The failed model of support which has permeated national systems and left ESL students labelled as learning-disabled, or with severe bilingual problems, must be removed from the educational vocabulary. School directors will be re-educated to promote this model throughout the world of international education, along with the realization that the majority of international students are emerging bilinguals and that there is a new paradigm in this increasingly globalized world. The reform will involve careful selection of staff for this new department, rigorous training for school leaders and department heads, awareness sessions for members of boards of governors that emphasize the equality of status of the ESL and mother tongue staff, and screening of each new staff member to ensure that they have professional training in linguistically responsive teaching. As already noted, this must be 'consistent, long-term training in ESL pedagogy and methodology. ... Quick and dirty 1-day, or 1-hour, in-service sessions simply cannot provide enough preparation and training for teachers expected to help ELLs succeed in their mainstream content classes in a new language' (Hansen-Thomas and Cavagnetto (2010: 263). School directors will reap rewards: they will notice a steady improvement in all ESL students, an interweaving of reading and writing processes among departments, more understanding of bilingual processes throughout the community, gratitude from parents, and improvement in grades and examination results.

That the language of each subject in the secondary school is the basis for second language students to make progress in the subject was pointed out in 1975 – over forty years ago:

> The core of the difficulty in the mathematics classroom is that the teacher often understands and takes for granted the whole register of mathematics, and thinks only of the mathematical aspects of these items ..., whereas for the learner they may also be unfamiliar *language* – they are 'peculiar' English. It is therefore desirable that the mathematics teacher should be aware of the register of mathematics as a sub-set of English .... To this end, mathematics educators and the English language teachers should collaborate in the production of guidelines, illustrative descriptions and teaching materials concerned with this problem.
>
> (UNESCO, 1975: 121–2)

What he writes about mathematics is of course equally and wholly applicable to every subject in the middle and upper school.

How research supports the arguments for an independent department responsible for teaching SLLs

We might do well ... to recall John T. Bruer's wise comment that one of the dangers of focusing on maturational issues in discussing learning is that it prompts us to pay too much attention to when learning occurs and too little attention to the conditions of learning.

(Singleton, 2014: 32)

It is generally accepted that learning a second language can be a fairly tough challenge, the demands of which no one is likely to take on willingly unless he/she wants or needs to.

(Cook, 2014b: 102)

This section contains a review of how the latest research on SLA and bilingualism supports our arguments for an independent department of professionals who will teach ESL in a sustainable framework. Many of the quotes are self-explanatory and point to a clear need for separate, focused instruction in the English language that ESL students need in order to study all school subjects for the curriculum.

Lenneberg (1967: 176) wrote that 'after puberty ... automatic acquisition from mere exposure to a given language seems to disappear ..., and foreign languages have to be taught and learned through a conscious and labored effort'; this is an indication that direct instruction is required – not support.

Singleton (2014: 50) notes that 'learners require constant attentiveness to their comprehension problems, ... and a generous supply of explicit explanations'.

ESL students must above all develop their writing skills: written work in all subjects is required at advanced levels in academic English. Speaking the language passably does not lead to advanced writing skills, or, as le Comte de Buffon said, 'Those who write as they speak, even though they speak well, write badly' (Cook, 2014a: 74). Some of the minefields of learning English spelling are given below. How many content teachers will be aware of these anomalies?

Sound correspondences for English vowel letters:

- a bait, wag, talkative, father, anaemia, daughter, many, aisle, boat, aerial, beauty, cauliflower, artistically (silent)
- e ten, cedar, be, kidney, offer, bureau, eight, lewd, pace (silent)
- i bit, bite, legible, auntie, sign, dirt, business (silent)
- o phone, dog, memoir, door, book, word, youth, ludicrous, cow, tough, flour, boy
- u but, fruit, burn, use, full, guest (silent)
- y yes, martyr, ratify, nylon, funny

(Cook, 2014a: 77)

When there is an ESL department, with fully trained professionals, these enthusiasts will not only know all the above facts but actually enjoy teaching them, as such matters are the life blood of applied linguistics; they will regularly introduce, explicate, and give opportunities for practice of, such English language quirks, perhaps also briefly introducing the historical reasons for them. In English, there are 26 letters in the alphabet to represent 44 phonemes, the basic units of the language's phonology.

Wolf (2008: 128) points out the need for children to be actively taught certain phonological and orthographic constituent parts of English. She gives an excerpt that contains common words that include the vowel pair 'ea' in its wide range of possible pronunciations: 'There once was a beautiful bear who sat on a seat near to breaking and read by the hearth about how the earth was created. She smiled beatifically, full of ideas for the realm of her winter dreams.'

In an international school setting there are students from almost every country in the world. They bring with them a variety of scripts, and also writing conventions. For many of them, learning a new script and style is a monumental task. As Cook points out (2014a: 80), 'The problem of recognising and writing the appropriate signs of the second writing system is largely unappreciated', to which I would add 'except by those trained in applied linguistics'.

Researchers describe the need for direct instruction of language

Students acquiring English need a sound, age-appropriate, content-based programme of SL instruction to a level which enables them to become socially and academically successful as quickly as possible, alongside a programme that enables them to maintain and develop their mother tongue. Often it is mistakenly thought, by non-ESL-qualified teachers and others, that a child who can communicate face to face has reached the level required. It can take between five and seven years for a second-language learner to acquire the necessary level of academic English to succeed in an English-medium school.

Davison writes:

> ESL learners have to acquire a whole new sound system, a new set of words and meanings, a new way of constructing sentences and a new set of discourse patterns. They must learn to express themselves clearly in a language that is appropriate for their age, their situation and their purpose. ... ESL students do not have a sound oral base in English on which to build their literacy skills and there are likely to be many gaps in their knowledge.
>
> (Davison, 1994: 89)

What follows are quotes from researchers on the need for direct L2 instruction and the ensuring advantages as opposed to the dangers of sink-or-swim policies:

> [K]nowing that young children may have a slow start when acquiring an L2 can be an important research-based argument against harmful attempts to promote so-called sink-or-swim educational policies that attempt to reduce or even completely withdraw the first and second language support that is to be provided to language minority children by schools. Such policies have been dangerously gaining ground ... for some time now.
>
> (Ortega, 2013: 28)

This extract points out the laissez-faire attitude to SL learners in many schools.

'For successful grammar acquisition, attention to form is probably necessary. This attentional focus on form can be externally achieved by instruction' (Ortega, 2013: 79). This is another call for direct instruction, particularly of grammar. 'Cognitive-interactionist researchers agree that negative feedback (or the implicit or explicit indication that some part of an utterance is ungrammatical) is better overall than entirely ignoring errors' (Ortega, 2013: 79–80). Here is an intervention that calls for mistakes to be corrected, not glossed over.

> Grammatical competence appears to evolve in ways that are less amenable to incidental benefits from the environment than other aspects of the language to be learned, such as vocabulary, discourse competence, and so on. It also seems to hold a special status in language acquisition. Specifically, grammar (a) requires more interest, attention and hard work than other aspects of the language to be learned; (b) may even require more time to simmer and deploy than the learning of other aspects of an L2; and (c) can act as a gatekeeper to development in other areas of the L2 beyond formulaic repertoires, particularly sociolinguistic competence.
>
> (Ortega, 2013: 80)

This is another call for grammar to be specifically taught to SL learners, and the following quote contains the same message as regards other aspects of language: 'Schmidt also proposes that nothing is free in L2 learning: "in order to acquire phonology, one must attend to phonology; in order to acquire pragmatics, one must attend to both linguistic forms and the relevant contextual features; and so forth" (1995, p. 17)' (Ortega, 2013: 96). The following three quotes all contain the same message, that SL learners need direct instruction, not 'support': 'L2 instruction has value. If instruction targets implicit processes, ... it can boost bottom-up induction of constructions by making exemplars in teaching materials more frequent, salient and consistent (Robinson and Ellis, 2008b)' (Ortega, 2013: 137); 'Instruction cannot override development, but it has been shown to result in clear benefits in the areas of accuracy and rate of learning for both syntax and morphology' (Ortega, 2013: 143); '[M]ost learners may benefit from external help via explanations and guided practice, provided these are well designed' (Ortega, 2013: 160). This last one emphasizes the need for a professionally drawn-up plan of study – a curriculum.

The following extracts point up the need for professional SL teachers:

> [I]nclusive pedagogies, unless properly resourced with appropriate teacher expertise and knowledge[,] may fail the very students they set out to support. Mismatches between the rhetoric of inclusion and the sometimes excluding practices of classroom life illustrate how linguistically diverse students learning English as an additional language might suffer.
>
> (Leung and Creese, 2010: xxi)

> Language at school has been described as the 'hidden curriculum' (Christie, 1985) as teachers and curriculum and assessment statements seldom make their expectations of language use explicit (Schleppegrell, 2004).
>
> (Monaghan, 2010: 24)

The extract below goes into the deeper aspects of language learning, showing that the lack of a well-taught language may lead to general difficulties with reasoning:

> As Schleppegrell (2004: 2) argues[,] 'Students' difficulties in "reasoning", for example, may be due to their lack of familiarity with the linguistic properties of the language through which the reasoning is expected to be presented, rather than to the inherent difficulty of the cognitive processes involved'.
>
> (ibid.)

Harper *et al.* (2010: 75) add, 'EAL students often need *language-sensitive content instruction* to facilitate their conceptual learning through academic English. They also need *content-based language instruction* to assist their development of the new language' (emphasis original). Once again, the basic requirements for an ESL programme are laid out.

> Teachers [need to] set objectives for English language and culture learning for their EAL students. The process includes identifying

and teaching the grammar and discourse structures that students need to understand and communicate important ideas in the content areas. It also means identifying and teaching key words and phrases that EAL students will need to learn in addition to the technical, content-specific words that will be new to all students.

(Echevarria *et al.*, 2004, quoted in Harper *et al.*, 2010: 77)

The above text is a further iteration of the basic needs of an SL programme.

[F]luent English speakers often hesitate to question or correct EAL speakers unless their meaning is unclear. Therefore, EAL learners at intermediate and higher levels of English proficiency typically receive insufficient feedback on their errors and have limited opportunities for English language development.

(Harper *et al.*, 2010: 84)

This is confirmation of a quote given above by Ortega on the need for feedback on errors.

Although many new words are learned through multiple exposures in everyday social settings outside schools, technical terms and their associated patterns of use in academic content areas are much less common and require more focused attention.

(ibid.: 85)

This extract requires a comment: a major difference between SLLs in national settings and those in international schools is that the latter usually have *no* exposure to English outside the school – another compelling reason for direct instruction of English.

[T]he placement of EAL students in mainstream classes without specialized EAL classes to support their English language development makes it extremely difficult for them to receive either the sheltered content instruction or the focused, content-based language and culture support that many need to succeed in school. In fact, we doubt that any individual teacher can provide sufficient support, and we believe that the old adage, 'It takes a whole village to raise a child', applies particularly well to EAL learners: 'It takes a whole school to educate a student.' This implies that all teachers (not just EAL specialists) must understand how language and culture influence learning in school.

(ibid.: 90)

Here we see evidence of the need for CPD for all staff on SL matters. The following quote reinforces the essential need for direct, professional instruction: 'Both first and second language vocabulary acquisition proceed in a context of input tuning of various kinds and are characterised by "special teaching" in the form of ostensive [clearly demonstrative] definitions' (Cook and Singleton, 2014: 50).

> [M]onolingualism is taken as the implicit norm, the reality of bi/multilingualism is made invisible, and linguistic ownership by birth and monolingual upbringing is elevated to an inalienable right and advantage …. Thus, the very goals of the discipline are led astray by the monolingual bias, and a subtractive bilingualism approach is uncritically embraced by SLA researchers.
>
> (Ortega, 2014: 36)

This shows how bi/multilingualism is sidelined, and even made 'invisible', which leads not only researchers but teachers and leadership to accept a subtractive bilingualism.

> If children have a limited command of the language of instruction, and of literacy, and no efforts are made to welcome them on their own terms, social stigma can be constructed, based on the 'implicit association between how well individuals express themselves and their intelligence' (Torres-Guzmán, 2002: 6).
>
> (Auleear Owodally, 2014: 4)

This quote reveals how SL learners can be relegated to the category of SEN without caring procedures.

> These exceptional learners [post-pubertal learners whose accents are not recognized as foreign even under close scrutiny in the laboratory] shared two features. *They had all received considerable amounts of high-quality L2 instruction* and they all self-reported high levels of motivation and concern to sound native-like.
>
> (Ortega, 2013: 23; emphasis added)

Another definitive argument for providing a good SL programme.

Finally, a clinching argument for the need for a designated ESL department with professional teachers comes from Ortega, who writes:

> While the value of language instruction regularly becomes the object of heated debates in scholarly and public policy circles,

supporters and sceptics often fail to pay sufficient attention to the fact that the accumulated evidence clearly shows accuracy and rate advantages for instruction. Simply put, instructed learners progress at a faster rate, they are likely to develop more elaborate language repertoires and they typically become more accurate than uninstructed learners.

(Ortega, 2013: 139)

Furthermore, 'Evidence of clear rate and accuracy advantages of instruction is also available for L2 morphology' (ibid.).

The above extracts from researchers present convincing evidence that L2 students benefit immensely from a professionally designed programme of instruction tailored to their needs, in addition to the evidence given by prominent researchers such as Cummins, Krashen, and Collier and Thomas discussed in previous chapters. They show the overwhelming arguments in favour of professional instruction by qualified teachers as opposed to support given by unqualified teaching assistants.

It is so obvious to ESL professionals that ESL students require all the trappings of programme delivery, curriculum and assessment geared to their needs that it is frustrating in the extreme to have to continually present arguments for their existence. Long-term stress is said to be the most debilitating, and in an already stressful (though rewarding) occupation, ESL teachers would be well served by international schools acknowledging their expertise and ensuring that optimal conditions are established for the healthy operation of their profession: a department structure, and recognition as a subject in its own right by curriculum and accreditation agencies.

The professionalization of ESL would also open career paths in the discipline. In the current support role, where ESL teachers are often teaching assistants, there is a permanent reinforcement of low expectations. Even good ESL teachers become disenchanted and demotivated, many changing discipline or even profession. I have seen excellent ESL teachers, well qualified, who in spite of being dedicated to their students have become unable to tolerate the steady downgrading of their profession and have moved into other areas. This is a huge loss for international education.

Length of time in the ESL programme

A key theme ... is the importance of adopting an explicitly positive view of bilingual learners, and their multiple linguistic repertoires, as the basis for their long-term educational success.

(May, 2014b: 24)

A particular focus needs to be on the length of time ESL students remain in the ESL programme; there is often undue haste in exiting them to the 'mainstream'. As Umansky and Reardon point out:

> In research and practice there is an implicit assumption that the more quickly students are reclassified, the better the academic and linguistic outcome. Faster reclassification, according to this underlying belief, implies more effective instruction and better-served English learners. This study shows that the speed with which students are reclassified is not necessarily a good indicator of how well students progress linguistically or academically. ...
>
> If exiting EL status is a de facto requirement for quality instruction and access to content, then EL students will continue to struggle in school with large achievement gaps between themselves and their non-EL counterparts (Callahan, 2005; Fry, 2007; Gándara & Contreras, 2009; Kanno & Kangas, 2014; Reardon & Galindo, 2009; Valdés, 1998). If, instead, EL students are ensured quality instruction and full access to content, longer periods spent in the EL classification could actually result in higher linguistic and academic outcomes by the end of high school.
>
> (Umansky and Reardon, 2014: 908)

Professional ESL teachers will be all too aware of the constant pressure from some parents and school leadership to move the ESL students out of the ESL programme; the above quote reinforces the arguments of why that is not a long-term solution.

Appropriate assessment models for SLLs

L2 users and L2 learners need to be assessed against successful L2 users, not against native speakers, as reflected in many contemporary examination systems.

(Cook, 2014c: 139)

A key problem of assessment ... stems from ... benchmarking performances in relation to inadequate or inappropriate descriptors. In the mainstream education context, the problems arise from using first language descriptors for assessing second language performance.

(Leung and Lewkowicz, 2008: 314)

The above statements raise many questions about the assessment of ESL students. Teachers in the Anglosphere and in international schools are familiar with a schedule of testing which appears to be being made more simplified, just as the level of diversity in student language repertoires becomes more varied and complex. Piccardo and Aden point out:

> [W]e can observe that, while on the one hand, new theoretical frameworks like complexity and sociocultural theory are increasingly being used for investigating the process of second language acquisition (Lantolf, 2000; Larsen-Freeman, 2002; Swain et al., 2011; van Lier, 2004, among others), on the other hand the idea that language proficiency can be described exclusively as a series of separate competences and organized in the form of lists of discrete items one can tick on a grid is more and more widespread, as shown by the multiplications of frameworks in all domains (above all in assessment but also competence specification, curriculum planning and quality assurance). This oversimplification is extended to all language features, including the cultural ones.
>
> (Piccardo and Aden, 2014: 236)

The process of simplification of assessment in the IBMYP is investigated by Hughes (2014), who makes the key point that when both grades and comments are given as feedback, comments are seen as more useful and constructive, but when a grade is given this is immediately seen as more 'important' and negates the value of the comment. He does not specifically mention ESL students – a notable omission – but their needs are especially well served by comments and ill served by grades, above all when these are given within the same scale as those for other students or subjects: in the case of the MYP this is foreign-language learners, not second language learners. Assessment needs to be adjusted for ESL students to ensure they are not demotivated by low grades. For ESL beginners, low grades can be almost automatically a result of combining ESL with Foreign Language, where there is an urgent need for reclassification.

ESL students require specific modes of assessment. The most suitable models are those which make use of multiple measures, including classroom grades, projects, and portfolios of student work. As pointed out by Boyle and Charles:

> The effectiveness of marks or written comments has also been investigated. There is evidence that providing written comments is more effective than providing grades ([R.] Butler, 1988; Crooks, 1988). Butler's research demonstrated that feedback through

comments alone led to learning gains whereas marks alone or comments accompanied by marks or giving praise, did not.

(Boyle and Charles, 2014: 111)

Formative assessment is the ideal solution for ESL students; it is also known as 'assessment for learning' (AfL). A definition given by Popham states, 'Formative assessment is not a test but a process that produces not so much a score but a qualitative insight into student understanding' (Popham, 2008: 6). In a comprehensive review of the subject, useful for both researchers and practitioners, Boyle and Charles write, of the situation in England:

> Formative assessment was legitimised and became part of the education policy makers' and teaching fraternity's lexicon through the seminal Task Group on Assessment and Testing report (DES 1988) which developed the assessment system for the National Curriculum encompassed by the 1988 Education Reform Act (DES, 1988). However, with the commencement of paper and pencil testing of the National Curriculum (the 'sats') in 1991, soon the only form of 'assessment' which mattered was summative and this was embodied in the end of key stage tests. These quickly became a 'high stakes' priority for schools who felt pressured by both Ofsted (Office for Standards in Education) and the government who used the test results as the principal (often, it appeared to teachers, the sole) measure of national standards and each school's success or failure.
>
> (Boyle and Charles, 2014: 8–9)

Thus formative assessment was sidelined in England, and summative assessment has become the deciding factor for education internationally:

> [I]nternationally assessment has become almost universally equated with high stakes scoring and testing (Hall et al. 2004; Shepard 2000, 2005; Twing et al. 2010) and teaching has consequently been reduced to servicing that metric (Guinier, 2003).
>
> (Boyle and Charles, 2014: 10)

Some benefits of summative assessment are given by Sternberg, but the accompanying negative effects are plain to see:

> IQs increased by about 30 points in the 20th century. Part of this increase may have been the result of increased standardized testing because testing improves the skills on which students are tested.

But although these practices may increase general intelligence, they may impede the development of creativity and wisdom. As a result, our society may be achieving short-term increases in well-being at the expense of long-term ones. Instruction and assessment need to better balance the development of intelligence, creativity, and wisdom.

(Sternberg, 2016: 66)

That assessment is not used to further the learning process but only to see 'whether change has occurred' is apparent from the following quote:

Assessment should always be feedback instruments that are integrated with and integral to teaching and learning – assessments are not 'add-ons' which 'round off' the process with a neat label or grade for the pupil. It is the feedback information and interpretations of children's learning locations, not the scores, levels and grades, that are important in the learning process. In too many cases, assessment is used synonymously with testing 'as the measure to judge whether change has occurred rather than as a mechanism to further enhance and consolidate learning by teachers and pupils' (Hattie and Timperley 2007, p. 104).

(Boyle and Charles, 2014: 114)

A clear summary of how assessment practices have developed is given below:

Paradigm one is the accountancy model, beloved of policy makers and at the core of the school effectiveness debate (Gorard 2010). It is best defined as 'teach to be measured', in which the sole purpose of teaching is to deliver or cover material that will later be tested; there is no involvement of the pupil in that learning process. Paradigm two is the banking model (Freire 1970) in which the teacher teaches and the pupils are taught and those are the fixed and immutable roles; there is no deregulation of the role (Allal & [Pelgrims] Ducrey 2000; Perrenoud 1998; Zimmerman 2000). In 'olden days' this was known as the 'topping up' model in which the child was the empty vessel and was topped up or filled up with knowledge, which she recited back to the teacher to prove that learning had taken place (Alexander 200[4], 2008; Tharp & Gallimore 1991 in Smith et al. 2004). Paradigm three is the 'testocracy' in which the metric is laid down and the teaching and learning process conforms to that testing metric. Its limitations and the humanistic and social implications ... are not even considered as flaws in the system: 'test scores correlate with parental income (and even grandparents' socio-economic status) rather than actual student performance ...' (Guinier & Torres 2003, p. 68). The fact that the testocracy reduces merit and a meritocracy to a meaningless predestined ordination is ignored. 'Test-centred techniques are used to ration access to elite higher education as appropriate measures of merit' (Guinier and Torres, 2003: 69) and '... at no point was any attempt made to reconcile this with an elitist rationing process' (p. 69).

(Boyle and Charles, 2014: 203–4)

This paints a bleak picture of assessment today, and one which needs to be understood and rejected above all by the ESL community:

> At four or five key points in the year (to be selected by the teacher without external interference) the teacher will carry out an analysis and write a detailed commentary on a piece of the child's assessed work. This commentary identifies the learning that the child has demonstrated in this specific piece of work and the further support or new learning which is required for the child's next step in the learning journey.
>
> (ibid.: 99)

This clarifies both how the formative assessment process can be carried out, and how it contributes to students' learning. It is easily applied to the SL learner. The advantages are:

> The teacher then has a progressive record across the year of the child's learning development, the learning issues and the scaffolding and support strategies which have been used in that period. This provides a full reportable record of each child's learning development for that year. The record is transferable to the next teacher and is an accurate document for reporting progress to parents, talking with the child and reporting externally to a range of accountability stakeholders. Each assessment piece reflects what has gone on in the classroom.
>
> (ibid.: 99)

Further benefits of formative assessment for ESL students can be seen from the following quotes: 'The core of formative assessment lies not in what teachers do but in what they see. The teacher has to have awareness and understanding of the pupils' understandings and progress' (ibid.: 10). ESL teachers have a close relationship with their students, and will be well placed to write comprehensively about their progress and learning needs. 'It is attention to pupil thinking that will cause the teacher to abandon his/her original plan for a lesson' (ibid.: 11), which shows the need for a 'negotiated syllabus' (see Carder, 1979). Also, 'formative assessment should be understood and presented as nothing other than genuine engagement with ideas, which includes being responsive to them and using them to inform next moves' (Coffey *et al.*, 2011: 1129, quoted in Boyle and Charles, 2014: 6). This points out that the teacher will use the assessment for future planning. Furthermore, 'The formative assessment activity must arise from current classroom practice (*not* externally produced tests, quizzes, work sheets for mass consumption and completion)' (Boyle and Charles, 2014: 7), which puts a definitive curb on mass-produced materials.

Practical examples of AfL would include:

> For example, if a teacher during a teaching session is assessing a learner's understanding of alphabetic principles (phonemes), we would not expect that teacher to present a worksheet focused on the 26 letters of the alphabet. Rather there would be multiple assessment routes for that concept, for example how the child reads, how the child writes, what form of code the child uses to write. These are all normal teaching activities with which the learner is comfortable (affective and conative domains)[;] however[,] they are also assessments.
>
> (Boyle and Charles, 2014: 13)

These are useful strategies for SL teachers. In conclusion:

> An assessment task should build on a learner's current experience. The task needs to be clearly, carefully and precisely constructed to enable the learner to demonstrate what he or she knows. Assessment needs to be understood as tightly integrated within teaching and learning.
>
> (ibid.)

This may look like common sense, but in reality how many content teachers would be willing to assess in this way for SL learners?

Assessment for ESL students in the middle school should be overseen by the ESL department. It should not be done in any way that diminishes the self-esteem of the students. Thus, in the IBMYP, for example, grades will not be given according to the language B/acquisition criteria as they have no relationship to the language needed for academic success. Portfolio work can be documented; there can be regular liaison between ESL and content teachers to decide on progress or the need for intervention.

Issues relating to assessment in a student's mother tongue are raised by Mahoney and MacSwan:

> We make a strong distinction between assessing a child's native-language ability and assessing a child's academic subject matter knowledge in his or her native language. The latter, like the assessment of children's knowledge of reading and writing in their native language, improves our understanding about the role that prior academic experience in the home language might play in students' ongoing educational experience. The former does not.
>
> (Mahoney and MacSwan, 2005: 38)

They continue:

> We advocate a child-study approach to assessment of ELL students, one that takes into account a wide range of evidence bearing on an individual child's specific needs and in which all stakeholders have a voice in important decisions. Local resources and program options are as important as the child's level of proficiency in the second language, and must also be taken into consideration. Criteria for identification might be rather different from those established for reclassification, and in no case should important decisions be ... based on one or more scores on standardized tests of language ability or academic achievement.
>
> (ibid.: 40)

Here is more confirmation that standardized tests should be avoided, in this case for SL learners' mother tongues.

Tangen and Spooner-Lane also address the issue of assessment, and the ensuing placement of students in appropriate classes. They write:

> Researchers have found that standardized testing for learning difficulties alone is inadequate and inappropriate to use with students who have EAL (Brown, 2004; Gunderson and Siegel, 2001; Limbos and Geva, 2001). As successful completion of such tests requires sufficient English language proficiency, it stands to reason that students who lack such proficiency will score poorly. In spite of the difficulties involved with testing, Vaughn, Bos and Schumm (2006) reported that there continues to be a disproportionately higher classification of learning

difficulties/disabilities and emotional/behavioural problems for students who have EAL than for those of the majority population group.

(Tangen and Spooner-Lane, 2008: 65)

Every trained and experienced ESL teacher knows about these issues with the testing of ESL students, and the need for more time. Standardized testing is simply not appropriate for them. There is a paradox in the current climate of education in the Anglosphere: as globalization becomes more pervasive there is increasing diversity of languages in the 'global mix'; but at the same time there is an increase in the demand for standardization of testing. There is a sense of a runaway train: the size, speed and complexity of so many issues require a firm hand to bring everything under control. What is needed is a sensitive and understanding approach to the needs of each individual, and this can be enabled by the professional ESL teachers overseeing the testing of ESL students, upon arrival in the school for appropriate placement, and thereafter by setting up school policies throughout grades 6–12 for assessing each ESL student's progression from class to class, or placement in suitable classes for best achievement. The focus will not be on what suits the framework of a politically and economically savvy curriculum provider, but on what is best for each ESL student's learning needs, and also on consideration for content teachers so that they can best provide for fluent English speakers.

We know that children learn at different rates, and we must use differentiation to reach a wide range of students and treat them as individuals, catering to their particular needs, and bringing them along. So why do we judge them all on standards that require that they all get the same skills at approximately the same pace? The irony seems to escape people. Attitudes to assessment have had a largely negative impact on ESL students. Harper and de Jong, discussing the No Child Left Behind Act of 2001 (NCLB; www.ed.gov/policy/elsec/leg/esea02/index.html, accessed 13 February 2018):

Unfortunately, expectations for grade-level achievement on standardised tests in English have resulted in the placement of ELLs into remedial reading classes alongside native English speakers who have been identified as poor readers (Harper, de Jong, and Platt 2008; Callahan 2006). It is assumed that the instruction in these intensive reading classes will meet their needs; however, the texts used in these classes are often too difficult for ELLs, and the curriculum is generally inappropriate for those whose reading difficulties in English lie in vocabulary development and reading comprehension, and not in the decoding and basic skills practice provided.

(Harper and de Jong, 2009: 140)

Here once again is evidence that SLLs are being wrongly placed with native speakers with learning difficulties, a situation that in my experience can be deeply demotivating for the SLLs and may even slow their advancement, but that takes place in many international schools.

Harper and de Jong write further about the inappropriateness of standardized tests for SL learners, and attest to:

the potential and very real negative consequences of standardised, grade-level tests in English for ELLs, including higher dropout rates and a narrowing of the curriculum as teachers focus on preparing students for the test. Further, although allowances for test 'accommodations' (such as bilingual dictionaries and additional time to take the tests) were later added as 'flexibilities' to NCLB accountability guidelines, research by Abedi (2002) and S. Wright (2005) indicates that such accommodations fail to adequately compensate for the language difficulty of the tests.

(ibid.)

It should by now be common knowledge that 'Teachers must provide CLD [culturally and linguistically diverse] students [with] content-specific academic language instruction to support their performance on content area assessments (Kieffer et al., 2009)' (Scanlan and López, 2012: 605). As O. García and Flores point out (2014: 161–2), 'For bilingual students it would be important to create language-proficiency assessments that assess their ability to perform academically in English, their heritage/home language, or a combination of both. In addition, it would be most important to develop valid and reliable assessments that separate language proficiency from content knowledge.'

Common-sense facts about the need for separate instruction for SLLs

Krashen (1982) has shown that an important factor in teaching ESL students is lowering the affective barrier. This implies that in order to encourage ESL students to feel confident, and not to feel restrained by making errors, the teacher should create an atmosphere of trust and freedom in which it is possible to speak out regardless of the consequences. Forty-two years of experience have provided me with conclusive proof that such a strategy bears fruit. Having taught them year after year, I have seen that ESL students aged 11 to 18 open up and gain confidence in a classroom in which they are encouraged to use whatever English language skills they have. A colleague posted a notice above his chalkboard to the effect that errors were to be seen as positive aspects of language learning which could be built on, discussed and improved. A mainstream teacher with many fluent English speakers in her class cannot create these conditions: the fluent speakers will lose patience; the ESL students will keep silent; they may even be teased or bullied by fluent speakers. The class teacher has a massive syllabus to get through; slowing down at every stage for the ESL students is not realistic, nor feasible, however much training may have been received (and for SL requirements it is usually minimal or non-existent).

If all the fluent speakers are graded, and the ESL students are given only comments – as is recommended in best practice – the ESL students, as teenagers, will come to see themselves as being in a separate category. This may persuade the content teacher to give them grades, which may be always lower than fluent speakers', which will discourage them, so that they get yet lower grades.

School administrators, and curriculum providers, need to be realistic about the needs of ESL students. They should not demand of teachers anything that they have not actually done themselves for a period of years. 'Curricula are largely determined by education ministries based on political decisions' (Conteh and Meier, 2014: 7), and teachers are often prevented from doing what they believe to be right because the mainstream curriculum or the hierarchy prevents them.

Tangen and Spooner-Lane comment:

> Students who have EAL very often experience an initial 'quiet period' (Igoa, 1995) as they come to grips with their new situation. There is no set time frame for these quiet periods but it has been observed that the younger the child, the longer the quiet period lasts. During this time, students may exhibit resistance to learning and being included in class activities. Teachers may interpret this reticence to engage in classroom activities as students being uncooperative and misbehaving. It is important for teachers to remember that students who have EAL experience incongruity in their home customs and practices while trying to adjust to their new culture (Singh Ghuman, 1994) and are often bewildered by

their new circumstances. Teachers who are unaware of students' underlying difficulties for learning may become focused on the product of students' work (correct spelling, grammar, reading pronunciation) rather than the process of learning (Nunan, 1999).

(Tangen and Spooner-Lane, 2008: 65–6)

This extract reveals that it is taken for granted that content teachers will not know about the quiet period experienced by ESL students. This is yet another indication that all teachers require CPD in linguistically responsive teaching, and staff who have not had such training should not be employed. Hayden and Thompson note:

Although programmes such as ESL in the Mainstream (Unlocking the World, 2013) have become increasingly popular in response to a need for support in this area, it is undoubtedly the case that too many international school teachers are expected to cope without specific training, and in some schools students may not be as well supported as they and their parents might expect to be the case.

(Hayden and Thompson, 2013: 10–11)

ESL in the Mainstream is no longer offered, and the website has moved to https://lexised.com/courses/teaching-esl-students-in-mainstream-classrooms/ (accessed 13 February 2018). It is interesting to note that these writers use the word 'cope', perhaps implying that this is the best that can be expected with ESL students.

Researchers Hansen-Thomas and Cavagnetto reported:

Many of the mainstream teachers ... reported the desire to learn techniques appropriate for ESL students, as well as to communicate more with the ESL teacher. This suggests a strong need to provide teachers with both time and opportunity to work with trained ESL professionals, through in-service professional development and through release time during the school day.

and:

Further, a partnership between well-trained ... teachers who are informed as to the linguistic demands of ... curriculum, texts, and assessments and other teachers (including those with ESL training) would greatly benefit the teachers and the students by conducting training and dissemination of appropriate information. It is therefore our view that consistent, long-term training in ESL pedagogy and methodology, as well as in the current dimensions of [content matter] and its language-rich requirements, will bring benefit to the teaching and learning of ELLs in content-area classes.

(Hansen-Thomas and Cavagnetto, 2010: 262)

The facts once again provide justification for setting up separate classes for ESL beginners so that they gain confidence in the hands of ESL specialists who are provided with the pedagogical tools and training to handle all aspects of the students' development.

Tangen and Spooner-Lane have also written:

Some teachers embrace the opportunity to work with students who have EAL, others may feel a cultural distance between themselves and their students (Gersten, 1999). Teachers who feel such a gulf may retreat into 'safe' teaching practices that involve little risk-taking for themselves and their students and that may mask what Wheatley (2002) describes as 'teacher doubt'. Teacher doubt may occur when a teacher feels that they are unable to differentiate between a learning difficulty and a difficulty in learning due to limited English language proficiency.

(Tangen and Spooner-Lane, 2008: 64–5)

Again, the need for specialist advice, and professional development training, is clear.

Tangen and Spooner-Lane go on to provide a brief recommendation on how all can be solved. Teachers should:

provide appropriate instruction for all students in the class. Such practices include developing strong communication ties with support personnel, accepting responsibility for including all students, partnering with parents, knowing when and who to ask for help and getting the most effective resources to do the job.

(Tangen and Spooner-Lane, 2008: 67)

Apparently simple, and of course well intentioned, each one of these precepts involves a massive number of obstacles. 'Developing strong communication ties with support personnel': does this mean ESL teachers? SEN teachers? ESL teachers will, in our model, be referred to as appropriate professionals. This whole concept of support continually subverts the professional status of all ESL teachers in the teaching profession. It plays straight into the hands of politicians who are out to de-skill the profession. It is yet another example of how ESL students in international schools are victims of a model designed by political forces in national systems to pander to the forces of nationalism and protectionism against immigrants.

'Accepting responsibility for including all students' is easy to pen, but impossible to realize for teachers who have no training or knowledge of ESL and no idea of what it is that makes the lessons challenging or inaccessible for ESL students; in a dynamic class in which a content teacher is keen to proceed with the syllabus, having to apply the brakes every tenth sentence in order to explain for ESL students is often not an option. This is where a parallel ESL class teaching the same content but at a different speed is the solution.

'Partnering with parents' is of course always recommendable, but issues of time again present themselves, especially if over 50 per cent of the students are SLLs. 'Knowing when and who to ask for help' sounds a little desperate; if there was an appropriate model of parallel ESL classes, in a framework in which ESL teachers had responsibility for parallel content, a mother-tongue programme and continuing professional development, 'help' would no longer be necessary. There might be occasions when extra advice on details was valued, but 'help' simply reveals the failure of the 'EAL as support' model.

Woolley assures us:

> There is, however, wide agreement that appropriate instruction for ESL learners should include explicit support in language and literacy and access to a balanced and challenging curricula associated with high but realistic teacher expectations (Geva & Verthoeven, 2000; Hammond, 2008; Lipka & Siegel, 2007; Ortiz et al., 2006).
>
> (Woolley, 2010: 90)

Again, a rather bland statement that covers a large number of issues that need to be addressed. 'Explicit support' in language and literacy: why not a professional programme of ESL instruction?

Woolley (2010) focuses on reading in ESL students, but, again, his recommendations are nothing that a professional ESL department would not quickly identify and remedy. For example, he writes:

> Although there is limited research on effective intervention practices for English-language learners the assertion is that many ESL learners with reading difficulties can achieve grade-level norms as a result of appropriate instruction (August & Shanahan,

2006; [S.] Baker, Gersten, Dimino, & Griffiths, 2004; Linan-Thompson et al., 2006; Snow, 2008; Tam et al., 2006).

(ibid.)

Once again, there is 'wide agreement that appropriate instruction for ESL learners should include explicit support in language and literacy', which will happen automatically where there is a professional ESL department to provide such instruction. The comments reported above highlight why international schools need to ensure that there is a professional ESL department staffed with qualified applied linguists who can advise content teachers on appropriate strategies, ensure that school directors only employ content teachers with appropriate training, and initiate such training in schools, but above all who can teach the ESL students in separate classes at carefully chosen times so that they can gain the confidence and skills required.

This leads us to issues surrounding ESL and SEN.

Issues relating to the misplacement of SLLs in SEN programmes

In schools in England 'EAL' and 'language support teachers' come under the aegis of special education needs (and disabilities) departments. This model has become ingrained to such an extent that it is barely questioned, and publishers reinforce it. A glance at a well-known publisher – Bloomsbury Publishing – shows how. On their website, www.bloomsbury.com/uk/education/ (accessed 13 February 2018), under 'Secondary', there is a list of 23 subjects. One of these is 'Special educational needs and EAL'. Of the pages that follow of books for this area, there is just one book on 'EAL', titled '100 ideas for supporting learners with EAL' (notice the 'supporting', not teaching), and the other books are on such subjects as psychological disorders, multiple disabilities, dyslexia, supporting deaf children, dyscalculia and such matters. 'Teaching modern foreign languages', of course, gets a separate link, even though this subject involves far less complexity than teaching a *second* language. There is no separate link for EAL. The negative effects of treating ESL students as SEN students have been documented throughout the literature on ESL students (e.g. Cummins, 1984), and have been touched on above.

The model from England had consequences for international schools: as already related, in 2002 the CIS reallocated ESL and put it in the same section as SEN in the Guide for Accreditation; in 2006 the IB devised a new post of Second Language Learning specialist, but appointed her under the SEN section. International schools in Europe are more affected by the proximity of the English experience, and many ESL teachers are British, bringing with them the experience of the English school curriculum. The result is often a docile acceptance that ESL/EAL will not be seen as a separate discipline, will be labelled EAL, and will be subsumed under the SEN umbrella.

Woolley (2010: 81) writes: 'In many countries the proportion of students learning English as their second language [L2] is increasing dramatically and presenting educators with greater challenges (Freebody, Maton, & Martin, 2008).' He continues (ibid.: 88), 'There is a growing international consensus in the literature that second-language (L2) learners have generally been underdiagnosed and overrepresented in special education classes.'

As mentioned above, Tangen and Spooner-Lane (2008: 65) address the issue of assessment, and the ensuing placement of students in inappropriate classes.

It is important to establish a clear differentiation between ESL students and those with genuine learning difficulties. Of course, such boundaries are not always clear, but they are not clear in any discipline when it comes to distinguishing students who are struggling with a particular subject, and the concern here is to provide a learning environment for SLLs which is geared to their potential and to avoid them being placed with a particular group of students, which might be seen as demotivating.

Some research articles on the ESL/SEN boundaries will be reviewed. What is interesting about these articles is that the authors appear to take it as a given that teachers will not have basic training in 'linguistically responsive teaching' of the type we recommended.

Tangen and Spooner-Lane write:

> There is a growing body of evidence to suggest that some students who have English as an additional language (EAL) are being misidentified by teachers as having learning difficulties when, in fact, some of these students may not have a learning difficulty at all (Artiles and Klingner, 2006; Brown, 2004; Gersten and Baker, 2003).
>
> (Tangen and Spooner-Lane, 2008: 63)

The reasons for this are related:

> [S.B.] Garcia and Ortiz (1988) suggested that one reason why students who have EAL may experience difficulties learning

is because they are often taught solely in English. Teachers who expect that these students should be keeping up with their peers may become frustrated teaching students who are EAL because they are not maintaining a similar learning pace (Byrnes et al., 1997). Teachers need to take into account that students who have EAL must learn new concepts in a new language within a new cultural reference. Teachers, therefore, must make accommodations in their teaching. Without adequate groundwork in developing learning activities to support their learning, students who have EAL may be missing out on important English language instruction due to limited teacher preparation and/or limited resources (Iredale [and Fox], 199[7]). Lo Bianco and Freebody (1997) described this deficit mode of teaching as a 'sink or swim' approach. Students who have EAL are placed in an English speaking classroom and are expected to learn in English while still learning the English language. While some students adapt and quickly learn the classroom protocol (swim), others struggle until the point of giving up (sink).

(Tangen and Spooner-Lane, 2008: 64)

These are strong statements of the situation of SL learners, and are ones that are frequently found in international schools.

Mahoney and MacSwan have another insight into the misclassification of ESL students as SEN:

Artiles, Rueda, Salazar, and Higareda (2005) report that ELL children assessed as lacking proficiency in their native language have a high likelihood of being classified (arguably incorrectly) as special education students. Although it has been argued that assessing children's native language provides supplemental information to help teachers and administrators better evaluate students' English-proficiency test results (CCSSO, 1991 [Council of Chief State School Officers]), we believe it is more likely to create an atmosphere of confusion and result in incorrect perceptions of children's learning situations.

(Mahoney and MacSwan, 2005: 38)

With the expert knowledge of ESL specialists the confusion could be resolved.

The following websites provide information on ways of differentiating ESL and SEN issues:

www.naldic.org.uk/teaching-learning/
https://naldic.org.uk/httpsealjournal-org20170320eal-pupils-with-special-needs-are-we-meeting-their-needs/
www.colorincolorado.org › *School Support* › *Special Education and English Language Learners*
https://bctf.ca/uploadedFiles/Publications/ESL-SpecialNeeds.pdf
www.education.vic.gov.au › ... › *Language Support*
www.assessmentforlearning.edu.au/verve/_resources/specialneeds.pdf (all sites above accessed 13 February 2018).

Realities and practicalities

Schools are places of tension and stress. Even in a school with no second language students there would still be the daily tasks of preparing, teaching, doing duties, attending meetings, liaising with other staff, correcting work, keeping up with the latest demands of the newest bureaucracy and the most up-to-date IT, informing parents – the list is endless. To add to this the creation of a new ESL and mother tongue department, with its declared role of educating all staff, leadership, parents and board members, will add a new dimension to the daily round. But it is essential that this new dimension be taken seriously and developed systematically, and this needs a guaranteed commitment from school heads. Without this commitment, and a comprehensive understanding of all the language and in-service issues involved, the new department will fail. It will be marginalized and deteriorate, and in all likelihood return to the status so long prevalent in national systems in which ESL students are seen as a problem in need of support, and the ESL teachers can look after them.

There is a real danger that the creation of a department seen to be responsible for bilingual matters will lead most of the other staff to shun their own responsibilities and defer all matters to the ESL staff. This of course would defeat the purpose of the exercise. Shaw's comment (2003: 104–5) that 'there is no collegiality in schools' and Davison's discussion (2006: 458) of 'contrived collegiality' need to be taken seriously. Sears (2015: 74) suggests that 'For teachers new to [the MYP], the most effective way forward is to build a good relationship with the ... MYP coordinators, who are appointed in every IB school to oversee the programmes and to support teachers.' Of course: but this won't help if the MYP coordinator does not have any answers about the learning and assessment needs of ESL students except for 'you must follow the language B/Acquisition programme', which has been shown to be working against their best interests. Tensions will arise. Maybe the head of English will intervene and say that the MYP rules must be followed at all costs, and that resistance to such a path will be referred to the head of school, with possibly dire consequences. These are not inventions but real case scenarios, and many ESL teachers end up in survival mode, hoping that someone somewhere will understand the wonderful potential of ESL students and provide a programme designed for their true learning needs rather than to suit a global curriculum body that wants to win the game. Therefore, no half measures will be enough. School heads and directors who are persuaded by the arguments in this book will need not only to set up the type of department advocated, but to back it all the way. Such departments will need strong, determined, qualified leaders, who can stand up to criticism in head of department meetings, make their case to boards of governors and to parent meetings, and employ enthusiastic, well-trained and flexible staff for the daily tasks of teaching ESL students, liaising with content teachers, running in-service programmes for all staff, and generally spreading the word about the potential and needs of ESL students.

ESL department heads will also need to have excellent organisational skills. Sears notes:

> Most specialist English teaching [i.e., ESL] … programmes have one thing in common: they tend to be logistically complex. It is common for teachers to have to consult numerous schedules and programme documents in order to understand the detail. The complexity arises because specialist English language and mother tongue provision (where an in-school programme exists) typically involve cross-class scheduling with classes at multiple levels. Newly arrived teachers in a school may need to consult year-level colleagues and specialist English language teachers in order to understand how the programme offerings affect the day-to-day running of an individual class.
>
> (Sears, 2015: 153)

Many years of experience of running a professional ESL programme support this statement, and contact with ESL in other international schools bears it out: one teacher told me that he always wore trainers in school as he spent so much time running around to talk to the various content teachers of the ESL students.

Implications for international schools, accrediting agencies and curriculum providers

When the recommendations outlined in this chapter are carried out there will be a need for a shake-up in international schools, accrediting agencies and curriculum providers.

In schools, directors will establish ESL and mother-tongue departments in middle schools and begin a process of cementing their centrality in the hierarchy. Only highly qualified and experienced ESL teachers will be employed: there is no lack of these, as many universities in the Anglosphere can corroborate, and there are countless NNESTs available. Unqualified ESL teachers and assistants offering support will be phased out. My experience of ESL teachers in many international schools is similar to that recounted by Pedalino Porter:

> I observed the haphazard assignment of ill-prepared teachers to teach ESL. In most cases, they had little idea at all of how to teach a foreign language – which is what English was to their students. My experience, once again, is representative. In the minds of school administrators, anyone who can speak English can teach English. ... [T]hey press-ganged all sorts of people into teaching limited-English students: high school English teachers and foreign language teachers, elementary classroom teachers, ... remedial reading teachers .... It was not unusual for small-group English lessons to be given in hallways, broom closets, cafeterias, and boiler rooms. ...
>
> Teachers who could not maintain discipline, who were not competent in teaching their subjects, or who, for various reasons, were functioning at a low level were sometimes given the job of working with ... children ... whose situations cried out for the most able teachers to work with them.
>
> (Pedalino Porter, 1990: 28–9)

Pedalino Porter also outlined, nearly thirty years ago, that a model ESL programme should have:

- Well-trained staff, skilled in second-language-teaching theory and methodology and in the school subjects, informed and sensitive to cultural differences, and with high expectations for the students

- Training for the whole school community – principals, mainstream teachers, and support staff – to recognize and understand cultural differences and to provide a reassuring, welcoming school atmosphere
- Strong, consistent communication with parents to enlist their understanding of and participation in the school's goals.

(ibid.: 129)

Schools will need an accelerating process of CPD in linguistic and cultural awareness techniques such as TESMC, which will be obligatory for all staff, regularly updated. Accrediting agencies such as the CIS will take the lead by carrying out the same process in their accrediting documentation: ESL will not come at the end of the documented requirements under support. Rather it will appear as the first subject item, carrying the most weight.

Curriculum providers such as the IB will make a clear distinction in the MYP between foreign language and second language. There will be extensive documentation specifically for second language, with details of the need for a well-constructed ESL programme and examples of the most appropriate types of assessment: the work has already been done with the SLA and MTD Guide. There will be workshops designed solely for teachers of ESL students, not combined with foreign-language workshops. If such changes are not forthcoming, alternatives to the MYP will need to be sought.

School heads will make clear to parents the issues associated with bilingualism, the principal ones being: the considerable length of time required for learning a second language to a high academic level; the fact that post-pubertal children will rarely acquire a native-like English accent; and the importance of maintaining and developing the mother tongue.

When all of the above processes are carried out school heads will experience improvements in many areas. Placing ESL teachers and their expertise at the centre of the departmental network will make all staff familiar with the many aspects of SLA and bilingualism. ESL students will benefit immensely and their parents will be enlightened and probably relieved to see the potential of bilinguals being unleashed. Monolingualism will no longer be seen as the norm. It is probable that IB examination results will improve across the spectrum.

But there is one large caveat: ESL professionals must be just that – professional. Having gained their new central status in the school and curriculum structure, they will be hardworking and outgoing, ready to deal with many issues beyond their teaching load: liaising with content teachers, communicating regularly with parents, sharing information about their students with the mother-tongue teachers, running CPD for content staff.

It will be vital to select a strong, knowledgeable, qualified and determined head of department and ensure that her department has the central status necessary to implement the strategies discussed, and to take a proactive stance with leadership if it does not understand or condone the central tenets of a professional ESL department. This person's most important tasks will be to ensure that all the ESL staff are trained and qualified ESL professionals, that there is a clear understanding that the department is of the same status as all other departments, that new staff have a university qualification focused on ESL and bilingualism, and that there is a comprehensive mother-tongue programme, and to take action when there is a lack in any area. Managing people is complex, but the responsibility is to the students, and ineffective and recalcitrant staff help no one.

There is a large body of research on the broad benefits of bilingualism, from neurological to economic advantages (Bialystok, 2011; Callahan and Gándara, 2014; Craik *et al.*, 2010; Engel de Abreu *et al.*, 2012; Hogan-Brun, 2017; Kovács and Mehler, 2009). Let international schools build on this in a professional manner, not on the rubble of national educational systems. As Fukuyama notes, 'The ability of societies to innovate institutionally ... depends on whether they can neutralize existing political stakeholders holding vetoes over reform' (Fukuyama, 2011: 456).

Chapter 9

The need for continuing professional development (CPD)

Patricia Mertin

The days when it was sufficient to train as a teacher then continue on the same path until retirement are long gone. Formerly it was often seen as a strength, and a sign of solid experience, when a teacher consistently maintained the same teaching approach, followed the same curriculum, and assigned the same homework tasks, tests and grading. However, this could be described as one year of experience followed by many years of repetition, rather than as a sign of developing knowledge. In the late twentieth and early twenty-first centuries the philosophy of education, and beliefs about teaching and learning, have undergone many changes. Practice is continually influenced by the latest research, with developing curricula and ever-changing examination requirements making it essential for educators to remain up to date.

Education has moved on from the twentieth-century emphasis on acquiring knowledge, facts and skills to a world in which facts are readily available through the internet, but the real expertise of analytical and critical thinking, together with deep understanding, is urgently required. There is a need for students to think for themselves, define and form opinions about problems and issues, find creative solutions, discuss, defend and debate ideas, listen to others and share knowledge.

In both national education systems and international education there is a growing awareness of global issues and their importance for the youth of today as the world becomes a smaller place. International schools in particular now use the term 'international-mindedness' to express a raft of ideas about the shared world we live in, and the development of intercultural understandings and linguistic proficiencies. A further idea which is reinforced by the IB is that we all, teachers and students, are or should be lifelong learners.

In addition to these developments in educational thinking, the world is changing around us, and across the globe people are becoming more mobile. In the past many people stayed in the same town, or at least the same area, for most of their lives. It often happened that children went to the same schools, even with the same teachers, as their parents did. Everyone spoke the same language, so that teaching students with a different mother tongue was seldom an issue. Now, however, in a world with increased mobility, more and more children are attending schools in which they must learn in one language but communicate in another, or others, at home. This change in society necessitates an additional set of skills, regrettably one seldom addressed in teaching colleges. This means that few teachers in international or national schools have been effectively trained and equipped to work with SL learners.

The current research on language acquisition has taken a new 'social turn' with the focus on social interaction as a key component of language acquisition (see Block, 2003). At the same time, more research is being undertaken into multilingualism and multilingual education. We now know that skills gained in the mother tongue are readily transferred to a second language. The need for qualified, experienced ESL teachers in international schools with a high percentage of SL learners is clear to any thinking educator. But there is also a need for mainstream classroom teachers, who are experts in their own special areas, to be given ongoing additional training to make their teaching accessible to the SL student's learning.

Just as teachers generally receive little training in working with SL speakers, they have even fewer opportunities to develop their ideas about and understanding of multilingualism.

> [M]any teachers struggle with the idea of legitimising multilingualism in their classrooms. Often, this is because they have had little opportunity to reflect on this during their teacher education, and to develop appropriate teaching strategies.
>
> (Conteh and Meier, 2014: 296)

Research has shown that the time taken for a SL learner to reach a native-speaker level of CALP is between five and seven years. During this period of time, after students have been given a solid grounding in the English language and have moved into full-time mainstream classrooms, they still require linguistically aware, thoughtful, knowledgeable teaching. That is teaching which will not only make the content and language of successful learning comprehensible but also equip students with the level of language required to demonstrate their knowledge and understanding.

The administration

In an international school, as in any school, the principal and the school leadership team play a crucial role and have responsibility for the provision of quality education for all students. However, as long as most administrators are from anglophone countries and monolingual, they may be led to believe that students who speak other languages at home present a problem, whereas these students are better seen as a source of linguistic and cultural learning experiences. Welcoming students from different cultural and linguistic backgrounds needs to be viewed as an exciting opportunity for all teachers and students: after all, these are the students who make an international school international.

It is essential that appropriately qualified and experienced administrators are hired, when possible from a variety of ethnic and linguistic groups which reflects the student population, and bring with them an understanding of the benefits of multilingualism and multiculturalism. Unless the situation of the majority of international students as SLLs is recognized and valued as a resource by those in leadership positions, little progress will be made. Monolingual educators often have difficulty accepting the idea of bilingualism or even multilingualism in the classroom, let alone the idea of using other languages to support content learning in English.

Practices in schools are always led from the top, and the climate of a school as a multilingual, multicultural, welcoming institution can only be determined through the demonstration of effective practices by the leadership team. If the leadership team and teachers are monolingual, from Anglosphere countries, with limited experience of working with SLLs in their classrooms, they are unlikely to understand the challenges facing SLLs, recognize their talents and abilities, or support their teachers in their efforts to teach. Cummins states in his discussion of why students choose to engage, or to withdraw from academic effort:

> [H]*uman relationships are at the heart of schooling.* All of us intuitively know this from our own schooling experiences. If we felt that a teacher believed in us and cared for us then we put forth much more effort than if we felt that she or he did not like us or considered us not very capable.
>
> (Cummins, 2000: 40; emphasis original)

August and Hakuta (1997) reviewed 33 studies of school effectiveness, and from this compiled a list of 13 attributes of effective schools. The second of these concerned the school leadership:

(2) *School leadership*. The principal of the school is seen as a key player in ELL students' academic achievement in most of the studies reviewed. She or he makes the achievement of ELL students a priority, monitors curricular and instructional improvement, recruits and keeps talented and dedicated staff, involves the entire staff in improvement efforts, and maintains a good social and physical environment.

...

(12) *Staff development*. August and Hakuta [(1997)] note that staff development for all teachers in the school, not just language specialists, was a significant component of many of the effective schools. All teachers were expected to know how to teach ELL students ... and were given the support to do so.

(Cummins, 2000: 264, 265)

The teachers

As explained in chapter 1, teachers tend to come from three groups: local hires, local expatriate hires, and foreign expatriate hires. The hiring of the best teachers is key to the quality of education in any school. Unfortunately, school directors or their principals who are responsible for hiring frequently have little training in the international aspects of the process.

Teachers new to international schools have rarely had the kind of training that prepares them for their new assignments, as their initial teacher training will have been based on their own national system. The biggest problem is that insufficient ESL teachers are being trained. Similarly, mainstream teachers are not being trained to teach the language of the curriculum or to respond to the challenges this presents to students as regards the language they need to express ideas, give information, answer questions, or complete any of the other tasks expected in a mainstream classroom. This problem is both a national and an international one, as reports in the British press demonstrate. Concerning the situation in England, Libby Purves wrote in *The Times*, in an article entitled 'Gift of language is what migrants need most'

For decades 'full-speed immersion' was a favoured local authority policy, pitching children into a mainstream class with a learning support assistant as if they had some mental or physical disability. Extroverts survived this, but other children felt humiliated and different, and never quite took to education thereafter.

She continued:

> In some places, 'immediate immersion' dribbles on for both
> economic and ideological reasons. One educationalist said that it
> doesn't much matter if children aren't saying much, they could be
> happy and 'picking up a lot'. But a child unable to express anything
> in the long school day is not, in my experience, particularly
> happy. Some schools rewrite lessons 'to accommodate low levels
> of English focusing on graphs and pictures'. That, like support
> assistants and relying on 'picked up' language, is far cheaper
> than hiring a qualified EAL teacher, if you can find one, to work
> alongside regular staff.
>
> (Purves, 2015)

Holderness writes:

> In 1998, Peel suggested that the task before international
> education was to ensure:
>
> • shared responsibility;
> • global standards in examinations;
> • training of teachers and examiners.
>
> Yet most newly appointed international teachers, leaving their
> home countries to enter the world of international schooling, are
> likely to have had little preparation for, or induction into, their
> new life.
>
> (Holderness, 2002: 86)

Many teachers hired to teach in international schools are young and
enthusiastic as they embark on this new adventure. They know they are
going to teach in a new country, but in many ways they are unprepared for
the challenges they will face. Many are the same challenges new students
at an international school face: living in a country where they may not
speak the language, growing accustomed to everyday life in an unfamiliar
environment, finding their place in a new school, finding friends, dealing with
a new curriculum, and more. In addition, new teachers have to work with
new bosses and colleagues in a different school system, but lack a network
of family and friends to support them. The familiar phases of culture shock
and assimilation are experienced by new teachers and students alike. The
question Cummins poses is relevant to international schools and teachers:

The need for continuing professional development (CPD)

> To what extent is it child abuse to send new teachers into
> classrooms (in multilingual cities such as Toronto, London, or
> New York) with minimal or no preparation on how to teach
> academic content to students who are in the process of learning
> English and whose cultural background differs significantly from
> that assumed by all of the structures of schooling (e.g. curriculum,
> assessment, and teacher preparation)?
>
> (Cummins, 2000: 14)

New teachers may have a working knowledge of a foreign language
themselves, but the ability to communicate in a foreign language is very
different from the ability to study, to understand academic content, or
to demonstrate knowledge and understanding of academic content in all
subject areas at the same level as native speakers. When students learn a
foreign language, as opposed to a second language, they may spend four
or five teaching periods in the foreign-language classroom per week. In
that time they are being actively taught the language. However, when they
leave the classroom at the end of the period they will probably not use the
language again until the next foreign-language class. They will not need to
use it to communicate with their peers on a daily basis and they will not
be studying science, maths, humanities or any other content area using this
foreign language.

Second language learners, on the other hand, spend the entire
school day listening, speaking, reading and writing in the second language.
Moreover, many international schools are situated in countries where
the environment presents a third language for SL students to master. The
challenges to succeeding academically are huge.

As most teachers have only learned a foreign language at school or
in their free time, it is difficult for them to appreciate the task of an SL
learner in their classroom. They often just do not know how to make the
language of their subject area accessible to SL learners. The content, the
specialist vocabulary, the language around it and the genres required are so
much part of the teacher's world, of who they are and what they do, that
when a student is unable to see through the language to grasp the content,
these teachers are often unable to understand the problem. The problem is
compounded when the students are unable to explain what it is that they
do not understand.

Leung notes:

> The mainstream (ordinary) curriculum is the place where a
> good deal of EAL teaching and learning is meant to take place,

> particularly for those students who are beyond the early stages of learning English ... in many English-speaking education systems.
>
> (Leung, 2010: 9)

If the mainstream teacher has not been trained to recognize the challenges and deal with them, the SL student is seriously disadvantaged. Often this leads the parents to hire private tutors who may or may not be familiar with the curriculum requirements of an international school: often the parents have neither the language nor the content knowledge to support their children. Native English-speaking parents are often able to provide more help, simply because they are more familiar, from their own school time, with the kind of material being learned.

Research has confirmed that bilingual students' perceptions of their teachers' appreciation of their mother tongue do indeed influence their bilingual cognitive advantages. Goriot *et al.* (2016) examined whether bilingual Dutch primary school students who spoke either German or Turkish at home differed in their perceptions of their teacher's appreciation of their home language, and also whether these differences could explain any differences between the two groups' performance in various skills. Their findings were that 'German-Dutch pupils perceived there to be more appreciation of their home language from their teacher than Turkish-Dutch pupils' (Goriot *et al.*, 2016: 700). This is more proof of the need for culturally and linguistically responsive teaching.

Varieties of in-service training
Induction

Many international schools offer a phase of induction to new teachers before the new term begins, but when basic problems such as where and how to do a daily shop, how to get to school each day, or how to deal with a new landlord, must be overcome, preparation for teaching may take second place. These teachers often need practical and even emotional support during the first weeks and months in a new school in an unfamiliar country when they face so many other challenges. This support must come from the administration, the department chair and departmental colleagues, all of whom are, hopefully, familiar with the details of daily life in school: the schedule, the curriculum, tasks to cover, the pace of teaching, assessment and more. In addition, new teachers are often unprepared for classes of highly motivated and engaged students whose parents are also successful and motivated.

These teachers may be surprised by the range of cultures and language levels which faces them from day one, so that the lesson plans and teaching methods which were successful in the past are inexplicably unsuccessful in their new situation. However, a one-week induction programme for new teachers cannot equip them with the skills they need to teach a linguistically and culturally diverse student population. Another challenge presented by international schools is the high level of motivation of many parents, who are themselves successful professionals and expect strong academic results from their children. SL learners are learning language and content simultaneously, and their academic results will influence their future prospects. This makes it essential for teachers to focus on the language of their subject as well as the content:

> The integration of content and language-learning objectives presents challenges for policy makers, program planners, curriculum designers, teachers, material writers, teacher educators, teacher supervisors, text writers, and learners.
>
> (Stoller, 2008: 65, quoted in Leung and Creese, 2010: xviii)

Professional development to deal with these challenges faced by new teachers needs to be a priority and has to be ongoing. The skills and strategies which teachers need to enable the SLLs to access the curriculum cannot be taught in an afternoon: there needs to be a process of in-service training in appropriate linguistically responsive techniques. Moreover, as the turnover of teaching staff is high in many international schools, this process has to be sustained over the years.

Professional development

One of the challenges facing international schools is which professional development should be offered to the faculty; there is a real danger that if too many initiatives are attempted at once the result will be overload and additional stress.

While the IB training for teachers is essential if the PYP, MYP and DP programmes are to be taught well, it is unfortunate that the IB fails to recognize the importance of a dedicated, qualified department to teach English to second language learners. Teachers who take part in the training, for MYP especially, find that ESL is considered to be language B/Acquisition, like other foreign languages studied at school. Those other languages, for example French, Spanish and Mandarin, are studied for an average of five periods each week. However, for SLLs, who leave the language classroom and use English to communicate socially and to study academic content across the curriculum for all of their studies – humanities, science, mathematics, etc. – the difference is considerable.

There are many other areas within a school which can be improved through professional development, and the key to this development is found when individual teachers can see the effect it has on both the effectiveness of their teaching and the learning demonstrated by students in their classrooms. There are many ways in which CPD can be encouraged and become an essential part of the culture of the school.

All-school professional development may be led by an outside expert who comes in for one or two days and presents to the full faculty. The danger with this form of PD is that one size does not necessarily fit all, and not everyone will see the value of the sessions. This external specialist may also work more specifically with small groups, but at the end of the day he or she will leave the school, and the old routines will return unless a concerted effort is made by the administration to develop the skills and strategies the visiting trainer has introduced.

Other professional development opportunities are presented at conferences, where individuals, who are permitted to attend by their school, can select the presentations they wish to hear and take back new ideas for their own teaching. This opportunity is often limited to a few individuals because of the cost, but the new knowledge and skills learned should, of course, be shared with colleagues wherever appropriate. A professional training course for teachers working with students who are learning English language and content in their mainstream classes is offered by the course TESMC (https://lexised.com, accessed 13 February 2018).

This is offered as a tutor-training course primarily for ESL teachers. A five-day, train-the-tutor professional development course is given to teachers who can go back to their schools and deliver professional training to the content teachers. The course for classroom teachers consists of 25 hours of instruction delivered in nine modules, plus readings and activities. This results in a total of 50 hours of professional development, which the teacher trained as a tutor can give to all their colleagues over a period of months. The course focuses on the language-related needs of ESL students, develops teacher awareness of cultural and linguistic difference, helps teachers try out strategies and to reflect on their own practice, and supports the development of collaborative working partnerships across subject areas and with the ESL department. The TESMC course is described as follows:

The programme claims the following outcomes:

- Identification of the language-related needs of ESL students and development of teaching practices that address their needs in a holistic and explicit manner.
- Development of teachers' awareness of how to accommodate the cultural and linguistic diversity and experiences of ESL students.
- Provision of a positive context for teachers to trial suggested strategies and reflect critically and openly on their teaching.
- Exemplification of how to develop collaborative working relationships between teachers (across subject areas) through a shared understanding of how to support ESL students.

(https://lexised.com/courses/teaching-esl-students-in-mainstream-classrooms/, accessed 13 February 2018)

The TESMC course is a development of ESL in the Mainstream (DECS, 1999), launched in 1987 in Australia, but no longer offered. Both Carder and I have been trained as tutors and led courses with colleagues from our schools. Experience shows that there is much enthusiasm for the course while it is running, but, so far, to the best of our knowledge, no research has been undertaken to measure the longer-term effects.

An initiative from the ECIS is the ITC, the International Teacher Certificate (www.ecis.org/learning/itc, accessed 13 February 2018), developed and examined by the University of Cambridge. Its main aim is to 'equip teachers with the global mind-set necessary for successful teaching in the 21st century'. This certificate has five standards, one of which focuses on the 'language dimension' of teaching and learning. The intercultural aspect of education in international schools is also addressed by the standards.

'George Mason University has been preparing educators to teach in international environments since 1990. Formerly called FAST TRAIN (Foreign Affairs Spouses Teacher TRAINing Program), Mason continues to offer high quality, convenient, and experience-driven graduate education to international educators worldwide' (https://gse.gmu.edu/teaching-culturally-diverse-exceptional-learners/international-cohorts/; accessed 18 September 2018). Teachers in the state of Colorado are now required to have a specific qualification for teaching ESL in content areas if they are working with middle-school students. A school that employs teachers from England will have to establish that ESL teachers have an MA in applied linguistics or TESOL, as there is no undergraduate or PGCE qualification.

A fundamental text for content teachers is *What Teachers Need to Know about Language* (Adger *et al.*, 2018), which has chapter headings such as 'Analyzing *themes*: Knowledge about language for explaining text structure', 'What educators need to know about academic language: Insights from recent research', and 'Language and instruction: Research-based lesson planning and delivery for English learner students'. The book, written by foremost researchers in the field, covers all aspects of what teachers need to know when teaching culturally and linguistically diverse students.

Cambridge International Examinations also offers routes that candidates can follow, from post-kindergarten stage through to university entrance. Cambridge University Press's provision includes support for teachers through publications, online resources, training, workshops and professional development. It offers examinations in ESOL at various levels of proficiency, and has centres throughout the world. Since it also offers training for teachers in ESOL it can be seen as a viable alternative to the IBMYP, which offers no dedicated course for ESL students or specific training workshops for ESL teachers. Recently, Cambridge University Press has published a book which focuses on content language for ESL students (T. Chadwick, 2012), and there is also a series of books on ESL for chemistry, biology and physics (Sang and Chadwick, 2014). I have written a book specifically for content teachers in international schools (Mertin, 2013).

If we are to put the 'continuing' into professional development the process must be continuing, ongoing and effective. There are many kinds of professional development, but the focus here has to be on the needs of teachers who are learning to work effectively with second-language students, 'effectively' meaning that the teachers are able to make the content comprehensible and accessible, while at the same time enabling the students to learn the language of their subject and develop their ability to listen, speak, read and write about their subject in English at grade level.

The array of subjects taught in international schools presents a huge range of content vocabulary, text structure, genre writing and expectations which students need to recognize and use correctly. A worthwhile activity for any teacher would be to spend a day shadowing an SL student and experience the range of language which confronts them as they struggle to master the language of maths, science, business studies, humanities, IT and other subject areas – a huge challenge.

One of the most effective ways of encouraging all-school PD is to promote the formation of small learning groups of teachers who identify their own areas of interest and undertake research to improve their teaching and learning. This can take many forms, for example observing colleagues and sharing observations, or reading and following up research in order to share and try out new ideas. A wealth of material on the subject of language acquisition is available, and of course the school's ESL department is a further valuable resource.

Creating small learning groups for PD has the advantage of engaging teachers in the areas they are interested in, and in which they can widen their areas of professional expertise. In this way, they are working towards a goal which they have identified, and so are engaged and active, rather than just passive receivers of information. At the same time, because the teachers have been active in choosing the research topics, they have a vested interest in the development. Final results can be published and shared in international school journals, which makes the research more meaningful.

As, probably, the biggest challenge to international schools is giving SLLs access to the curriculum, research groups can be formed, either by subject area or by grade levels, that include the ESL teachers. Through discussions about many aspects of language acquisition, the difference between academic and social language, and the challenges of specific language for certain areas of the curriculum, the ESL teachers can support and guide the classroom and subject-area teachers while the latter learn more about the linguistic demands which confront students in each area of the curriculum. Enabling the ESL students to be successful, by clarifying the demands of academic language, has to be the responsibility of the whole faculty.

Chapter 10

The importance of maintaining mother tongue development

Patricia Mertin

Wer fremde Sprachen nicht kennt, weiss nichts von seiner eigenen.
(Goethe, 1821)

The nature of an international school is that many of its students are not mother-tongue speakers of English, which is usually the language of instruction. These students not only need to learn English but also to learn *in* English, which is an enormous challenge. As SLLs make up a high percentage of the students, it is a key responsibility of the boards, the administrators and all teachers to ensure that they are taught English in such a way that they benefit socially and academically and can continue their education with as little interruption as possible. As SLLs may stay for only a few years before either moving on to another international school or returning to their home country, to continue school or higher education or to pursue their careers, the importance of an effective ESL programme cannot be ignored. The students' time in an international school may begin at any stage of their education, from kindergarten to high school, but it is essential that during this period their academic study continues successfully; their whole future depends on this.

The parents of these students entrust their children to international schools in the belief that the administration and teachers know how to teach their children English to the level required for academic success. This makes the maintenance and development of the mother tongue to an age-appropriate level of vital importance for their continuing academic success.

The role of English in the lives of SLLs is unusual in several ways. The language they must learn, English, is often not the language of the environment, so there may be little linguistic input outside the school environment. A further language is often used in the environment, so that students have no opportunities to practise their English while shopping, reading local papers or magazines, watching local TV, or reading road signs or advertisements in the street. This is a fundamental difference from the situation of SLLs in Anglosphere countries: English is not heard being used by the local population. Their fellow students may speak a wide variety of other languages, so that much of the language practice will be undertaken between English language learners and users with varying levels of proficiency, rather than with fluent native speakers.

The mother tongues spoken by students in international schools need to be valued as of equal status and importance with English. This contrasts with SLLs in national systems where assimilation is the goal and other mother tongues are ignored.

Recognition of the mother tongues in the classroom

Students who speak languages other than English in the home become English language learners and users in international English-medium schools. They bring with them their cultural capital: a wealth of knowledge about the world, their previous learning, educational experience, culture and their language. All of these can contribute to enriching learning experiences for everyone who comes into contact with them if they are given opportunities to share. When their language, their culture and their previous knowledge and experiences are recognized and accepted, the students' own feelings of worth are increased. However, as Cummins states:

> [W]hen students' language, culture and experience are ignored or excluded in classroom interactions, students are immediately starting from a disadvantage. Everything they have learned about life and the world up to this point is being dismissed as irrelevant to school learning; there are few points of connection to curriculum materials or instruction and so students are expected to learn in an experiential vacuum. Students' silence and non-participation under these conditions have frequently been interpreted as lack of academic ability or effort, and teachers' interactions with students have reflected a pattern of low expectations which become self-fulfilling.
>
> (Cummins, 1996: 2–3)

Similarly, Reeves writes:

> The use of bilingualism in the classroom is an important educational tool. The Cox Report (1989) followed in the footsteps of the Swann Report (1985) in stating that the emphasis in the primary classroom should be firmly on the development of a good command of English. At the same time the Cox Report

asserted that 'the evidence shows that children will make greater progress in English if they know that their knowledge of their mother tongue is valued'.

(Reeves, 1994: 61)

Unfortunately, while the students are learning English, less attention tends to be paid to their mother tongue; consequently, parents and teachers need to be informed about the importance of maintaining and developing students' mother tongues.

Clearly mother-tongue maintenance is important for social reasons: maintaining contact with extended family and friends, and making new friends who speak the same language at school. It is also important for academic and professional reasons: deepening and extending students' understanding of the material studied, enabling them to discuss their learning with family members, and facilitating their return to their home countries to continue their education before beginning their careers. Students who maintain their mother tongue while learning English, and so become balanced bilinguals, have major advantages when they begin their careers, as the increasingly globalized world requires speakers of more than one language who can communicate across borders. Additive bilingualism brings clear professional advantages.

The importance of the mother tongue is not a new idea: Cummins quotes an example in which Gaelic is the mother tongue and English the target language:

[N]ot all regions in Scotland had schools, even well into the nineteenth century. And where schools existed, students and educators alike faced another dilemma: largely for political reasons, English was the preferred medium of instruction, despite obvious problems in communication. Worse, many schools ignored Gaelic entirely, both because it was politically expedient and because there were no Gaelic texts to use. Fortunately, by the early nineteenth century, attitudes had softened somewhat; the Scots had not risen against the English recently, and educators discovered that Gaelic students learned to read English more easily if they had a basic grounding in Gaelic grammar and literature.

(Thompson, 1998: x–xi, quoted in Cummins, 2000: 173)

This extract underlines the relevance of the mother tongue to learning a second language, and many studies have shown that cognitive and academic development in L1 has a strong, positive effect on L2 development for academic purposes. Cummins states:

> There are close to 150 empirical studies carried out during the past 30 or so years that have reported a positive association between additive bilingualism and students' linguistic, cognitive, or academic growth. The most consistent findings among these research studies are that bilinguals show more developed awareness of language (metalinguistic awareness) and that they have advantages in learning additional languages.
>
> (Cummins, 2000: 37)

Cummins's threshold hypothesis has been discussed already; it highlights the idea that if a student's mother tongue is not supported, and they are required to focus only on learning English, they will reach a stage where they become unable to function academically in either English or their mother tongue. In English the language to explain the concepts is missing, and in the mother tongue both concepts and language have been neglected, so that the student lacks the language to think, reason, understand or discuss effectively in either language. This means that if the mother tongue is not developed in parallel with the second language and so remains at a lower level, proficiency in the second language will be negatively affected.

In a large-scale research project Thomas and Collier (2002) show that the longer students are educated using both English and the language of the home, the better the results, and this is of course encouraging for bilingual schools. However, international schools are generally not bilingual schools. The range of languages spoken by students can be extensive, and the presence of up to 100 languages is not unusual. This makes educating students consistently through English *and* their first language extremely difficult, if not impossible. However, it remains essential that schools support all students' mother-tongue development and growth, and there are a number of ways in which this can be facilitated by school administrators, teachers and parents working together.

Informing the students and their parents

Parents need to be informed of the importance of students maintaining and developing their mother tongue, and schools must do all they can to support both students and parents. Most of the parents will have had little or no experience of learning in a different language, and so support and advice given by the school are essential if they are to feel confident in and knowledgeable about the process.

Few teachers or administrators in international schools are themselves bilingual, which often means that their understanding of the process involved and the challenges students face is limited. Consequently, these challenges are frequently underestimated or ignored. The process of language acquisition is outside the area of expertise of most administrators. They should consult and be advised by the language acquisition experts in their ESL departments. These teachers will have specialist knowledge, training and experience. But all too often their voices are not heard and decisions are made from administrators' desks. These can have negative effects on the academic success of SL learners.

The academic success of SL learners of English who complete their education in international schools is often demonstrated by their IB Diploma results. Over many years of teaching in international schools, we have often seen these L2 students outperform the native English speakers. This indicates that the students have experienced a solid programme of English as a second language, but also that their mother tongue development has continued.

Factors that influence bilingual development

Yamamoto (2001: 19) reviewed a number of studies of the factors which influence children's bilingual development and the families' use of language; she summarizes these factors under three main headings: linguistic and environmental, sociocultural, and familial. The linguistic and environmental factors which influence bilingual development include the parents' language choice. The parents may speak different languages, or communicate with each other in just one language. They can make a conscious choice of which language or languages to use with their children. The quantity and quality of linguistic exposure which the children receive is an important factor, as is the style and quality of parent–child interaction. Yamamoto names patterns of language use and parental discourse strategies towards language mixing as key factors. The language of formal instruction in school is also of vital importance.

Sociocultural factors which influence bilingual development include the attitude of the parents towards bilingualism, the status of the language (the mother tongue), and the input of both parents and other members of society.

Familial factors include the need or desire for communication with the extended family, which is often important to international families. Yamamoto identifies the existence of siblings as a factor which may influence the use of the native language. For example, if siblings attend a school in which English is used throughout the day, they may continue to speak English to each other outside school, rather than the language of the home.

The importance of mother-tongue maintenance and development should be clear to educators who understand the importance of building on the students' previous knowledge and experience. A positive culture of recognition and appreciation of the range and value of students' mother tongues communicates to parents and students that bilingualism is a desirable aspect of life which all should strive for. The expectation that the student will leave their language and their culture at the school gate should be unacceptable. Raising the awareness of parents, administrators and teachers of the importance of mother-tongue development remains essential, as the turnover of families, administrators and teachers means that the understanding may be lost if it is not a central part of the philosophy of the school.

Some of the benefits of bilingualism

Some of the benefits of additive bilingualism are now well known. In particular, the research of Bialystok is often described in the popular press; it shows a positive link between bilingualism and a delay in the onset of dementia (Bialystok *et al.*, 2007).

Bilingualism affects the brain and improves the *executive function*. This is the command system, also called *cognitive control*, which allows humans to pay selective attention, to avoid being distracted, to concentrate on problem solving, to stay focused, and to hold information; the improvement seems to result in a heightened ability to monitor the environment in bilinguals. In addition, and of great relevance to education, cognitive and linguistic development in the first language transfers positively to the second language. Students are also more aware of language and have increased flexibility in thinking and understanding. Other researchers describe the benefits of bilingualism in more general terms. Bilingualism is thought to result in the ability to think more divergently and creatively, and to access a greater number of learning strategies and be more adaptable (Sears, 1998: 44).

Mehisto describes a number of benefits of bilingualism for individuals: they include increased mental processing capacity, greater control over information processing, improved memory, greater metalinguistic awareness, increased mental flexibility, improved health, improved intercultural skills and opportunities for increased income (Mehisto, 2012: 6–8).

The goal

The goal will be additive bilingualism, in which the new language is added to the existing language, not subtractive bilingualism, in which the new language replaces the old. For academic study in an international school, the second-language student will aim at a level of proficiency which allows them to function with a high level of competence in both languages. The challenge for teachers is to integrate the mother tongue into the students' learning so that both languages grow and develop.

Research-based developments

In the past it was believed that the best way to learn a new language was to completely separate the mother tongue and the language to be learned, as if these were two separate entities. In the classroom, students were told only to use the target language in order to avoid interference from their mother tongues. To quote Cenoz and Gorter:

> The ideology of language separation is well rooted in education and the teaching practices that date from the Direct Method and avoids translation and interaction between languages. There is a strong idea of separating the target language from the student's L1 or from other languages in the curriculum. Thus, only the target language is expected to be used so as to avoid interference from the other languages. The idea that languages have to be kept as separate containers has been referred to as 'parallel monolingualism' (Heller, 1999: 271), 'two solitudes' (Cummins, 2005: 588) or 'separate bilingualism' ([Creese and Blackledge], 2010).
>
> (Cenoz and Gorter, 2015b: 4–5)

Research has shown that using the first language as a resource is an excellent strategy, especially when the content and the language level are complex. The term 'translanguaging' is used to describe the way emerging bilinguals work with both languages to the best possible effect.

Wei explains:

> The term 'translanguaging' is often attributed to Cen Williams (1994, ...) who first used it to describe a pedagogical practice in bilingual classrooms where the input (e.g. reading and listening) is in one language and the output (e.g. speaking and writing) in another language.
>
> (Wei, 2015: 178)

For example, a text relating to new material in class may be read in the mother tongue, possibly on the internet, but then the student may read a similar text in English before answering questions or writing a response in English. However, the term is also used in a much broader sense which can describe a variety of ways in which a student uses his or her languages to make sense of information.

Wei continues:

> [T]he act of translanguaging is transformative in nature; it brings together different dimensions of multilingual speakers' linguistic, cognitive and social skills, their knowledge and experience of the social world and their attitudes and beliefs, and in doing so, it develops and transforms their skills, knowledge, experience, attitudes and beliefs, thus creating a new identity for the multilingual speaker.
>
> (ibid.: 179)

This transfers easily into the classroom. In the early stages of learning English, students can use their mother tongues to research the topics being studied and produce work for the class. Working in both the mother tongue and English creates opportunities for the students to discuss their work with other speakers of the same language, including their parents, of course, and so develop a deeper understanding of the material and language used.

The interdependence hypothesis makes clear the advantages of being literate in the mother tongue:

> [A]cademic language proficiency transfers across languages such that students who have developed literacy in their L1 will tend to make stronger progress in acquiring literacy in L2.
>
> (Cummins, 2000: 173)

and:

> 'Focus on multilingualism' considers that the metalinguistic awareness and communicative competence acquired in previously learned languages can be actively used to learn the target language in a more efficient way.
>
> (Cenoz and Gorter, 2015b: 8)

To date there has been little research on translanguaging in the secondary school. Cummins's work on identity texts focuses primarily on the second language acquisition of students in the elementary years. Mazak and Carroll (2017) published, in *Translanguaging in Higher Education*, a collection of accounts from all over the world, but the secondary school area has been neglected so far. This is surprising, as the level of understanding of cognitive academic language required for success is a challenge for many second language students. The implementation of translanguaging in all subject areas across the secondary school will bear fruit for bilingual students (see Mertin et al., 2018).

Responsibility for mother tongue maintenance and development
Administration and board of governors

The maintenance and development of all students' mother tongues need to be explicitly encouraged and supported by the leadership in international schools. There are a variety of ways in which this can be achieved, for example through having language policies which support mother tongues and through educating staff and parents about the huge benefits to be gained from bilingualism and the dangers which can arise if the students' mother tongues are ignored. Regular CPD must be planned for staff, especially as in a typical international school there is a rapid turnover of teachers. Many teachers are monolingual and will have had little experience of what it means to be fully bilingual. As a result, they have little understanding of how to achieve additive bilingualism or of the benefits it brings. This means that the teachers are unable to work effectively with the SL learners. Professional development should include a focus on the key role of the mother tongue in learning, the process and stages of language acquisition, and the advantages of second language acquisition. New teachers should be encouraged to learn a new language themselves, as this will give them some insight into the challenges students face. Often, lessons are offered to teachers keen to learn the language of the host country.

The leadership should raise the profile of the mother tongues used in the school, as they are essential elements of internationalism and multiculturalism. For example, the school website, brochures, handbooks, flyers and other sources of information for interested parties should have sections in a variety of mother tongues, not only in English. The variety of languages used in the school should be visible in the building wherever English is being used, for example on signs: 'Director's office', 'High School secretary's office', 'Nurse's room', and so on. Samples of children's work that highlight the range of languages spoken in the school are also a positive example of international and multiculturalism in practice. The admissions information should be available in all of the main languages of the school. Information about teaching programmes should also be available in mother tongues. The weekly bulletins which most schools produce for parents can be produced in various mother tongues as well as English. Many of these documents could be contributed by older students as part of their community service work. The administration can support the development of mother-tongue resources in the school, for example through developing collections of library books, newspapers, magazines, videos and other resources. Resources which explain and offer information on bilingualism are also helpful for parents new to the situation.

Parents

> *If you talk to a man in a language he understands, that goes to his head. If you talk to him in his language, that goes to his heart.*
>
> (Attributed to Nelson Mandela)

Parents especially need to be informed about the process of becoming bilingual, and the importance of their support for their children. Such communication should be part of the school's programme of informing and advising new parents, and reminding present parents of the importance of the mother tongue and the advantages of additive bilingualism. Unfortunately, parents, and indeed teachers, often fail to understand that learning a foreign language at school is very different from learning a language which will be the main source of academic learning; the latter means not only learning the language but, critically, learning to learn in the second language.

These information sessions for parents need to take place regularly. Many parents have little idea of how or why they should support their children's growth towards balanced bilingualism. It is not easy to arrange mother-tongue classes in a wide variety of languages, but with the support of parents, embassies and the local community it can be done. In some situations, classes may take place within the school day; alternatively, after-school classes can be offered. Parents often have the best contacts for finding other parents and children who share the same mother tongue, and can establish playgroups, encourage friendships and share resources. Through such networks, parents can also find mother-tongue teachers of their language. Where mother-tongue classes are held at the end of the day, this will add depth and intensity to the practice of the mother tongue, and students will benefit from the additional exposure to academic language at the appropriate age level. Some languages may be taught in private supplementary schools in the evenings or at the weekends. The educational authorities of some countries, for example the Netherlands and Sweden, offer professionally organized classes for their citizens living abroad, at which students work on the home-country curriculum content.

All of these activities make a valuable contribution to the academic success of second language students in the mainstream classes, as the skills, content knowledge and language acquired in the mother tongue are resources which are transferable and support English language acquisition. More detailed information on how to set up a mother-tongue department is to be found in Carder, 2007a, chapter 4.

Parents often believe that they can support their children's progress in school best by using English at home. This, of course, will be counterproductive, as the student loses the chance to develop their mother tongue age-appropriately, and other benefits of bilingualism are at risk. The parents of SL learners are usually English-language learners themselves, and although their level of proficiency may be high it is important that discussions, explanations and conversations with their children are held with competent, native-level speakers of the mother tongue.

The mother tongue is an important part of a child's identity: it is who they are. From birth, or even before birth, the sound of this language plays a key role in a child's emotional development. This is the language of parental and family love and affection, the language of the first nursery rhymes and stories, the language of family rituals and practices and the basis of all the learning which the child will receive in the future. It is a responsibility of the parents to maintain and develop that language within the home as far as possible. The books read, the discussions enjoyed, the talk around the dinner table, should all be in the mother tongue. At the same time, of course, the parents will continue to develop the child's mother-tongue competence by extending the vocabulary and increasing the complexity of the language and the child's ability to discuss, reason and argue in depth.

Examples of negative practice concerning mother tongues in international schools

At one of the few international schools that had a proactive policy for mother tongues, within a few months of the director responsible for that policy leaving the school, the new director initiated a policy which stated, 'Our mother tongue programme is a "point of difference"', 'the use of mother tongue by our students will not be permitted where it excludes others; students and teachers', and 'all teachers are expected to promote the use of English'.

Many of these students certainly feel excluded for most of the time in an English-speaking environment, as they do not understand all the words and nuances that are spoken. The school head was presumably reacting to the concerns of some staff or parents, or his own monolingual outlook.

Understandable though this may be, the new policy imposes a blanket silence on the central aspect of these students' identities. These students will in any case continue to use their own mother tongue in their heads, but they will feel silenced and thus stigmatized. Mother-tongue English speakers in international schools are never subjected to such policies, and the edict reveals a lack of knowledge about students' identities, social behaviour and ways of learning. In addition, to say that a mother-tongue programme is a 'point of difference' is the exact opposite of what needs to be said; the aim of such a programme is to integrate all students' languages, not to stigmatize them by calling them 'different'. Again, the fact that such a statement could be made in a school with a well-developed mother-tongue and ESL programme emphasizes two points: the continuing in-built sense that 'English is above all other languages', and that decisions on languages are taken by those who are in power and are mother-tongue English speakers.

As documented by Young:

> Refusing to authorise a child to use her/his home language as a cognitive tool for learning is effectively an act of discrimination. UNESCO underlines language as a human right, stating that the integration of migrant 'children should be facilitated by teaching the language in use in the school system' ... (UNESCO, 2003: 16–17).
>
> (Young, 2014: 97)

In addition:

> [MRG (1994)])] proposes five reasons as to why minority language children should develop their home language including maintaining communication between grandparents, parents and children, promoting a positive self-image and supporting the learning of the second language.
>
> (ibid.)

In a study of head teachers' views on bilingualism carried out by Young (2014: 90), only one out of 46 mentioned the cognitive benefits of bilingualism: this was also the only head that referred to research findings. Of course, school heads are busy, but the responsibility for the education of the hundreds of children in their care lies with them, and they should be up to date with what has become the reality in international schools: most of the students do not have English as their mother tongue. Cruickshank (2014: 60) writes: 'It is "surreal" that the day schools often have no knowledge of which of their students are learning in community languages schools or of the language practices and cultural knowledge they have acquired and use in contexts outside day school'. Young writes:

> It has been acknowledged that as a direct result of our increasingly globalised world, many school populations now include a greater number of pupils with a wider variety of home languages which are not languages of instruction (OECD, 2010). This places additional strain on teachers, who very often have received little or no training to prepare them to support these pupils (Cajkler & Hall, 2012; Murakami, 2008; Wiley, 2008).
>
> (ibid.: 93)

Young's next statement about the language knowledge of the teachers in his study resonates with the situation in international schools:

> Given that the majority of teachers in France are not from a migration background (Charles & Legendre, 2006) and have only a school-based experience of languages, how are they supposed to understand complex issues such as bilingualism, biliteracy, multiple identities and intercultural communication with little personal experience and training?
>
> (Young, 2014: 96)

The argument for training and careful recruitment is evident.

Advice for parents

Parents should be encouraged to talk to their children about the day at school from the very early stages of learning in a second language right up to the high school. The content of lessons can be supplied by the teacher so that parents can access the same information in the mother tongue. For example, if the child is studying the water cycle at school, the water cycle can be researched on the internet in the mother tongue and shared with the child. The topic can be discussed, and the child can explain it and give additional information which may have been learned in school. In this way, through the transfer of language, competence in both languages is further developed. Older children can be encouraged to research topics on the internet using mother-tongue resources. This will develop their academic vocabulary and deepen their understanding of the content matter. It will also make it possible for parents to discuss the content with their children, so that the students benefit from opportunities to talk around the subject, and question, challenge and confirm their understanding.

Reading is a key resource for supporting, developing and maintaining the child's mother tongue. For younger children, after a tiring day at school, being read to in the mother tongue will be an enjoyable, relaxing experience. Similarly, through technology and the internet, stories, songs, cartoons and films can be enjoyed, shared and discussed in the mother tongue.

Some languages may be taught in private supplementary schools in the evenings or at the weekends. These activities make a valuable contribution to the academic success of SLLs in the mainstream classes, as the skills, content knowledge and language acquired in the mother tongue are all resources which are transferable, and support English language acquisition.

If a student joins an international school, for example in grade 5, and then uses only English until they return to their home country – a frequent scenario in international schools – they will not have acquired the necessary academic vocabulary and language to express knowledge and key concepts and so to continue to study successfully in their mother tongue. Students who continue their studies up to grade 12 using only English and then wish to enter university in their home countries often find that they lack the academic language and the ability to explain concepts and express their higher-level thinking through lack of language, fluency, experience or practice. They may be left with the vocabulary and language style of a much younger student, which will not come up to the standards of academic study or help them to make new friends.

Teachers

The teachers are the people who spend the most time with the students during the school year, making their role in recognizing the vital importance of mother-tongue maintenance and development, and encouraging and supporting them, of prime importance.

International teachers and students change schools more frequently than those based in their home countries and attending national schools. Those first days at a new school are always stressful for new teachers and students, but at least the teachers speak the language and are familiar with the cultural norms of schools. It is their responsibility to make the new student's first hours and days comforting. For students who do not speak the language of the school fluently the level of stress is magnified and may become almost unbearable. Students have to cope with a day in a new school where they cannot understand what is being said, they do not have friends, and their language, their culture, in fact everything which is important to them, becomes irrelevant in this incomprehensible new environment. Teachers who recognize the challenges these children face can help them in many ways. Often schools have a 'buddy' system, whereby an established student takes the new student through the school day and is an instant friend for the first few weeks. If the buddy is a speaker of the same language the level of comfort and reassurance given is great. The system is simple but can prevent untold misery. Buddies can explain the schedule, help locate classrooms and the toilets, be a friend at break- or lunchtime and introduce the new student to after-school activities.

Teachers should make a point of knowing which students are coming into the school, where they have come from, which language(s) they speak, their level of English, and most importantly how to pronounce their names correctly. It is also important that the student knows the teacher's name, how to pronounce it correctly, and how to spell it. Just as the student's name may be challenging for the teacher, so may the teacher's name be unfamiliar and confusing.

In the classroom

The teachers in the lower grades spend more time with the students than teachers in upper grades, so they have more opportunities to support the mother tongues of their students. For example, the students could teach expressions in their mother tongues, which would add to their confidence and self-worth by allowing their own special abilities to be recognized. Not only greetings and phrases but also the language used in science or other topic areas can be shared. In this way students can learn to appreciate linguistic similarities and differences and extend their interest in and understanding of their own languages. As long as they are unable to express their ideas in English and are given no alternative avenues to do so, students' identities, abilities, creativity and originality are ignored and thus appear to count for nothing. The work of Cummins and Early on 'identity texts' (Cummins and Early, 2011) has been shown to bring many advantages to young students whose mother tongue is not English. Through writing texts, stories and poems in their mother tongue and having them translated into English, the students confirm their own identities. These texts can be translated by classroom friends who are further along the bilingual continuum, or by older students or relatives. The translation process is also supportive of the new student's second language development. The samples of creative work which are truly their own can be shared outside school with relatives and friends to demonstrate their growing bilingualism.

Parents may read or tell stories in the mother tongue to groups of children or talk to the whole class, in English, or in the mother tongue with a translator, about their home country and language, using artefacts to make the talk come alive: pictures, clothes, music and so forth. The mother tongue can be explained, simple words taught, and the written language shared. The teacher can take a language each week to share, and the students can teach their classmates new words and phrases, maybe even a rhyme or a song. Weekly assemblies can also be used to focus on one of the many mother tongues in any school. Students who share the same mother tongue can be given opportunities to discuss the content of lessons in that language, or work together to produce texts, charts and posters in their mother tongue related to the work being done in class. Students can be given opportunities to explain and share their work, and so to demonstrate to everyone the importance and relevance of other languages. These experiences enrich the learning of all students. Some teachers may fear a loss of control – see the quote below – and thus be reluctant to allow students to discuss in their mother tongues, but if the students are later asked to report on their discussion in English this can be avoided.

> Language teachers who ban the students' first language from the classroom might be shattered to know how much it is being used in the privacy of the students' minds.
>
> (Cook and Singleton, 2014: 9)

Teachers in upper grades can create situations which give students opportunities to discuss their work in their mother-tongue groups. Students can also be encouraged to use the internet to research the topics studied in their mother tongue. Students who are beginning to learn English should be given alternative ways to demonstrate understanding, for example by making charts or diagrams, which could easily be labelled in the mother tongue and to which the English terms could be added later. Through CPD given by experienced, qualified ESL colleagues, classroom teachers can begin to comprehend the challenges SL learners are facing, and learn skills and techniques to enable these students to access the curriculum and to succeed, using their mother tongues and English.

Chapter 11

Advice and guidance for school leaders, teachers and parents

All of this reinforces the fundamental conservatism of human societies, because mental models of reality once adopted are hard to change in the light of new evidence that they are not working.

(Fukuyama, 2011: 443)

Obstacles to instituting the proposed model

What is needed in international schools is that leaders have the courage to recognize that language policies based on research serve the students and their parents and will affect the quality of their long-term future. Individual components of the international schools network – curriculum providers and accreditation agencies, school heads, boards of governors, and teachers – may argue against change. But the burgeoning numbers of ESL students in international schools demand that change occurs, so there needs to be an agenda about how to manage that change fairly and equitably. Those who resist such a change, or who claim that it is totally unexpected, should explain why, after obvious trends over many years, and the number of publications pointing out the demographic linguistic shift, they have not already shown their competence as leaders, seen the clear picture approaching, and admitted that they were simply not doing their job.

As Wolin warns, there is a:

> paucity of intellectual proposals that deviate from the current orthodoxies. This reflects a quiet but paradigmatic change: a shift in intellectual and ideological influence from academia to think tanks, the vast majority of which were conservative and dependent upon corporate sponsorship. Whereas the former had on occasion housed and nurtured deviants, 'impractical dreamers' of new paradigms and challengers of orthodoxy, the think-tank inmates are committed to influencing policy makers and hence their horizons are restricted by the demands of practicality

and constricted by the interests of their corporate sponsors to proposing mitigative changes.

(S.S. Wolin, 2008: xv)

This shows the influence of well-financed corporate bodies on those who come up with proposals that might offer sensible, academically supported ways forward.

Higgs (2014) traces the subtle infiltration of the language of obfuscation, the spread of public relations (PR) and the various tactics used by politicians and corporations to oppose the scientific facts about 'global warming', a phrase which was one of the first victims of their campaign; the more acceptable 'climate change' was their proposal. Higgs writes, for example, of how some anti-environmentalist businessmen set up a 'wise use' umbrella organization. Higgs reports a 1991 conversation between John Krakauer and the businessman Ron Arnold, who was the vice-president of the Center for the Defense of Free Enterprise:

'Wise use' itself was 'a marvellously ambiguous expression. ... Symbols register most powerfully in the subconscious when they're not perfectly clear. ... Facts don't really matter. In politics, perception is reality.' 'Wise use' was perfect. It smacked of good judgment and responsibility and could have meant almost anything.

(Higgs, 2014: 234)

It is possible to trace the influence of PR and wise use on the IB decision to phase out language A2 in the Diploma Programme, to merge second language and foreign language into 'language acquisition', and to dispose with the SLA and MTD guide.

Another area addressed by Higgs is 'doubt'. By sowing the seeds of doubt about second language issues, educational organizations can claim that 'there is no consensus on the best method', thereby laying the ground for whatever suits their needs best. As reported by Higgs:

We are operating in a political world from which morality has been banished .... In its place ... we find simple greed masked by the euphemisms of 'management' and 'efficiency'.

(Middleton *et al.*, 1993: 4, 11, quoted in Higgs, 2014: 129)

Further insights into why more effective SL programmes have not been instituted

Understanding *why* effective policies and programmes for ESL students have not been put in place in international schools will help educators to ensure that the situation can be reversed. Many of the underlying reasons for such failure have so far in this book been traced to the politics of national educational policies; now some insights drawn from research by cognitive psychologists and sociologists will be presented.

Language is something that people take for granted, and believe that they own. English speakers especially are owners of the world's current lingua franca and the great majority see no need to learn another language. Even though it might be expected that in the field of education a more objective, scientific approach to this essential element of schooling would be taken, especially in an international context where many languages are represented among the student body, this is often not the case.

Tame and wicked problems

Cognitive psychologists talk about two types of problems: tame, or simple, problems, and wicked problems. Simple problems have defined causes, objectives and outputs; wicked problems are multifaceted and constantly changing: they are complex, demanding a continuous process of evaluation and redefinition. There are obvious attempts by governments in some English-speaking countries to 'simplify' education generally. It is easier to control a simple mechanism. When an issue to do with state education defies a clear definition it becomes frustrating, as it keeps evolving as various solutions are tried. When, as with our issue of language and languages, it impinges on our basic comfort zone, 'our' English language, it is easiest to proclaim that students should just get on with it, especially when parents mostly demand that their offspring should learn it quickly and get good grades in it. But language, in fact bilingualism, for that is what is involved, is an educational problem, a human rights problem, a social justice problem, a governance problem, and an ideological battle between contending factions.

To solve tame problems, the solution is first to understand the problem, then to gather information, collect it together, and work out and apply solutions. If students are not all equally good at maths, put them in different sets. This is precisely what happens in most international schools at some stage. For wicked problems, you have to know all about their context; however, it is often the case that you have to delve deep to discover the roots of the problem, and the solution may prove elusive.

Many – most? – international schools treat bilingualism and ESL issues as somewhere between a tame and a wicked problem. The purpose of this book has been to show that they should be treated as a tame problem: we have understood the problem, gathered information, collected it together and worked out solutions, and are waiting for the international educational community to apply them by setting up the structures we have recommended. We have known about the solutions for some time, but issues have intervened that can be categorized as political, which have made the problem a wicked one. So rather than actively addressing the bilingual learning needs of the many, many students who could have far better programmes of instruction and assessment than they are currently receiving, we actively shift attention away from them, keeping them permanently on the edge of our pool of worry (see Rittel and Webber, 1973).

A compelling narrative is key to managing a school, a curriculum body or an accrediting agency. Research has shown that this is best done by including a cause, an effect, a perpetrator, and a motive. What is seen about the way that ESL students (the cause) are treated is often that the governing body/agency/school (the perpetrators) justify the peripheralization of ESL students in order to marginalize them and so save the effort of devising appropriate programmes (the motive). The result (the effect) is that ESL students are often marginalized and not given the means to achieve their full potential. A gripping story, even when we know that it is factually wrong, is often more emotionally compelling than the truth. Among a large body of mostly monolingual English-speaking staff, and parents who are keen – sometimes desperate – to have their children in an English-speaking school, the emotional narrative of 'putting them all in the mainstream with "support"' is not so hard to sell. Parents can see that their children are in the regular classes, even if they don't understand much and their writing skills in content areas leave much to be desired.

Different types of bias

There are also issues of 'bias'. Many people interpret language questions in the light of their own assumptions and prejudices: they may prefer a certain accent, or insist that a particular point of grammar is wrong. If they believe that English-only is the natural way forward, they see speakers of other languages who learn to speak it, and lose their mother tongue, as proof that assimilation is the only solution; if they accept that bilingualism can bring advantages, they see successful bilinguals as proof of the benefits of bilingualism. Psychological researchers call such conclusion-drawing 'bias'. Those who cherry-pick evidence that fits their world view are showing 'confirmation bias'. For example, if a student has been diagnosed as an ESL student by ESL specialists, but has been determined by non-specialists to be 'fluent' as she can talk quite fluently about her wish to be in the content classes rather than in a parallel ESL class, the non-specialist will claim that the student has perfectly good English and her wishes should be followed, showing confirmation bias. Further testing of written proficiency, however, may show that the student's writing skills are a long way behind her speaking ability. If there is no ESL specialist to confirm this, or no dedicated ESL programme, the student will commence a long decline of reading and writing skills.

There are also situations in which we modify new information to fit in with our world view; this is called 'biased assimilation'. For example, the parents of the student described above may bring in reports from a previous school in another country that show good writing skills in English. The non-specialist will proclaim, 'Here is the evidence', but the ESL specialists may produce current evidence that shows insufficient writing skills.

Attitudes towards language can become very heated and polarized: a teacher from, for example, the English department may say that the student in question has given very good presentations in class, but then backtrack and say, 'Well, the writing skills were not so good today'. Making one's mind up on the spot in this way, on the basis of easily available evidence, is called 'availability bias'. This kind of decision making happens frequently to students with language issues in schools which do not assess in depth the verifiable language abilities of every student – their speaking and writing abilities in both their mother tongue and English – and provide the appropriate programme. Teachers in such scenarios are not doing their duty as educators.

All of these 'biases' are common human foibles, but there should be no place for them in the professional environment of international schools. Language is the basis of everything students do in schools, and with a complex multilingual student body it is essential first to evaluate the possible language skills of each student in all of their languages, and then to provide the appropriate programme of instruction.

Rationality versus irrationality

A book that became a bestseller contains useful advice on these issues. In *Thinking, Fast and Slow* (Kahneman, 2012), the author writes about human rationality and irrationality. He shows that people obtain their information through those they think they can trust, and the reason they accept or do not accept an issue is to do not with the information on the subject, but with the 'cultural coding'. So in our case, in an international school where English is the language of the curriculum and the majority of the teachers are monolingual and from the Anglosphere, a rational discourse from ESL specialists on the best programme for a second-language student can lose against a compelling story that speaks to people's core values, such as 'We know English, we can see that this girl has fluent English, so she can join our regular English department class'. If all the surrounding teachers and administrators are also monolingual English speakers, the ESL specialist can give all the rational arguments in the world for setting up a dedicated ESL programme, with a mother-tongue programme to back it up, but communications from peers can have far more influence than the advice of experts. A reminder: in a school where the ESL teachers are in 'support' mode and have no professional standing, their case will be even weaker.

Native speakers versus non-native speakers

Then there is 'self-categorization theory', by which people not only identify strongly with their own social group but believe that it has a distinctive identity that makes it superior to other groups. Thus in schools where a board of governors may, apparently with good intentions, have insisted on recruiting only native English speakers, perhaps even only British teachers (seen in some international schools), there will be a body that will be wide open to confirmation bias and the white man effect. For ESL specialists, to stand up to this, day after day, is a gruelling experience: science and maths teachers do not have to justify their decisions in their subject area, case by case, on a daily basis. This can lead to 'pluralistic ignorance', which happens when people – teachers, for us – misread the social norm and suppress their own views, which further widens the divide, and may create an atmosphere in which the majority of teachers keep silent because they fear they are in a minority. I have seen this in action in many instances.

When school heads or boards of governors make such decisions – to employ only native English speakers – they are unwittingly doing exactly the wrong thing, as potentially bilingual ESL students will see only monolingual English speakers as their teachers and take that as the ideal. School heads must understand what is at stake and speak forcefully to governors and parents so that they understand how much better the ESL students would progress if they could see that their teachers were bilinguals, like them, that their chances of developing a native-like English accent after puberty were minimal, and that there are more SL speakers of English than native speakers in the world. We have noticed the professionalism and competence of SL English speakers who are teachers of ESL; they compare favourably with the too often seen amateurism of 'native speakers', who are frequently poorly qualified. Indeed, native English speakers can actually be worse communicators than SL speakers of English: Morrison (2016) writes, 'often you have a boardroom full of people from different countries communicating in English and all understanding each other and then suddenly the American or Brit walks into the room and nobody can understand them'. The reason for this is that 'The non-native speakers … speak more purposefully and carefully, typical of someone speaking a second or third language. Anglophones … often talk too fast for others to follow, and use jokes, slang and references specific to their own culture.' Morrison quotes Jenkins: '"Native speakers are at a disadvantage when you are in a lingua franca situation," where English is being used as a common denominator, says Jennifer Jenkins, professor of global Englishes at the UK's University of Southampton. "It's the native English speakers that are having difficulty understanding and making themselves understood."'

In schools whose ESL teachers come from a system like that of England, in which they are not given professional status and have become inured to being in a support role, it is likely that content teachers who see them and may believe that there might be something that they could do about the situation, do not speak out as they are more likely to be victim to the 'bystander effect', by which the more that people have seen of a problem and the way it is dealt with, the more likely they are to ignore their own judgement. This is a strong factor working against ESL teachers in a British-style international school. With globalization, language has become an issue needing a global response, and is thus particularly prone to the bystander effect. People look around to see what others are doing and saying, or more pertinently what they are not doing or saying. Social conformity is a strong behavioural instinct built into people's core psychology, as in earlier stages of human development not doing the same as others around us could entail ostracism or abandonment. There are often risks involved in holding views that are not in step with your social group. In addition, if an ESL teacher is repeatedly out of step with the English-speaking peer-group majority, the threat of dismissal is always present; the choice is to speak out on the issues and be fired, or be silent, swallow, and sit in classes in a support role. ESL teachers have written to me about precisely this scenario, in real fear of losing their jobs.

It needs repeating that the monolingual English teachers and administrators are the ones who are out of step, as the student body is usually multilingual. Since experiments on social conformity have shown that people conform even when there is a real threat, a strong school leader will be needed who is determined to maintain a professional ESL department. Another potential problem is that the board may feel that such a strong leader does not have the backing of the staff, or is upsetting them, so will not renew her contract. English speakers, when in a majority on a school staff, face two risks: accepting bilingualism, possibly a perceived risk, compared with the certain and very personal risk of opposing the norm of English-only, or keeping a support ESL programme instead of having a professional ESL and mother-tongue programme.

Lynskey affirms:

> Humans do not instinctively enjoy changing their minds. Admitting that you were wrong, especially when the original decision has huge ramifications, is a painful and destabilising experience that the brain tends to resist. Research into this kind of denial has given us concepts such as cognitive dissonance and confirmation bias.
>
> 'When you have a strong view about something, you're likely to reject information that's contrary to your view, reject the source of the information and rationalise the information,' says Jane Green, professor of political science at the University of Manchester .... 'We select information that's consistent with our views, because it's more comfortable and reaffirming.' In fact, it's physically pleasurable. Some recent studies of confirmation bias indicate that consuming information that supports our beliefs actually produces a dopamine rush.
>
> (Lynskey, 2017)

Further examples of how large organizations are unable to adapt to a more appropriate path are given by Meek:

> [We live in] an era where large corporations' trappings of openness – bright, friendly, content-rich websites and well-staffed PR operations – turn out to be facades for gagged workforces, denial of corporate history and a refusal to engage with sceptical questions.
>
> (Meek, 2015: 266)

Unfortunately, requesting the setting up of a professional ESL and mother-tongue department as the centre of each international school is likely to be seen as a sceptical question.

Solutions

How can we counter these tendencies? The solution is to use words that promote the main ideas of bilingualism and inhibit those of monolingual smugness. Once words become engrained in common usage they perpetuate their message. Ideally this will lead to international school leaders maintaining a message of the centrality of a professional *ESL* department, promoting students' *mother tongues*, and the benefits of *additive bilingualism*. They will talk down the terms EAL and support, and all the language that contributes to the demotivation of SLLs. They will point out that EAL has no professional status in England. If teachers do not understand the theory behind the advantages of bilingualism, school leaders will talk about it over and over again. Kahneman (2012) has shown that the division between the emotional brain and the rational brain (he calls them 'system 1' and 'system 2') runs deep in our culture, and this 'cultural mistake' should have no place in an education system. But it does. Unfortunately, extensive research evidence shows that information does not change people's attitudes, and since the emotional brain leads in decision making, its initial impressions will sway subsequent decisions; there are plenty of examples from recent world events that show how lies, repeated between peers, can gain social acceptance. Leaders can create the impression that something is being done while preventing anything from happening, or do the reverse – do something that is not welcome among the populace while creating the impression that it is for their benefit. Education has the care of children in its hands: there really should be no place for deception or for not doing what is known, on the basis of solid research and good practice, to be the best. If school leaders see their job as making a sales pitch, getting parents hooked on promises of native English teachers only in order to promote the numbers of entrants, their motives for their career choice should be questioned: treating the care of young children as a market opportunity is not an option.

Unrealistic pretensions of having a 'native' accent

Parents are naturally keen for their children to become fluent in English. It is the globalized world's lingua franca, and fluency is considered to offer considerable benefits. Indeed, it is safe to say many opportunities and career paths will not be available to someone without competence in English. However, it is important that parents understand that their children are unlikely to acquire an impeccable native accent, especially if they commence learning the language after puberty.

Some examples will illustrate how far false expectations can lead, and the views that adults can hold of the importance of having a native accent. Stephen Krashen recounted (at the ECIS ESL and MT conference, Geneva, in 2008) how in South Korea many parents believed that their ethnic background included having a physical characteristic that precluded them from speaking English 'native-like'. They therefore took their children for operations that involved cutting away certain tissues around the tongue. No perceivable benefit was reported.

The argument that being taught English by a native speaker is the only way to be sure of gaining a native-like accent has many flaws, not the least of which is that SL speakers of English far outnumber native speakers, so SL learners are far more likely to spend their lives conversing with other SL speakers than with native speakers. A thorough investigation of this issue is made by Cook (2014c), who states (p. 134), 'If you ask L2 learners what they want to become in a second language, the answer is . . .: they want to be native speakers.' However, he points out that 'A *native speaker* is usually said to be "a person who has spoken a certain language since early childhood."' He adds, 'most people seem to believe that the only person who speaks a language properly is a native speaker. But, if the definition above is correct, *no* L2 user could ever become a native speaker: it's far too late. The only ones to make the grade would be children brought up from the very beginning in two languages' (ibid.: 135). The result can be that 'Consequently most L2 users consider themselves failures for not sounding like native speakers, something they could never be – by definition' (ibid.). In a summary of a thorough analysis of the matter, Cook writes, 'Many L2 learners and L2 users aspire to be as similar as possible to a native speaker. Yet it is hard to pin down what an ideal native speaker might be. This native speaker goal cannot be achieved because they already have one language in their minds. L2 users and L2 learners need to be assessed against successful L2 users, not against native speakers as reflected in many contemporary examination systems' (ibid.: 139).

The need to inform parents

These facts need to be distributed among the parent body and the school faculty. Through CPD, teachers should be aware of these facts. But parents, too, need to understand them, so that their expectations are realistic. Schools should have notice boards and newsletters and websites where all these facts are widely available.

It is important that parents are made aware of what their children are involved in through booklets and information evenings. An informative website on all aspects of bringing up children bilingually is www. multilingualliving.com (accessed 13 February 2018).

Many parents are so grateful to have their children in an international school that they will accept any type of programme, and the 'promise of English', the world language and the key to success, may blind them to the vast task of language learning and the personal stress awaiting their children (Krashen, 2006). Unfortunately, unscrupulous or unknowing international school boards and school leaders are frequently party to attracting parents to a school with poorly designed provision for ESL students.

School leaders need to ensure they employ well-qualified ESL staff, and listen to their advice. This is possible, as I found in my former school. Although in the USA in 2002 'only … 18% [of ELLs' teachers] were certified in … English as a second language' (Crawford and Krashen, 2007: 14), and in England there is no statutory provision for an EAL qualification, I always insisted that ESL teachers had an MA in ESL, TESOL, applied linguistics, or similar: there are plenty of such teachers out there looking for employment in international schools. I wrote in 1990 (almost thirty years ago), 'An ESL department is generally seen as the hub of the school, with the spokes leading out to the other departments' (Kalinowski and Carder, 1990: 81). Some schools have managed to maintain and develop such a model, notably the Frankfurt International School (www.fis.edu/, accessed 13 February 2018) which, by offering the IBPYP and the IBDP but not the IBMYP (they have created their own programme), overcomes the negative effects of that programme on ESL students already noted.

Many years of regular contact with parents in international schools have cast light for me on matters which are of a sensitive nature, but which have to be discussed if there is to be any chance of improving the language education of their children. A useful introduction may be in the form of an anecdote. A director new to the international school, who had heard that there could be 'tricky' situations with parents, recounted that she was quite ready to deal with any encounter, as in her previous school (in the English state system) an angry parent had threatened to dump a lorryload of earth at the school gates if certain conditions were not met. The director recounted how she had dealt with the matter successfully. After a year at the international school the director realized that dealing with the more sophisticated complaints and detailed requests of the professional class of parents at the school was more time-consuming and complex. As mentioned above, Bourdieu (1984) recounts in *Distinction*, at great length and with well-chosen examples, that those in privileged classes are unwilling to challenge the authority of the dominant power directly: rather, they expect what they consider to be sensible decisions as regards their children's education to be taken on their behalf as soon as they air them, but often prefer to pursue their agendas covertly, in discussions with other parents, or by contacting teachers or heads of school. As professionals, they may not wish to speak openly at school meetings on matters of concern to them – often financial issues – but they will pursue their agendas in other ways.

Parents are often not cognizant of the factors which go towards making their child able to master English at an academic level. When school directors are not aware of such factors either, as recounted throughout this book, poor models of instruction are often accepted. A group of Brazilian businessmen, for example, came to Europe looking for a teacher to set up a new school in a large city, but wanted 'only British teachers' as there was an anti-American mood at that time. It should by now be clear that SLLs will usually not develop native-like proficiency or accents after puberty, and will in all likelihood acquire the 'mid-Atlantic' accent common to most international school students worldwide.

The marketization of professionalism versus commitment

Research has shown (Carder, 2011) the diverse responses of parents to maintaining their children's mother tongue to an academic level. In a school in which every effort was made to promote the importance of every child keeping up and developing their mother tongue literacy, the issue of payment for mother-tongue classes became political. The department responsible for mother-tongue classes had a policy of approving each mother-tongue teacher and drawing up a recommended payscale for such teachers to ensure a professional standing for the teachers. One language group protested about this as they had found a teacher who charged less than the published rate:

> [Parent]: Well, what's the advantage of the mother-tongue programme? As opposed to tutoring our kids on the side, for instance?
>
> (Carder, 2011: 110)

This area is discussed by Sennett under the heading of 'craftsmanship'. He writes:

> The educational system ... favors facility at the expense of digging deep. ... [C]raftsmanship has a cardinal virtue missing in the new culture's idealized worker, student, or citizen. It is commitment.
>
> (Sennett, 2006: 194, 195)

However:

> Commitment poses a more profound question about the self-as-process. Commitment entails closure, forgoing possibilities for the sake of concentrating on one thing. You might miss out. The emerging culture puts enormous pressure on individuals not to miss out.
>
> (ibid.: 196)

Mother-tongue teachers at the school in question were committed professionals working in a situation that isolated them and left them vulnerable to 'market forces'. The director responded:

> [This] school is unique, I believe, quite unique in offering a programme of such variety and such size here in the school. Many IB schools simply say to students: '*You* sort that out. *You* arrange your own tutors. *You* do that out of school. You do that privately. We don't want to know.' OK? [This] school has taken a very different approach, and I believe a very, very successful approach and we measure that success by the benefit to the students; by the number of bilingual diplomas; by the success rate in the diploma programme and by the fantastic success rate in getting those young people to the universities of their choice.
>
> (Carder, 2011: 111)

The IB coordinator intervened and commented:

> I'm a teacher and an English speaker but I would not like to teach my own children English because the approach to learning a language from a linguistic viewpoint is very different from just speaking at home; so the literary skills, the analysis it involves at the IB level, it absolutely has to be taught by, well, as far as possible it should be taught by a trained teacher, and I can imagine that that goes right down the line. And there are so many families that don't have the opportunity to be able to develop all the language, that the programme that the school offers reminds people that they should be approaching the programme in an organized way and gives those parents the facility to have it done for them in school.
>
> (ibid.: 238–9)

These extracts highlight what schooling is about: it is about in-depth learning and knowledge. In an age of the instant fix directors will need to reinforce this message constantly. Language issues are complex, and having a department at the centre of the school structure which has a *commitment* to manage them will take a weight off the school leadership, and provide students with a deep knowledge of their own language *and* of English, which will benefit them in all subjects and in their final examinations.

Linguistic and cultural diversity is increasing worldwide. Against the background of a huge influx of refugees to the EU in September 2015, a spokesman reported:

> 'Any society, anywhere in the world, will be diverse in the future – that's the future of the world .... So [Central European countries] will have to get used to that. They need political leaders who have the courage to explain that to their population instead of playing into the fears.'
>
> (V. Chadwick, 2015)

Given the linguistic diversity globalization is bringing to international schools, school leaders and board members need to be equally courageous in explaining to their communities the complexity of the issues surrounding bilingualism, and to set up the comprehensive structures recommended in this book: such action can only improve the lives of ESL students and the whole student body. Baetens Beardsmore writes in the foreword to a book for school principals in bilingual schools:

> Principals, teachers, students, parents must share the aims of a common goal where two or more distinct languages form the foundation of a process seen as a long-term commitment. Such programmes cannot succeed if based on tactics and strategies built upon hit-and-miss improvisation.
>
> (Baetens Beardsmore, 2012: v)

This statement could usefully appear at the head of all the mission statements and accreditation and curriculum documents of international schools.

Chapter 12

The challenges ahead

Maurice Carder and Patricia Mertin

International schools across the world, with their multilingual, multicultural communities, are increasing in numbers at an enormous rate. The great range of varieties of international schools has already been discussed, and their geographical locations are spreading from the Western world to the East. However, most of these schools follow a largely Western style of education, with Western curricula and Western ways of learning, understanding and expressing ideas. The IB, with the PYP, MYP and DP range of subjects which lead to examinations, tends strongly towards the Western view of education. Similarly, the IB Learner Profile and its attributes actually embody a Western approach, which ignores the fact that not all cultures encourage children to be, for example, questioners and risk-takers.

At the same time as international schools are growing in number the population of the world is becoming more mobile, with the result that students in state schools across the globe are no longer all speakers of that state's official language, and nor do they necessarily share the cultural norms of the nation state in which they live.

International schools have been working with diverse groups for many years and so should be models of multilingual and multicultural understanding. But the truth is that in many schools the leadership fails to take advantage of this immense resource, and much more importantly fails to give every student equal opportunities through equal access to the curriculum.

The mother tongues of the students are often ignored, and students are not given the chance to learn English (when that is the language of instruction in the school) effectively.

International schools have so many advantages which could be used to demonstrate how they could be operating in the globalized world, and when a variety of languages and cultures exist in close proximity, peacefully and successfully.

International schools are financially advantaged, the school population comes from a relatively well-off sociocultural group, and the parents of the students are financially and professionally successful. As a result, the parents have high expectations of the schools, which sadly are often not met with regard to SL learners.

What should an international school be aiming for?

International schools are all set and fully equipped to be world leaders in education, *where* they have SL programmes which cater to the needs of SLLs. Unfortunately, many have not taken advantage of this, as they adhere to models created in and for national systems, with the residue of the political detritus that sticks to them.

School heads and directors who are persuaded by the arguments in this book will need not only to set up the model advocated, but to back it all the way. Such a move will mature into the solid establishment of equitable and professional programmes for SLLs. Policies are not enough: they need consistent implementation. Given the complexity of sound provision for SLLs it is reasonable to insist on professional courses for teachers, in line with other disciplines. Professionalism at all levels – ESL qualifications, ESL training, ESL programmes, CPD, access to mentor figures and leaders in the field – needs to be recognized as necessary in order to cement the profession for the long-term benefit of SL students.

School leaders should be familiar with the core knowledge base regarding: trajectories of school language acquisition among new students, including the time taken to learn a second language – five to seven years (Thomas and Collier, 1997) – and the need to employ well-qualified SL teachers; the positive role of students' L1 in facilitating L2 development; and the instructional strategies required to teach academic content effectively to students who are in the process of developing academic English proficiency, and therefore the need for content teachers to be trained in these techniques.

SL and mother-tongue programmes are developed according to a specialized body of knowledge – about bilingualism, second language acquisition and teacher training. Decisions affecting such programmes need to be considered in the light of the situation in international schools where ESL students are frequently in a majority.

School leaders will be able to counter parents who want the quick fix, and unaware managers from national systems who want to label ESL 'support'; they will recognize the need to employ graduate ESL teachers, regardless of whether they are native speakers, who are qualified in their speciality with more than a diploma, as experts in all matters relating to ESL and bilingualism, and who can act as centres of expertise for all staff, parents and students. They will make this move in the light of the information made explicit in this book, emphasizing that collegiality actually doesn't happen that much in schools (the more usual path being a contrived collegiality or a managed collegiality), which is a principal reason for setting up an ESL department.

ESL teachers will have to work hard in their new role. They will be highly qualified, and will at first have to struggle to cement their new status as repositories of all matters bilingual and as being responsible for the continuing training of all staff in linguistically responsive teaching. They will expect 100 per cent support from leadership (the true meaning of support), and their enthusiasm and energy for delivering the SL programmes demanded by the linguistic make-up of the student body will be unceasing. They will work tirelessly at developing a mother-tongue programme, and encourage all SLLs to take lessons in their mother tongue.

They will deliver sessions on SL learning to staff and parents on: the importance of students maintaining their mother tongue at an academic level; the fundamental difference between *second* language and *foreign* language; and the time taken to learn a second language. They will broadcast information about native-speaker accent and non-native-speaker accent so that parents do not have false expectations, saying that a native-speaker accent is largely unattainable after puberty, or even before; they will promote school-wide understanding about the way in which academic knowledge is transferred from the mother tongue to the second language so that all teachers can draw on this resource.

The ESL department will set in motion the programme of CPD through which content teachers will acquire a deeper understanding of the ways in which bilinguals have a different knowledge base from monolinguals so that even their mother tongue may be affected by their second language(s), and these should be assessed against other second-language measures, not first-language ones. Assessment for these students is best given not in grades, but through comments, portfolios and formative class work, not summative tests, i.e., tests given at the end of a period of study to evaluate students' work.

There will be a school-wide encouragement of 'critical vigilance' on all second-language matters, which will be continually talked up by those in positions of responsibility, at least as much as on other discriminatory issues such as race. All new entrants will be screened in depth by the ESL department, especially on their academic writing abilities, and attention will be given to probing whether weaknesses are largely linguistic or may include a special educational needs element. There will be separation of the ESL and SEN departments and personnel. Each student will be profiled on their language background and given a language passport, updated every year to show their achievement in each of their languages in speaking and writing skills (see, for example, the Common European Framework of Reference for Languages: Learning, Teaching, Assessment (CEFR) of the Council of Europe: www.coe.int/en/web/portfolio/the-language-passport, accessed 13 February 2018). All of this information on each student will be available to all content teachers.

Today's world has many challenges; many observers point to the negative aspects of the internet. In *Proust and the Squid* (Wolf, 2008), on the origins of reading, how the brain adapted itself to the process, and how reading enables the reader to build on previously learned knowledge to acquire a deeper development of their intellectual potential, Wolf presents evidence that the assumption that thinking faster and having more information is better requires vigorous questioning. She delves into the concerns of Socrates about the effect of reading and writing on our critical faculties, and considers today's society of internet decoders of information. Socrates feared that the permanence of the written language would mean less searching for true knowledge, which would lead to the death of human virtue. Wolf concludes by writing, 'I fear that many of our children are in danger of becoming ... a society of decoders of information, whose false sense of knowing distracts them from a deeper development of their intellectual potential. It does not need to be so, if we teach them well' (p. 226). The solution she presents is to teach children to switch between different presentations of written language and different modes of analysis 'to preserve the capacities of two systems and appreciate why both are precious' (ibid.: 229). In a section on the effects of bilingualism on reading (ibid.: 105–7), Wolf describes it as 'an extraordinary, complicated cognitive investment for children', albeit one that represents an ever-increasing reality for huge numbers of students. She points out that the advantages are greater than the possible 'up-front costs', with the important proviso that the child learns each language well.

Woolley writes that a positive school climate for SLLs is a major factor in promoting good reading habits:

> A number of researchers have emphasized that for any reading program to be effective, educators must find ways to embed the cultural interests and competencies of ESL students into classroom programs and routines (Craig, Hull, Haggart and Perez-Selles, 2000).
>
> (Woolley, 2010: 91)

This is a must-have in an international school, and the ESL department will be ever vigilant to ensure each incoming director keeps up such practices.

Closing comments

Only by adopting the model and policies outlined in this book can the subtractive bilingual tendency that is routine in so many international schools be turned around. School leaders need to be aware of the link between nationalism and nation building that promotes monolingualism as the norm and leads to monolingual educational policies. Anglosphere countries are particularly prone to this mindset, so school boards of governors could usefully be on the lookout for heads of school who are second-language speakers of English.

Obviously, the task would be much more straightforward if the CIS, the IB and other agencies changed their policies and approach; in any school, teachers have to follow the curriculum and rules handed out from above and outside. Given the facts set out in this book about those agencies, school heads will have to take tough decisions: international schools, from being the leaders in developing the IB, now find themselves in a minority. The IB has some excellent programmes, but has set its sights on the national US market, thereby becoming less concerned about the international schools' constituency in matters related to SL learners, in the middle school especially. Schools which had good ESL programmes in middle schools have sometimes seen these diminished in efficacy, or even dissolved. Schools that offer the PYP, jump the MYP and develop their own programmes but still offer the IB Diploma have, to the contrary, shown the way (see http://esl. fis.edu/index.htm, accessed 13 February 2018). What is the purpose of the 'international' in the IB if appropriate language-development programmes, according to the latest research, are not provided to all students who are not literate in the language of instruction? As already related, 'Will the programmes of the IB continue to be fit for the purpose of international education, as practised in international schools?' (Cambridge, 2013: 201). For ESL students, they certainly will not.

This is equally true of the CIS: this organization is not, as far as is known, aiming to secure a niche in a national system in the same way as the IB (though its close partner, the NEASC, is), so it can focus its efforts on providing a genuinely fair and supportive model of accreditation for ESL students that is international, no longer relegating them to the end of the accreditation documents under support services, and removing the language of the disabled: support.

We, the authors of this book, have lived our lives through ESL and MT issues. Researchers and academics have been of enormous assistance as they have provided a bedrock on which to base our programmes. But the daily experience of teaching ESL students, providing the best programmes and tuition, talking to the parents, explaining painstakingly to school heads who have come from national systems and are soon replaced – all these factors have convinced us that a good SL programme in the middle school will not only enable SLLs to better develop their English for schooling, but will change the very nature of the school teaching force and the school ethos, thereby delivering a model for the globalized world we inhabit. International school leaders need to take bold decisions, to accept the reality that current models, and the organizations that provide or oversee them, are not fulfilling their potential, and to urgently institute the model outlined in this book.

Appendix: Useful websites for SLLs in international schools

Bilingual Family Newsletter archives: www.multilingualmatters.com/bilingual_family_archive.asp (accessed 13 February 2018).

Common European Framework of Reference for Languages: Learning, Teaching, Assessment (CEFR): www.coe.int/en/web/common-european-framework-reference-languages (accessed 18 September 2018).

Frankfurt International School, ESL: http://esl.fis.edu/ (accessed 13 February 2018).

Institute for Language and Education Policy: www.elladvocates.org/ (accessed 13 February 2018).

International English Language Testing System test (IELTS): www.ielts.org (accessed 13 February 2018). 'The IELTS Academic test is suitable for entry to study at undergraduate or postgraduate levels, and also for professional registration purposes. It assesses whether you are ready to begin studying or training in an environment where English language is used, and reflects some of the features of language used in academic study.' Free practice tests: https://takeielts.britishcouncil.org/prepare-test/free-practice-tests (accessed 13 February 2018).

Thomas and Collier: www.thomasandcollier.com (accessed 13 February 2018).

Language Web Site & Emporium (DiversityLearningK12): www.languagepolicy. net/ (accessed 18 September 2018).

Maurice Carder: www.mauricecarder.net (accessed 13 February 2018).

EAL-time (Joris Van Den Bosch): www.eal-time.com (accessed 18 September 2018).

Multilingual Living: www.multilingualliving.com (accessed 13 February 2018).

Stephen Krashen: www.sdkrashen.com/ (accessed 13 February 2018).

Jim Cummins's web page with resources: www.iteachilearn.com/cummins/ (accessed 13 February 2018).

The Council of Europe Autobiography of Intercultural Encounters (AIE): www.coe.int/en/web/language-policy/the-autobiography-of-intercultural-encounters-aie- (accessed 3 September 2018).

The Council of Europe platform of resources and references for plurilingual and intercultural education: www.coe.int/en/web/platform-plurilingual-intercultural-language-education/home (accessed 3 September 2018).

Teaching ESL students in mainstream classrooms (TESMC): https://lexised. com/courses/teaching-esl-students-in-mainstream-classrooms/ (accessed 13 February 2018).

ESL Resource Guide: www.wiseoldsayings.com/esl-guide/ (accessed 13 February 2018).

References

Abedi, J. (2002) 'Assessment and accommodations of English language learners: Issues, concerns, and recommendations'. *Journal of School Improvement*, 3 (1), 83–9.

Adesope, O.O., Lavin, T., Thompson, T. and Ungerleider, C. (2010) 'A systematic review and meta-analysis of the cognitive correlates of bilingualism'. *Review of Educational Research*, 80 (2), 207–45.

Adger, C.T., Snow, C.E. and Christian, D. (eds) (2018) *What Teachers Need to Know about Language*. 2nd ed. Bristol: Multilingual Matters.

Adorno, T. (2005) 'Education after Auschwitz'. In *Critical Models: Intervention and catchwords*. New York/Chichester: Columbia University Press, 191–204. Online. https://signale.cornell.edu/text/education-after-auschwitz (accessed 18 September 2018).

Alexander, R. (2004) 'Still no pedagogy? Principle, pragmatism and compliance in primary education'. *Cambridge Journal of Education*, 34 (1), 7–33.

Alexander, R. (2008) *Education for All, the Quality Imperative and the Problem of Pedagogy* (CREATE Pathways to Access Research Monograph 20). London: Consortium for Research on Educational Access, Transitions and Equity.

Allal, L. and Pelgrims Ducrey, G. (2000) 'Assessment of – or in – the zone of proximal development'. *Learning and Instruction*, 10 (2), 137–52.

Allan, M. (2002) 'Cultural borderlands: A case study of cultural dissonance in an international school'. *Journal of Research in International Education*, 1 (1), 63–90.

Apple, M. (1986) *Teachers and Texts: A political economy of class and gender relations in education*. New York: Routledge and Kegan Paul.

Arkoudis, S. (2003) 'Teaching English as a second language in science classes: Incommensurate epistemologies?' *Language and Education*, 17 (3), 161–73.

Arkoudis, S. (2006) 'Negotiating the rough ground between ESL and mainstream teachers'. *International Journal of Bilingual Education and Bilingualism*, 9 (4), 415–33.

Arkoudis, S. and Creese, A. (2006) 'Introduction', in 'Teacher–teacher talk: The discourse of collaboration in linguistically diverse classrooms', special issue of *International Journal of Bilingual Education and Bilingualism*, 9 (4), 411–14.

Artiles, A.J. and Klingner, J.K. (2006) 'Forging a knowledge base on English language learners with special needs: Theoretical, population, and technical issues'. *Teachers College Record*, 108 (11), 2187–94.

Artiles, A.J., Rueda, R., Salazar, J.J. and Higareda, I. (2005) 'Within-group diversity in minority disproportionate representation: English language learners in urban school districts'. *Exceptional Children*, 71 (3), 283–300.

Atkinson, K. (2013) *Life after Life*. London: Doubleday.

Auer, P. (2009) 'Bilingual conversation'. In Coupland, N. and Jaworski, A. (eds) *The New Sociolinguistics Reader*. Basingstoke: Palgrave Macmillan, 490–511.

August, D. and Hakuta, K. (eds) (1997) *Improving Schooling for Language-Minority Children: A research agenda*. National Research Council, Institute of Medicine, National Academy Press.

References

August, D. and Shanahan, T. (eds) (2006) *Developing Literacy in Second-Language Learners: Report of the National Literacy Panel on Language Minority Children and Youth*. Mahwah, NJ: Lawrence Erlbaum Associates.

August, D. and Shanahan, T. (eds) (2008) *Developing Reading and Writing in Second-Language Learners: Lessons from the report of the National Literacy Panel on Language-Minority Children and Youth*. New York: Routledge.

Auleear Owodally, A.M. (2014) 'Socialized into multilingualism: A case study of a Mauritian pre-school'. In Conteh, J. and Meier, G. (eds) *The Multilingual Turn in Languages Education: Opportunities and challenges*. Bristol: Multilingual Matters, 17–40.

Azadi, S. (1987) *Out of Iran: One woman's escape from the Ayatollahs*. London: Macdonald.

Baetens Beardsmore, H. (2003) 'Who's afraid of bilingualism?' In Dewaele, J.-M., Housen, A. and Wei, L. (eds) *Bilingualism: Beyond basic principles: Festschrift in honour of Hugo Baetens Beardsmore*. Clevedon: Multilingual Matters, 10–27.

Baetens Beardsmore, H. (2012) 'Foreword'. In Mehisto, P. *Excellence in Bilingual Education: A guide for school principals*. Cambridge: Cambridge University Press, v–vi.

Baker, C. (2003) 'Language planning: A grounded approach'. In Dewaele, J.-M., Housen, A. and Wei, L. (eds) *Bilingualism: Beyond basic principles*. Clevedon: Multilingual Matters, 88–111.

Baker, C. (2006) *Foundations of Bilingual Education and Bilingualism*. 4th ed. Clevedon: Multilingual Matters.

Baker, C. (2011) *Foundations of Bilingual Education and Bilingualism*. 5th ed. Bristol: Multilingual Matters.

Baker, C. and Prys Jones, S. (eds) (1998) *Encyclopedia of Bilingualism and Bilingual Education*. Clevedon: Multilingual Matters.

Baker, S., Gersten, R., Dimino, J.A. and Griffiths, R. (2004) 'The sustained use of research-based instructional practice: A case study of peer-assisted learning strategies in mathematics'. *Remedial and Special Education*, 25 (1), 5–24.

Barnett, R. (2001) 'Managing universities in a supercomplex age'. In Cutright, M. (ed.) *Chaos Theory and Higher Education: Leadership, planning, and policy*. New York: Peter Lang, 13–32.

Becher, T. and Trowler, P.R. (2001) *Academic Tribes and Territories: Intellectual enquiry and the culture of disciplines*. 2nd ed. Buckingham: Society for Research into Higher Education and Open University Press.

Belich, J. (2011) *Replenishing the Earth: The settler revolution and the rise of the Anglo-world, 1783–1939*. Oxford: Oxford University Press.

Bentley, K. (2010) *The TKT Course: CLIL module*. Cambridge: Cambridge University Press.

Ben-Zeev, S. (1977) 'The influence of bilingualism on cognitive strategy and cognitive development'. *Child Development*, 48 (3), 1009–18.

Bernstein, B. (1990) *The Structuring of Pedagogic Discourse* (Class, Codes and Control 4). London: Routledge.

Bernstein, B. (2000) *Pedagogy, Symbolic Control and Identity: Theory, research, critique*. Lanham, MD: Rowman and Littlefield.

Bialystok, E. (ed.) (1991) *Language Processing in Bilingual Children*. Cambridge: Cambridge University Press.

Bialystok, E. (2004) 'The impact of bilingualism on language and literacy development'. In Bhatia, T.K. and Ritchie, W.C. (eds) *The Handbook of Bilingualism*. Malden, MA: Blackwell Publishing, 577–601.

Bialystok, E. (2010) 'Global-local and trail-making tasks by monolingual and bilingual children: Beyond inhibition'. *Developmental Psychology*, 46 (1), 93–105.

Bialystok, E. (2011) 'Reshaping the mind: The benefits of bilingualism'. *Canadian Journal of Experimental Psychology*, 65 (4), 229–35.

Bialystok, E., Craik, F.I.M. and Freedman, M. (2007) 'Bilingualism as a protection against the onset of symptoms of dementia'. *Neuropsychologia*, 45 (2), 459–64.

Blackledge, A. (ed.) (1994) *Teaching Bilingual Children*. Stoke-on-Trent: Trentham Books.

Blandford, S. and Shaw, M. (2001) 'The nature of international school leadership'. In Blandford, S. and Shaw, M. (eds) *Managing International Schools*. London: RoutledgeFalmer, 9–28.

Block, D. (2003) *The Social Turn in Second Language Acquisition*. Edinburgh: Edinburgh University Press.

Bourdieu, P. (1984) *Distinction: A social critique of the judgement of taste*. Trans. Nice, R. London: Routledge and Kegan Paul.

Bourne, J. (1989) *Moving into the Mainstream: LEA provision for bilingual pupils*. Windsor: NFER-Nelson.

Boyle, B. and Charles, M. (2014) *Formative Assessment for Teaching and Learning*. London: SAGE Publications.

Brown, C.L. (2004) 'Reducing the over-referral of culturally and linguistically diverse students (CLD) for language disabilities'. *NABE Journal of Research and Practice*, 2 (1), 225–43.

Brummitt, N. and Keeling, A. (2013) 'Charting the growth of international schools'. In Pearce, R. (ed.) *International Education and Schools: Moving beyond the first 40 years*. London: Bloomsbury Academic, 25–36.

Bunnell, T. (2008) 'The International Baccalaureate in England and Wales: The alternative paths for the future'. *Curriculum Journal*, 19 (3), 151–60.

Bunnell, T. (2011) 'The growth of the International Baccalaureate diploma program: Concerns about the consistency and reliability of the assessments'. *Educational Forum*, 75 (2), 174–87.

Butler, R. (1988) 'Enhancing and undermining intrinsic motivation: The effects of task-involving and ego-involving evaluation on interest and performance'. *British Journal of Educational Psychology*, 58 (1), 1–14.

Butler, Y.G., Orr, J.E., Gutiérrez, M.B. and Hakuta, K. (2000) 'Inadequate conclusions from an inadequate assessment: What can SAT-9 scores tell us about the impact of Proposition 227 in California?' *Bilingual Research Journal*, 24 (1–2), 141–54.

Byrnes, D.A., Kiger, G. and Manning, M.L. (1997) 'Teachers' attitudes about language diversity'. *Teaching and Teacher Education*, 13 (6), 637–44.

Cajkler, W. and Hall, B. (2012) 'Multilingual primary classrooms: An investigation of first year teachers' learning and responsive teaching'. *European Journal of Teacher Education*, 35 (2), 213–28.

References

Callahan, R.M. (2005) 'Tracking and high school English learners: Limiting opportunity to learn'. *American Educational Research Journal*, 42 (2), 305–28.

Callahan, R.M. (2006) 'The intersection of accountability and language: Can reading intervention replace English language development?' *Bilingual Research Journal*, 30 (1), 1–21.

Callahan, R.M. and Gándara, P.C. (eds) (2014) *The Bilingual Advantage: Language, literacy and the US labor market*. Bristol: Multilingual Matters.

Calvet, L.-J. (1987) *La Guerre des langues: Et les politiques linguistiques*. Paris: Payot.

Cambridge, J. (2006) 'Book review: *Education Management in Managerialist Times: Beyond the textual apologists*'. *Journal of Research in International Education*, 5 (3), 369–72.

Cambridge, J. (2013) 'Dilemmas of international education: A Bernsteinian analysis'. In Pearce, R. (ed.) *International Education and Schools: Moving beyond the first 40 years*. London: Bloomsbury Academic, 183–204.

Carder, M. (1979) 'The negotiated syllabus'. Unpublished MA thesis, University of Lancaster.

Carder, M. (1991) 'The role and development of ESL programs in international schools'. In Jonietz, P.L. and Harris, D. (eds) (1991) *International Schools and International Education* (World Yearbook of Education). London: Kogan Page, 108–24.

Carder, M. (1993) 'Are we creating biliterate bilinguals?' *International Schools Journal*, 26, Autumn, 19–27. Reprinted in Murphy, E. (ed.) (2003) *ESL: Educating non-native speakers of English in an English-medium international school* (International Schools Compendium, 1). Saxmundham: Peridot Press.

Carder, M. (1995) 'Language(s) in international education: A review of language issues in international schools'. In Skutnabb-Kangas, T. (ed.) *Multilingualism for All*. Lisse: Swets and Zeitlinger, 113–57.

Carder, M. (2005) 'Bilingualism and the Council of International Schools'. *International Schools Journal*, 24 (2), 19–27.

Carder, M. (2006) 'Bilingualism in International Baccalaureate programmes, with particular reference to international schools'. *Journal of Research in International Education*, 5 (1), 105–22.

Carder, M. (2007a) *Bilingualism in International Schools: A model for enriching language education*. Clevedon: Multilingual Matters.

Carder, M.W. (2007b) 'Organization of English teaching in international schools'. In Cummins, J. and Davison, C. (eds) *International Handbook of English Language Teaching: Part 1*. New York: Springer, 379–89.

Carder, M. (2008a) 'The development of ESL provision in Australia, Canada, the USA and England, with conclusions for second language models in international schools'. *Journal of Research in International Education*, 7 (2), 205–31.

Carder, M. (2008b) 'The language repertoires of students in the Vienna International School: Issues relating to the importance of maintaining fluency and literacy in their mother tongue'. Unpublished Institution Focused Study, as element of EdD (International), Institute of Education, London, 57–60.

Carder, M. (ed.) (2009a) 'International schools', special issue of *NALDIC Quarterly*, 7 (1). www.naldic.org.uk/eal-publications-resources/Shop/shop-products/nq71.html.

Carder, M. (2009b) 'ESL or "EAL"? Programme or "support"? The baggage that comes with names'. *International Schools Journal*, 29 (1), 18–25.

Carder, M.W. (2011) 'Challenging the English-only orthodoxy: Linguistic pluralism, recognition and diversity rather than assimilation'. Unpublished EdD (International) thesis, Institute of Education, University of London.

Carder, M. (2013a) 'International school students: Developing their bilingual potential'. In Abello-Contesse, C., Chandler, P.M., López-Jiménez, M.D. and Chacón-Beltrán, R. (eds) *Bilingual and Multilingual Education in the 21st Century: Building on experience*. Bristol: Multilingual Matters, 275–98.

Carder, M. (2013b) 'English language teaching: The change in students' language from "English only" to "linguistically diverse"'. In Pearce, R. (ed.) *International Education and Schools: Moving beyond the first 40 years*. London: Bloomsbury Academic, 85–106.

Carder, M. (2014a) 'Managerial impact on programmes for second language learners in international schools'. Online. http://mclanguage.tripod.com/ webonmediacontents/Managerial%20impact%20on%20second%20 language%20learners%20in%20international%20schools.pdf (accessed 18 June 2018).

Carder, M. (2014b) 'Tracing the path of ESL provision in international schools over the last four decades: Part 1'. *International Schools Journal*, 34 (1), 85–96.

Carder, M. (2015) 'Tracing the path of ESL provision in international schools over the last four decades: Part 2'. *International Schools Journal*, 34 (2), 59–67.

Carder, M. (2017a) 'EAL in the rear-view mirror'. Keynote speech given at the COBIS British School of Bucharest, Romania, 16 February. Online. http:// mclanguage.tripod.com/webonmediacontents/EAL%20in%20the%20rear-view%20mirror,Bucharest,2017.pdf (accessed 18 June 2018).

Carder M. (2017b) 'Solution: The professionalization of ESL'. Keynote speech given at the COBIS British School of Bucharest, Romania, 17 February. Online. http://mclanguage.tripod.com/webonmediacontents/EAL%20in%20the%20 rear-view%20mirror,Bucharest,2017.pdf (accessed 18 June 2018).

Carder, M. (2017c) 'ESL departments as centres of expertise in international middle and upper schools: Exposing myth-information about second-language issues'. Presentation given at the CIS Symposium, Amsterdam, 10 March. Online. http://mclanguage.tripod.com/webonmediacontents/ESL%20 Departments%20as%20Centres%20of%20Expertise,CIS,2017.pdf (accessed 18 June 2018).

Cenoz, J. and Gorter, D. (eds) (2015a) *Multilingual Education: Between language learning and translanguaging*. Cambridge: Cambridge University Press.

Cenoz, J. and Gorter, D. (eds) (2015b) 'Towards a holistic approach in the study of multilingual education'. In Cenoz, J. and Gorter, D. (eds) *Multilingual Education: Between language learning and translanguaging*. Cambridge: Cambridge University Press, 1–15.

Chadwick, T. (2012) *Language Awareness in Teaching: A toolkit for content and language teachers*. Cambridge: Cambridge University Press.

Chadwick, V. (2015) 'Timmermans: Central Europe has "no experience with diversity"'. *Politico*, 24 September. Online. www.politico.eu/article/migration-news-diversity-timmermans/ (accessed 13 February 2018).

References

Charles, F. and Legendre, F. (2006) *Les Enseignants issus des immigrations: Modalités d'accès au groupe professionnel, représentations du métier et de l'école.* Paris: Sudel.

Cherng, H.-Y.S. and Halpin, P.F. (2016) 'The importance of minority teachers: Student perceptions of minority versus white teachers'. *Educational Researcher,* 45 (7), 407–20.

Christian, D. and Genesee, F. (eds) (2001) *Bilingual Education.* Alexandria, VA: Teachers of English to Speakers of Other Languages.

Christie, F. (1985) 'Language and schooling'. In Tchudi, S.N. (ed.) *Language, Schooling and Society.* Upper Montclair, NJ: Boynton/Cook, 21–40.

CIS/NEASC (2014) 'Journey to excellence in international education: The main guide to school evaluation and accreditation'. 8th ed. (version 8.2), September. Online. https://cie.neasc.org/sites/cie.neasc.org/files/Downloads_pdf/Main%20 Guide%20-%20CIS-NEASC%20-%208th%20Ed%20%28V8%202%29%20 Sept%202014_1.pdf (accessed 25 August 2018).

Clark, E.V. (1978) 'Awareness of language: Some evidence from what children say and do'. In Sinclair, A., Jarvella, R.J. and Levelt, W.J.M. (eds) *The Child's Conception of Language.* Berlin: Springer, 17–43.

Clarke, J. (1995) 'Doing the right thing? Managerialism and social welfare'. Paper presented at the ESRC 'Professionals in Late Modernity' seminar, Imperial College, London, 26 June.

Clarke, J. and Newman, J. (1997) *The Managerial State: Power, politics and ideology in the remaking of social welfare.* London: SAGE Publications.

Coetzee-Van Rooy, S. (2006) 'Integrativeness: Untenable for world Englishes learners?' *World Englishes,* 25 (3–4), 437–50.

Coffey, J.E., Hammer, D., Levin, D.M. and Grant, T. (2011) 'The missing disciplinary substance of formative assessment'. *Journal of Research in Science Teaching,* 48 (10), 1109–36.

Coïaniz, A. (2001) *Apprentissage des langues et subjectivité.* Paris: L'Harmattan.

Collier, V.P. (1989) 'How long? A synthesis of research on academic achievement in a second language'. *TESOL Quarterly,* 23 (3), 509–31.

Collier, V.P. (1992) 'A synthesis of studies examining long-term language minority student data on academic achievement'. *Bilingual Research Journal,* 16 (1–2), 187–212.

Collier, V.P. (1995a) *Acquiring a Second Language for School.* Washington, DC: National Clearinghouse for Bilingual Education.

Collier, V.P. (1995b) *Promoting Academic Success for ESL Students: Understanding second language acquisition for school.* Woodside, NY: Bastos Educational Publications.

Collier, V.P. (1995c) 'Second language acquisition for school: Academic, cognitive, sociocultural, and linguistic processes'. In Alatis, J.E., Straehle, C.A., Gallenberger, B. and Ronkin, M. (eds) *Linguistics and the Education of Language Teachers: Ethnolinguistic, psycholinguistic, and sociolinguistic aspects* (Georgetown University Round Table on Languages and Linguistics). Washington, DC: Georgetown University Press, 311–27.

Collier, V.P. (2003) 'Foreword'. In Murphy, E. (ed.) *ESL: Educating non-native speakers of English in an English-medium international school* (International Schools Journal Compendium 1). Saxmundham: Peridot Press, 7–8.

Collier, V.P. and Crawford, J. (1998) 'Policy and programs'. In Ovando, C.J. and Collier, V.P. *Bilingual and ESL Classrooms: Teaching in multicultural contexts.* 2nd ed. Boston: McGraw-Hill, 27–61.

Collier, V.P. and Thomas, W.P. (1999a) 'Making US schools effective for English language learners: Part 1'. *TESOL Matters*, 9 (4), 1, 6.

Collier, V.P. and Thomas, W.P. (1999b) 'Making US schools effective for English language learners: Part 2'. *TESOL Matters*, 9 (5), 1, 6.

Collier, V.P. and Thomas, W.P. (1999c) 'Making [US] schools effective for English language learners: Part 3'. *TESOL Matters*, 9 (6), 1, 10.

Collier, V.P. and Thomas, W.P. (2007) 'Predicting second language academic success in English using the prism model'. In Cummins, J. and Davison, C. (eds) *International Handbook of English Language Teaching: Part 1.* New York: Springer, 333–48.

Collier, V.P. and Thomas, W.P. (2017) 'Validating the power of bilingual schooling: Thirty-two years of large-scale, longitudinal research'. *Annual Review of Applied Linguistics*, 37, 203–17.

Conteh, J. and Meier, G. (eds) (2014) *The Multilingual Turn in Languages Education: Opportunities and challenges.* Bristol: Multilingual Matters.

Cook, V. (2014a) 'How do people learn to write in a second language?' In Cook, V. and Singleton, D. *Key Topics in Second Language Acquisition.* Bristol: Multilingual Matters, 73–88.

Cook, V. (2014b) 'How do attitude and motivation help in learning a second language?' In Cook, V. and Singleton, D. *Key Topics in Second Language Acquisition.* Bristol: Multilingual Matters, 89–108.

Cook, V. (2014c) 'What are the goals of language teaching?' In Cook, V. and Singleton, D. *Key Topics in Second Language Acquisition.* Bristol: Multilingual Matters, 125–41.

Cook, V. and Singleton, D. (2014) *Key Topics in Second Language Acquisition.* Bristol: Multilingual Matters.

Corrie, L. (1995) 'The structure and culture of staff collaboration: Managing meaning and opening doors'. *Educational Review*, 47 (1), 89–99.

Coupland, N. and Jaworski, A. (eds) (2009) *The New Sociolinguistics Reader.* Basingstoke: Palgrave Macmillan.

Coyle, D., Hood, P. and Marsh, D. (2012) *CLIL: Content and language integrated learning.* Cambridge: Cambridge University Press.

Craig, S., Hull, K., Haggart, A.G. and Perez-Selles, M. (2000) 'Promoting cultural competence through teacher assistance teams'. *Teaching Exceptional Children*, 32 (3), 6–12.

Craik, F.I.M., Bialystok, E. and Freedman, M. (2010) 'Delaying the onset of Alzheimer disease: Bilingualism as a form of cognitive reserve'. *Neurology*, 75 (19), 1726–9.

Crandall, J. (ed.) (1987) *ESL through Content-Area Instruction: Mathematics, science, social studies.* Englewood Cliffs, NJ: Prentice-Hall.

Crawford, J. (2000) *At War with Diversity: US language policy in an age of anxiety.* Clevedon: Multilingual Matters.

Crawford, J. and Krashen, S. (2007) *English Learners in American Classrooms: 101 questions, 101 answers.* New York: Scholastic.

Creese, A. (2002) 'The discursive construction of power in teacher partnerships: Language and subject specialists in mainstream schools'. *TESOL Quarterly*, 36 (4), 597–616.

Creese, A. (2005) *Teacher Collaboration and Talk in Multilingual Classrooms*. Clevedon: Multilingual Matters.

Creese, A. and Blackledge, A. (2010) 'Translanguaging in the Bilingual Classroom: A pedagogy for learning and teaching?' *Modern Language Journal*, 94 (1), 103–15.

Crooks, T.J. (1988) 'The impact of classroom evaluation practices on students'. *Review of Educational Research*, 58 (4), 438–81.

Crotty, M. (1998) *The Foundations of Social Research: Meaning and perspective in the research process*. London: SAGE Publications.

Cruickshank, K. (2014) 'Exploring the -lingual between bi and mono: Young people and their languages in an Australian context'. In Conteh, J. and Meier, G. (eds) *The Multilingual Turn in Languages Education: Opportunities and challenges*. Bristol: Multilingual Matters, 41–63.

Crystal, D. (1997) *English as a Global Language*. Cambridge: Cambridge University Press.

Cummins, J. (1979) 'Cognitive/academic language proficiency, linguistic interdependence, the optimum age question and some other matters'. Working Papers on Bilingualism 19. Ontario Institute for Studies in Education, Toronto.

Cummins, J. (1984) *Bilingualism and Special Education: Issues in assessment and pedagogy*. Clevedon: Multilingual Matters.

Cummins, J. (1991) 'Interdependence of first- and second-language proficiency in bilingual children'. In Bialystok, E. (ed.) *Language Processing in Bilingual Children*. Cambridge: Cambridge University Press, 70–89.

Cummins, J. (1993a) 'Empowerment through biliteracy'. In Tinajero, J.V. and Ada, A.F. (eds) *The Power of Two Languages: Literacy and biliteracy for Spanish-speaking students*. New York: Macmillan/McGraw-Hill, 1–17.

Cummins, J. (1993b) 'Bilingualism and second language learning'. *Annual Review of Applied Linguistics*, 13, 51–70.

Cummins, J. (1996) *Negotiating Identities: Education for empowerment in a diverse society*. Ontario: California Association for Bilingual Education.

Cummins, J. (2000) *Language, Power and Pedagogy: Bilingual children in the crossfire*. Clevedon: Multilingual Matters.

Cummins, J. (2001a) *An Introductory Reader to the Writings of Jim Cummins*, ed. Baker, C. and Hornberger, N.H. Clevedon: Multilingual Matters.

Cummins, J. (2001b) 'The influence of bilingualism on cognitive growth: A synthesis of research findings and explanatory hypotheses'. In Cummins, J. *An Introductory Reader to the Writings of Jim Cummins*. Clevedon: Multilingual Matters, 26–55. 1976, Working Papers on Bilingualism 9. Ontario Institute for Studies in Education, Toronto.)

Cummins, J. (2001c) 'Linguistic interdependence and the educational development of bilingual children'. In Cummins, J. *An Introductory Reader to the Writings of Jim Cummins*. Clevedon: Multilingual Matters, 63–95. (Originally published in 1979, *Review of Educational Research*, 49 (2), 222–51.)

Cummins, J. (2001d) 'The entry and exit fallacy in bilingual education'. In Cummins, J. *An Introductory Reader to the Writings of Jim Cummins.* Clevedon: Multilingual Matters, 110–38. (Originally published in 1980, *NABE Journal*, 4, 25–60.)

Cummins, J. (2001e) 'Tests, achievement, and bilingual students'. In Cummins, J. *An Introductory Reader to the Writings of Jim Cummins.* Clevedon: Multilingual Matters, 139–47. (Originally published in 1982, *FOCUS*, February, 9, 1–7.)

Cummins, J. (2001f) 'Empowering minority students: A framework for intervention'. In Cummins, J. *An Introductory Reader to the Writings of Jim Cummins.* Clevedon: Multilingual Matters, 175–94. (Originally published in 1986, *Harvard Educational Review*, 56 (1), 18–36.)

Cummins, J. (2001g) 'The role and use of educational theory in formulating language policy'. In Cummins, J. *An Introductory Reader to the Writings of Jim Cummins.* Clevedon: Multilingual Matters. (Originally published in 1988, *TESL Canada Journal*, 5 (2), 11–19.)

Cummins, J. (2005) 'A proposal for action: Strategies for recognizing heritage language competence as a learning resource within the mainstream classroom'. *Modern Language Journal*, 89 (4), 585–92.

Cummins, J. (2008) 'Foreword'. In Gallagher, E. *Equal Rights to the Curriculum: Many languages, one message.* Clevedon: Multilingual Matters, x–xii.

Cummins, J. and Early, M. (eds) (2011) *Identity Texts: The collaborative creation of power in multilingual schools.* Stoke-on-Trent: Trentham Books.

Cummins, J. and Gulutsan, M. (1974) 'Some effects of bilingualism on cognitive functioning'. In Carey, S.T. (ed.) *Bilingualism, Biculturalism and Education.* Edmonton: University of Alberta Press, 129–36.

Cummins, J. and Hornberger, N.H. (eds) (2008) *Encyclopedia of Language and Education. Volume 5: Bilingual education.* 2nd ed. New York: Springer.

Dale, L. and Tanner, R. (2012) *CLIL Activities with CD-ROM: A resource for subject and language teachers.* New York: Cambridge University Press.

Davison, C. (1992) 'Look out: Eight fatal flaws in support and team teaching'. *TESOL in Context*, 2 (1), 39–41.

Davison, C. (1994) 'Integrating ESL into the mainstream: An Australian perspective'. In Blackledge, A. (ed.) *Teaching Bilingual Children.* Stoke-on-Trent: Trentham Books.

Davison, C. (2001a) 'ESL in Australian schools: From the margins to the mainstream'. In Mohan, B., Leung, C. and Davison, C. (eds) *English as a Second Language in the Mainstream: Teaching, learning and identity.* Harlow: Longman, 11–29.

Davison, C. (2001b) 'Current policies, programs and practices in school ESL'. In Mohan, B., Leung, C. and Davison, C. (eds) *English as a Second Language in the Mainstream: Teaching, learning and identity.* Harlow: Longman, 30–50.

Davison, C. (2006) 'Collaboration between ESL and content teachers: How do we know when we are doing it right?' *International Journal of Bilingual Education and Bilingualism*, 9 (4), 454–75.

Day, C. (1987) 'Professional learning through collaborative in-service activity'. In Smyth, J. (ed.) *Educating Teachers: Changing the nature of pedagogical knowledge.* London: Falmer Press, 7–15.

References

De Avila, E.A. and Duncan, S.E. (1979) 'Bilingualism and the metaset'. *NABE Journal*, 3 (2), 1–20.

DECS (South Australian Department of Education and Children's Services) (1999) 'ESL in the mainstream'. Hindmarsh, South Australia: Department of Education and Children's Services.

de Lotbinière, M. (2009) 'Stark lessons in mother tongues'. *The Guardian*, 9 December. Online. www.theguardian.com/education/2009/dec/09/tefl-southafrica (accessed 14 June 2018).

de Mejía, A.-M. (2002) *Power, Prestige and Bilingualism: International perspectives on elite bilingual education*. Clevedon: Multilingual Matters.

DES (Department of Education and Science) and the Welsh Office) (1988) *National Curriculum Task Group on Assessment and Testing: A report*. London: Department of Education and Science and the Welsh Office. Online. www.educationengland.org.uk/documents/pdfs/1988-TGAT-report.pdf (accessed 13 February 2018).

Dewaele, J.-M., Housen, A. and Wei, L. (eds) (2003) *Bilingualism: Beyond basic principles*. Clevedon: Multilingual Matters.

Diamond, C.T.P. (1991) *Teacher Education as Transformation: A psychological perspective*. Milton Keynes: Open University Press.

Doherty, C. (2009) 'The appeal of the International Baccalaureate in Australia's educational market: A curriculum of choice for mobile futures'. *Discourse: Studies in the Cultural Politics of Education*, 30 (1), 73–89.

Dolson, D.P. (1985) 'Bilingualism and scholastic performance: The literature revisited'. *NABE Journal*, 10 (1), 1–35.

Dörnyei, Z. and Ushioda, E. (eds) (2009) *Motivation, Language Identity and the L2 Self*. Bristol: Multilingual Matters.

Duncan, C. (2015) 'If "speak Australian" is the standard set in the Senate, what hope is there for the rest of us?' *The Guardian*, 17 September. Online. www.theguardian.com/commentisfree/2015/sep/17/if-speak-australian-is-the-standard-set-in-the-senate-what-hope-is-there-for-the-rest-of-us (accessed 13 February 2018).

Dutcher, N. (2001) *The Use of First and Second Languages in Education: A review of international experience*. 2nd ed. Washington, DC: Center for Applied Linguistics.

Echevarría, J. and Graves, A. (2014) *Sheltered Content Instruction: Teaching English-language learners with diverse abilities*. London: Pearson Education.

Echevarría, J., Vogt, M. and Short, D.J. (2004) *Making Content Comprehensible for English Learners: The SIOP model*. 2nd ed. Boston: Allyn and Bacon.

Edwards, J. (2004) 'Foundations of bilingualism'. In Bhatia, T.K. and Ritchie, W.C. (eds) *The Handbook of Bilingualism*. Malden, MA: Blackwell Publishing, 7–31.

Edwards, V. (2004) *Multilingualism in the English-Speaking World: Pedigree of Nations*. Malden, MA: Blackwell Publishing.

Edwards, V. (2009) *Learning to be Literate: Multilingual perspectives*. Bristol: Multilingual Matters.

Edwards, V. (2010) 'Foreword'. In Leung, C. and Creese, A. (eds) *English as an Additional Language: Approaches to teaching linguistic minority students*. London: SAGE Publications, xiii.

Ellwood, C. and Davis, M. (2009) *International Mindedness: A professional development handbook for international schools.* London: Optimus Education.

Engel de Abreu, P.M.J., Cruz-Santos, A., Tourinho, C.J., Martin, R. and Bialystok, E. (2012) 'Bilingualism enriches the poor: Enhanced cognitive control in low-income minority children'. *Psychological Science*, 23 (11), 1364–71.

European Commission (2017) *Education and Training Monitor 2017* (European Commission Staff Working Document). Luxembourg: Publications Office of the European Union. Online. https://ec.europa.eu/education/sites/education/files/monitor2017_en.pdf (accessed 18 June 2018).

Ezra, R. (2003) 'Culture, language and personality in the context of the internationally mobile child'. *Journal of Research in International Education*, 2 (2), 123–49.

Facella, M.A., Rampino, K.M. and Shea, E.K. (2005) 'Effective teaching strategies for English language learners'. *Bilingual Research Journal*, 29 (1), 209–21.

Fathman, A.K., Quinn, M.E. and Kessler, C. (1992) *Teaching Science to English Learners, Grades 4–8.* Washington, DC: National Clearinghouse for Bilingual Education.

Fennes, H. and Hapgood, K. (1997) *Intercultural Learning in the Classroom: Crossing borders.* London: Cassell.

Ferguson, G. (2006) *Language Planning and Education.* Edinburgh: Edinburgh University Press.

Feuerstein, R. (1979) *The Dynamic Assessment of Retarded Performers: The learning potential assessment device, theory, instruments, and techniques.* Baltimore: University Park Press.

Fishman, J.A. (1966) *Language Loyalty in the United States: The maintenance and perpetuation of non-English mother tongues by American ethnic and religious groups.* The Hague: Mouton.

Fishman, J.A. (1970) *Sociolinguistics: A brief introduction.* Rowley, MA: Newbury House.

Fishman, J.A. (2004) 'Language maintenance, language shift, and reversing language shift'. In Bhatia, T.K. and Ritchie, W.C. (eds) *The Handbook of Bilingualism.* Malden, MA: Blackwell Publishing, 406–36.

Fishman, J.A. (2009) 'Language, ethnicity and racism'. In Coupland, N. and Jaworski, A. (eds) *The New Sociolinguistics Reader.* Basingstoke: Palgrave Macmillan, 435–46.

Franson, C. (1999) 'Mainstreaming learners of English as an additional language: The class teacher's perspective'. *Language, Culture and Curriculum*, 12 (1), 59–71.

Freebody, P., Maton, K. and Martin, J.R. (2008) 'Talk, text, and knowledge in cumulative, integrated learning: A response to "intellectual challenge"'. *Australian Journal of Language and Literacy*, 31 (2), 188–201.

Freire, P. (1970) *Pedagogy of the Oppressed.* Trans. Ramos, M.B. New York: Continuum.

Freire, P. (1972) *Cultural Action for Freedom.* Harmondsworth: Penguin.

Fry, R. (2007) *How Far Behind in Math and Reading are English Language Learners?* Washington, DC: Pew Hispanic Center.

Fukuyama, F. (2011) *The Origins of Political Order: From prehuman times to the French Revolution.* London: Profile Books.

Gallagher, E. (2008) *Equal Rights to the Curriculum: Many languages, one message*. Clevedon: Multilingual Matters.

Gándara, P. and Contreras, F. (2009) *The Latino Education Crisis: The consequences of failed social policies*. Cambridge, MA: Harvard University Press.

García, O. and Flores, N. (2014) 'Multilingualism and common core state standards in the United States'. In May, S. (ed.) *The Multilingual Turn: Implications for SLA, TESOL and bilingual education*. New York: Routledge, 147–66.

García, O., Skutnabb-Kangas, T. and Torres-Guzmán, M.E. (2006) 'Weaving spaces and (de)constructing ways for multilingual schools: The actual and the imagined'. In García, O., Skutnabb-Kangas, T. and Torres-Guzmán, M.E. (eds) *Imagining Multilingual Schools: Languages in education and glocalization*. Clevedon: Multilingual Matters, 3–47.

Garcia, S.B. and Ortiz, A.A. (1988) 'Preventing inappropriate referrals of language minority students to special education'. Occasional Papers in Bilingual Education 5. National Clearinghouse for Bilingual Education, Silver Spring, MD. Online. https://eric.ed.gov/?id=ED309591 (accessed 13 February 2018).

Gardner, R.C. and Lambert, W.E. (1959) 'Motivational variables in second-language acquisition'. *Canadian Journal of Psychology*, 13 (4), 266–72.

Gavin, C. (2015) *The Times*, 24 June. www.thetimes.co.uk/article/headteachers-and-poor-classroom-behaviour-cjhggs7qvmr (accessed 13 February 2018).

Genesee, F. (1987) *Learning through Two Languages: Studies of immersion and bilingual education*. Cambridge, MA: Newbury House.

Genesee, F. (ed.) (1994) *Educating Second Language Children: The whole child, the whole curriculum, and the whole community*. New York: Cambridge University Press.

Genesee, F. (2004) 'What do we know about bilingual education for majority-language students?' In Bhatia, T.K. and Ritchie, W.C. (eds) *The Handbook of Bilingualism*. Malden, MA: Blackwell Publishing, 547–76.

Gersten, R. (1999) 'Lost opportunities: Challenges confronting four teachers of English-language learners'. *Elementary School Journal*, 100 (1), 37–56.

Gersten, R. and Baker, S. (2003) 'English-language learners with learning difficulties'. In Swanson, H.L., Harris, K.R. and Graham, S. (eds) *Handbook of Learning Disabilities*. New York: Guilford Press, 94–100.

Geva, E. and Verhoeven, L. (2000) 'Introduction: The development of second language reading in primary children – research issues and trends'. *Scientific Studies of Reading*, 4 (4), 261–6.

Ghuman, P.A.S. (1994) *Coping with Two Cultures: British Asian and Indo-Canadian adolescents*. Clevedon: Multilingual Matters.

Gibbons, P. (2002) *Scaffolding Language, Scaffolding Learning: Teaching second language learners in the mainstream classroom*. Portsmouth, NH: Heinemann.

Gibbons, P. (2006) *Bridging Discourses in the ESL Classroom: Students, teachers and researchers*. London: Continuum.

Goethe, J.W. von (1821) 'Maximen und Reflexionen'. *Kunst und Altertum*, 3 (1).

Goldenberg, C. and Coleman, R. (2010) *Promoting Academic Achievement among English Learners: A guide to the research*. Thousand Oaks, CA: Corwin.

Goodenough, F.L. (1926) 'Racial differences in the intelligence of school children'. *Journal of Experimental Psychology*, 9 (5), 388–97.

Goodson, I.F. and Hargreaves, A. (eds) (1996) *Teachers' Professional Lives*. London: Falmer Press.

Gorard, S. (2010) 'Serious doubts about school effectiveness'. *British Educational Research Journal*, 36 (5), 745–66.

Goriot, C., Denessen, E., Bakker, J. and Droop, M. (2016) 'Benefits of being bilingual? The relationship between pupils' perceptions of teachers' appreciation of their home language and executive functioning'. *International Journal of Bilingualism*, 20 (6), 700–13.

Graddol, D. (2006) *English Next: Why global English may mean the end of 'English as a Foreign Language'*. London: British Council.

Greene, J.P. (1998) 'A meta-analysis of the effectiveness of bilingual education'. Tomas Rivera Policy Institute, University of Texas at Austin.

Grosjean, F. (1989) 'Neurolinguists, beware! The bilingual is not two monolinguals in one person'. *Brain and Language*, 36 (1), 3–15.

Guinier, L. (2003) 'Admissions rituals as political acts: Guardians at the gates of our democratic ideals'. *Harvard Law Review*, 117 (1), 113–24.

Guinier, L. and Torres, G. (2003) *The Miner's Canary: Enlisting race, resisting power, transforming democracy*. Cambridge, MA: Harvard University Press.

Gunderson, L. and Siegel, L.S. (2001) 'The evils of the use of IQ tests to define learning disabilities in first- and second-language learners'. *Reading Teacher*, 55 (1), 48–55.

Hakuta, K. (1986) *Mirror of Language: The debate on bilingualism*. New York: Basic Books.

Hakuta, K. and Diaz, R.M. (1985) 'The relationship between degree of bilingualism and cognitive ability: A critical discussion and some new longitudinal data'. In Nelson, K.E. (ed.) *Children's Language*, vol. 5. Hillsdale, NJ: Lawrence Erlbaum Associates, 319–44.

Halliday, M.A.K. and Martin, J.R. (1993) *Writing Science: Literacy and discursive power*. London: Falmer Press.

Hammond, J. (2008) 'Intellectual challenge and ESL students: Implications of quality teaching initiatives'. *Australian Journal of Language and Literacy*, 31 (2), 128–54.

Hansen-Thomas, H. and Cavagnetto, A. (2010) 'What do mainstream middle school teachers think about their English language learners? A tri-state case study'. *Bilingual Research Journal*, 33 (2), 249–66.

Harber, K.D., Gorman, J.L., Gengaro, F.P., Butisingh, S., Tsang, W. and Ouellette, R. (2012) 'Students' race and teachers' social support affect the positive feedback bias in public schools'. *Journal of Educational Psychology*, 104 (4), 1149–61.

Hargreaves, A. (1994) 'Collaboration and contrived collegiality: Cup of comfort or poisoned chalice?' In Hargreaves, A. *Changing Teachers, Changing Times: Teachers' work and culture in the postmodern age*. London: Cassell, 186–211.

Hargreaves, A. and Macmillan, B. (1994) 'The balkanization of teaching: Collaboration that divides'. In Hargreaves, A. *Changing Teachers, Changing Times: Teachers' work and culture in the postmodern age*. London: Cassell, 212–40.

References

Harper, C. with Cook, K. and James, C.K. (2010) 'Content-language integrated approaches for teachers of EAL learners: Examples of reciprocal teaching'. In Leung, C. and Creese, A. (eds) *English as an Additional Language: Approaches to teaching linguistic minority students*. London: SAGE Publications, 75–96.

Harper, C.A. and de Jong, E.J. (2009) 'English language teacher expertise: The elephant in the room'. *Language and Education*, 23 (2), 137–51.

Harper, C.A., de Jong, E.J. and Platt, E.J. (2008) 'Marginalizing English as a second language teacher expertise: The exclusionary consequence of No Child Left Behind'. *Language Policy*, 7 (3), 267–84.

Harris, J.L. (2003) 'Prologue: Toward an understanding of literacy issues in multicultural school-age populations'. *Language, Speech, and Hearing Services in Schools*, 34 (1), 17–19.

Hattie, J. and Timperley, H. (2007) 'The power of feedback'. *Review of Educational Research*, 77 (1), 81–112.

Hayden, M. (2006) *Introduction to International Education: International schools and their communities*. London: SAGE Publications.

Hayden, M. and Thompson, J. (2000) 'Quality in diversity'. In Hayden, M. and Thompson, J. (eds) *International Schools and International Education: Improving teaching, management and quality*. London: Kogan Page, 1–12.

Hayden, M. and Thompson, J. (2013) 'International schools: Antecedents, current issues and metaphors for the future'. In Pearce, R. (ed.) *International Education and Schools: Moving beyond the first 40 years*. London: Bloomsbury Academic, 3–24.

Hayden, M., Thompson, J. and Walker, G. (eds) (2002) *International Education in Practice: Dimensions for national and international schools*. London: Kogan Page.

Haynes, J. (2002) *Children as Philosophers: Learning through enquiry and dialogue in the primary classroom*. London: RoutledgeFalmer.

Hébert, R. (1976) *Rendement académique et langue d'enseignement chez les élèves franco-manitobains*. Saint-Boniface, Manitoba: Centre de Recherches du Collège universitaire de Saint-Boniface.

Hedges, C. (2009) *Empire of Illusion: The end of literacy and the triumph of spectacle*. New York: Nation Books.

Heller, M. (1999) *Linguistic Minorities and Modernity: A sociolinguistic ethnography*. London: Longman.

Hélot, C. and de Mejía, A.-M. (eds) (2008) *Forging Multilingual Spaces: Integrated perspectives on majority and minority bilingual education*. Bristol: Multilingual Matters.

Herman, E.S. and Chomsky, N. (2002) *Manufacturing Consent: The political economy of the mass media*. London: Vintage.

Higgs, K. (2014) *Collision Course: Endless growth on a finite planet*. Cambridge, MA: MIT Press.

Hill, I. (2000) 'Internationally-minded schools'. *International Schools Journal*, 20 (1), 24–37.

Hoff, K. and Pandey, P. (2004) 'Belief systems and durable inequalities: An experimental investigation of Indian caste.' World Bank Policy Research Working Paper 3351. Washington, DC.

Hofstede, G. (1980) *Culture's Consequences: International differences in work-related values*. Beverly Hills, CA: SAGE Publications.

Hogan-Brun, G. (2017) *Linguanomics: What is the market potential of multilingualism?* London: Bloomsbury Academic.

Holderness, J. (2002) 'The role of continuing professional development in the improvement of international schools'. In Hayden, M., Thompson, J. and Walker, G. (eds) *International Education in Practice: Dimensions for national and international schools*. London: Kogan Page, 83–98.

Hu, G. and McKay, S.L. (2014) 'Multilingualism as portrayed in a Chinese English textbook'. In Conteh, J. and Meier, G. (eds) *The Multilingual Turn in Languages Education: Opportunities and challenges*. Bristol: Multilingual Matters, 64–88.

Hughes, C. (2014) 'A critical analysis of the International Baccalaureate's Middle Years Programme assessment design with particular focus on feedback'. *Journal of Research in International Education*, 13 (3), 203–17.

Hurst, D. and Davison, C. (2005) 'Collaboration on the curriculum: Focus on secondary ESL'. In Crandall, J. and Kaufman, D. (eds) *Case Studies in TESOL: Teacher education for language and content integration*. Alexandria, VA: Teachers of English to Speakers of Other Languages, 41–66.

Igoa, C. (1995) *The Inner World of the Immigrant Child*. Mahwah, NJ: Lawrence Erlbaum Associates.

International Baccalaureate Organization (2004) *Second-Language Acquisition and Mother-Tongue Development: A guide for schools*. Geneva: International Baccalaureate Organization.

International Baccalaureate Organization (2005–18) *IB Learner Profile*. Geneva: International Baccalaureate Organization. Online. www.ibo.org/benefits/learner-profile/ (accessed 13 February 2018).

International Baccalaureate Organization (2008a) 'Guidelines for developing a school language policy'. Cardiff: International Baccalaureate Organization.

International Baccalaureate Organization (2008b) 'Learning in a language other than mother tongue in IB programmes'. Cardiff: International Baccalaureate Organization.

International Baccalaureate Organization (2011) 'Language and learning in IB programmes'. Cardiff: International Baccalaureate Organization.

International Baccalaureate Organization (2014) 'Programme standards and practices'. Cardiff: International Baccalaureate Organization.

International Baccalaureate Organization (2015) 'What is an IB education?' Cardiff: International Baccalaureate Organization. Online. www.ibo.org/globalassets/digital-tookit/brochures/what-is-an-ib-education-en.pdf (accessed 13 February 2018).

Iredale, R. and Fox, C. (1997) 'The impact of immigration on school education in New South Wales, Australia'. *International Migration Review*, 31 (3), 655–69.

Janzen, J. (2008) 'Teaching English language learners in the content areas'. *Review of Educational Research*, 78 (4), 1010–38.

Jones, O. (2015) *The Establishment: And how they get away with it*. London: Penguin Books.

Jonietz, P.L. (2003) 'Trans-language learners: A new terminology for international schools'. In Murphy, E. (ed.) *ESL: Educating non-native speakers of English in an English-medium international school* (The International Schools Journal Compendium 1). Saxmundham: Peridot Press, 52–6.

Jonietz, P.L. and Harris, D. (eds) (1991) *International Schools and International Education* (World Yearbook of Education). London: Kogan Page.

Kahneman, D. (2012) *Thinking, Fast and Slow*. London: Penguin Books.

Kalinowski, F. and Carder, M. (1990) 'Features of the programme'. In Murphy, E. (ed.) *ESL: A Handbook for Teachers and Administrators in International Schools*. Clevedon: Multilingual Matters, 72–90.

Kanno, Y. and Kangas, S.E.N. (2014) '"I'm not going to be, like, for the AP": English language learners' limited access to advanced college-preparatory courses in high school'. *American Educational Research Journal*, 51 (5), 848–78.

Kenny, M. and Pearce, N. (2015) 'The rise of the Anglosphere: How the right dreamed up a new conservative world order'. *New Stateman*, 10 February. www.newstatesman.com/politics/2015/02/rise-anglosphere-how-right-dreamed-new-conservative-world-order (accessed 13 February 2018).

Kieffer, M.J., Lesaux, N.K., Rivera, M. and Francis, D.J. (2009) 'Accommodations for English language learners taking large-scale assessments: A meta-analysis on effectiveness and validity'. *Review of Educational Research*, 79 (3), 1168–201.

Kovács, Á.M. and Mehler, J. (2009) 'Cognitive gains in 7-month-old bilingual infants'. *Proceedings of the National Academy of Sciences*, 106 (16), 6556–60.

Krashen, S.D. (1982) *Principles and Practice in Second Language Acquisition*. Oxford: Pergamon Press.

Krashen, S.D. (2006) *English Fever*. Taipei: Crane Publishing.

Krashen, S. and Biber, D. (1988) *On Course: Bilingual education's success in California*. Sacramento: California Association for Bilingual Education.

Kusuma-Powell, O. (2004) 'Multi-lingual, but not making it in international schools'. *Journal of Research in International Education*, 3 (2), 157–72.

Lamb, M. (2004) 'Integrative motivation in a globalizing world'. *System*, 32 (1), 3–19.

Lambert, W.E. (1974) 'Culture and language as factors in learning and education'. In Aboud, F.E. and Meade, R.D. (eds) *Cultural Factors in Learning and Education*. Proceedings of the 5th Western Washington Symposium on Learning, 15–16 November 1973. Bellingham, WA: Western Washington University, 91–122.

Lambert, W.E. and Tucker, G.R. (1972) *Bilingual Education of Children: The St. Lambert experiment*. Rowley, MA: Newbury House.

Landry, R.G. (1974) 'A comparison of second language learners and monolinguals on divergent thinking tasks at the elementary school level'. *Modern Language Journal*, 58 (1–2), 10–15.

Langford, M. (2001) 'Global nomads, third culture kids and international schools'. In Hayden, M. and Thompson, J. (eds) *International Education: Principles and practice*. London: Kogan Page, 28–43.

Lantolf, J.P. (ed.) (2000) *Sociocultural Theory and Second Language Learning*. Oxford: Oxford University Press.

Larsen-Freeman, D. (2002) 'Language acquisition and language use from a chaos/complexity theory perspective'. In Kramsch, C. (ed.) *Language Acquisition and Language Socialization: Ecological perspectives*. London: Continuum, 33–46.

Lenneberg, E.H. (1967) *Biological Foundations of Language*. New York: Wiley.

Leopold, W.F. (1939–49) *Speech Development of a Bilingual Child: A linguist's record*. 4 vols. Evanston, IL: Northwestern University Press.

Leopold, W.F. (1961) 'Patterning in children's language learning'. In Saporta, S. (ed.) *Psycholinguistics: A book of readings*. New York: Holt, Rinehart and Winston, 350–8.

Leung, C. (2001) 'Evaluation of content-language learning in the mainstream classroom'. In Mohan, B., Leung, C. and Davison, C. (eds) *English as a Second Language in the Mainstream: Teaching, learning and identity*. Harlow: Longman, 177–98.

Leung, C. (2004) 'Integrating EAL learners into mainstream curriculum'. *NALDIC Quarterly*, 2 (1), 3–10.

Leung, C. (2007) 'Integrating school-aged ESL learners into the mainstream curriculum'. In Cummins, J. and Davison, C. (eds) *International Handbook of English Language Teaching: Part 1*. New York: Springer, 249–69.

Leung, C. (2010) 'Communicative language teaching and EAL: Principles and interpretations'. In *English as an Additional Language: Approaches to teaching linguistic minority students*. London: SAGE Publications, 1–14.

Leung, C. (2013) 'Second/additional language teacher professionalism – what is it?' *Symposium 2012: Lärarrollen I svenska som andrapråk*. Stockholm: Stockholms universitets förlag, 11–27.

Leung, C. and Creese, A. (eds) (2010) *English as an Additional Language: Approaches to teaching linguistic minority students*. London: SAGE Publications.

Leung, C. and Franson, C. (2001a) 'England: ESL in the early days'. In Mohan, B., Leung, C. and Davison, C. (eds) *English as a Second Language in the Mainstream: Teaching, learning and identity*. Harlow: Longman, 153–64.

Leung, C. and Franson, C. (2001b) 'Mainstreaming: ESL as a diffused curriculum concern'. In Mohan, B., Leung, C. and Davison, C. (eds) *English as a Second Language in the Mainstream: Teaching, learning and identity*. Harlow: Longman, 165–76

Leung, C. and Franson, C. (2001c) 'Curriculum identity and professional development: System-wide questions'. In Mohan, B., Leung, C. and Davison, C. (eds) *English as a Second Language in the Mainstream: Teaching, learning and identity*. Harlow: Longman, 199–214.

Leung, C., Harris, R. and Rampton, B. (1997) 'The idealised native speaker, reified ethnicities, and classroom realities'. *TESOL Quarterly*, 31 (3), 543–60.

Leung, C. and Lewkowicz, J. (2008) 'Assessing second/additional language of diverse populations'. In Shohamy, E. and Hornberger, N.H. (eds) *Encyclopedia of Language and Education. Volume 7: Language testing and assessment*. 2nd ed. New York: Springer, 301–17.

Limbos, M.M. and Geva, E. (2001) 'Accuracy of teacher assessments of second-language students at risk for reading disability'. *Journal of Learning Disabilities*, 34 (2), 136–51.

References

Linan-Thompson, S., Vaughn, S., Prater, K. and Cirino, P.T. (2006) 'The response to intervention of English language learners at risk for reading problems'. *Journal of Learning Disabilities*, 39 (5), 390–8.

Lindholm-Leary, K.J. (2001) *Dual Language Education*. Clevedon: Multilingual Matters.

Lindholm-Leary, K. and Borsato, G. (2006) 'Academic achievement'. In Genesee, F., Lindholm-Leary, K., Saunders, W.M. and Christian, D. (eds) *Educating English Language Learners: A synthesis of research evidence*. Cambridge: Cambridge University Press, 176–222.

Lindholm-Leary, K. and Genesee, F. (2010) 'Alternative educational programs for English learners'. In California Department of Education, *Improving Education for English Learners: Research-based approaches*. Sacramento: California Department of Education, 323–82.

Lindholm-Leary, K. and Howard, E.R. (2008) 'Language development and academic achievement in two-way immersion programs'. In Fortune, T.W. and Tedick, D.J. (eds) *Pathways to Multilingualism: Evolving perspectives on immersion education*. Clevedon: Multilingual Matters, 177–200.

Lipka, O. and Siegel, L.S. (2007) 'The development of reading skills in children with English as a second language'. *Scientific Studies of Reading*, 11 (2), 105–31.

Little, J.W. (1990) 'Teachers as colleagues'. In Lieberman, A. (ed.) *Schools as Collaborative Cultures: Creating the future now*. London: Falmer Press, 165–93.

Lo Bianco, J. (1998) 'ESL: Is it migrant literacy? Is it history?' *Australian Language Matters*, 6 (2), 1, 6–7. (Also available in ACTA Background Papers No. 2, Literacy, ESL, broadbanding, benchmarking', pp. 15–21.)

Lo Bianco, J. and Freebody, P. (1997) *Australian Literacies: Informing national policy on literacy education*. Melbourne: Language Australia.

López, L.M. and Greenfield, D.B. (2004) 'The cross-language transfer of phonological skills of Hispanic Head Start children'. *Bilingual Research Journal*, 28 (1), 1–18.

Lüdi, G. and Py, B. (2009) 'To be or not to be … a plurilingual speaker'. *International Journal of Multilingualism*, 6 (2), 154–67.

Lynskey, D. (2017) '"I thought I'd put in a protest vote": The people who regret voting leave'. *The Guardian*, 25 November. Online. www.theguardian.com/politics/2017/nov/25/protest-vote-regret-voting-leave-brexit (accessed 13 February 2018).

MacKenzie, P. (2003) 'Bilingual education: Who wants it? Who needs it?' In Murphy, E. (ed.) *ESL: Educating non-native speakers of English in an English-medium international school* (The International Schools Journal Compendium 1). Saxmundham: Peridot Press, 49–56.

Mahoney, K.S. and MacSwan, J. (2005) 'Reexamining identification and reclassification of English language learners: A critical discussion of select state practices'. *Bilingual Research Journal*, 29 (1), 31–42. DOI: 10.1080/15235882.2005.10162822.

Matthews, M. (1989a) 'The scale of international education: Part I'. *International Schools Journal*, 17, 7–17.

Matthews, M. (1989b) 'The uniqueness of international education: Part II'. *International Schools Journal*, 18, 22–33.

Matthews, M. (2009) 'Challenging the IB: A personal view, post-Seville'. *International Educator*, 24 (2), 19–20.

May, S. (1994) *Making Multicultural Education Work*. Clevedon: Multilingual Matters.

May, S. (ed.) (2014a) *The Multilingual Turn: Implications for SLA, TESOL and bilingual education*. New York: Routledge.

May, S. (2014b) 'Disciplinary divides, knowledge construction, and the multilingual turn'. In May, S. (ed.) *The Multilingual Turn: Implications for SLA, TESOL and bilingual education*. New York: Routledge, 7–31.

May, S. and Hill, R. (2005) 'Māori-medium education: Current issues and challenges'. *International Journal of Bilingual Education and Bilingualism*, 8 (5), 377–403.

Mazak, C.M. and Carroll, K.S. (eds) (2017) *Translanguaging in Higher Education: Beyond monolingual ideologies*. Bristol: Multilingual Matters.

McArthur, T. (1986) 'Comment: Worried about something else'. *International Journal of the Society of Language*, 60, 87–91.

McCaig, N. (1994) 'The expatriate parent: Issues and options for internationally mobile parents'. In McCluskey, K.C. (ed.) *Notes from a Traveling Childhood: Readings for internationally mobile parents and children*. Washington, DC: Foreign Service Youth Foundation, 38–42.

McGilchrist, I. (2009) *The Master and His Emissary: The divided brain and the making of the Western world*. New Haven and London: Yale University Press.

McLaughlin, B. (1984) 'Early bilingualism: Methodological and theoretical issues'. In Paradis, M. and Lebrun, Y. (eds) *Early Bilingualism and Child Development*. Lisse: Swets and Zeitlinger, 19–46.

Meek, J. (2015) *Private Island: Why Britain now belongs to someone else*. London: Verso.

Mehisto, P. (2012) *Excellence in Bilingual Education: A guide for school principals*. Cambridge: Cambridge University Press.

Meier, G. (2014) 'Our mother tongue is plurilingualism: A framework of orientations for integrated multilingual curricula'. In Conteh, J. and Meier, G. (eds) The *Multilingual Turn in Languages Education: Opportunites and challenges*. Bristol: Multilingual Matters, 132–57.

Meisel, J.M. (2004) 'The bilingual child'. In Bhatia, T.K. and Ritchie, W.C. (eds) *The Handbook of Bilingualism*. Malden, MA: Blackwell Publishing, 91–113.

Mertin, P.A. (2006) 'The role of culture in second language learning with special reference to the Japanese students at the international school of Düsseldorf'. Unpublished PhD thesis, Goldsmiths College, University of London.

Mertin, P. (2013) *Breaking through the Language Barrier: Effective strategies for teaching English as a second language (ESL) students in secondary school mainstream classes*. Woodbridge: John Catt Educational.

Mertin, P., Van Den Bosch, J. and Daignault, P. (2018) *Translanguaging in the Secondary School*. Woodbridge: John Catt Educational.

Middleton, N., O'Keefe, P. and Moyo, S. (1993) *The Tears of the Crocodile: From Rio to reality in the developing world*. London: Pluto Press.

Mill, J.S. (1861) *Considerations on Representative Government*. London: Parker, Son, and Bourn. Online. https://books.google.bg/books?id=emABAAAAYAAJ&pg=PR3&hl=bg#v=onepage&q&f=false (accessed 13 February 2018).

References

Mill, J.S. (1869) *On Liberty*. 4th ed. London: Longman, Roberts and Green. Online. www.econlib.org/library/Mill/mlLbty2.html# (accessed 13 February 2018).

Ministry of Education (1963) 'English for immigrants'. London: HMSO.

Mohan, B., Leung, C. and Davison, C. (eds) (2001) *English as a Second Language in the Mainstream: Teaching, learning and identity*. Harlow: Longman.

Monaghan, F. (2010) 'Mainstream participatory approaches: From slipstream to mainstream'. In Leung, C. and Creese, A. (eds) *English as an Additional Language: Approaches to teaching linguistic minority students*. London: SAGE Publications, 15–32.

Morrison, L. (2016) 'Native English speakers are the world's worst communicators'. *BBC Capital*, 31 October. Online. www.bbc.com/capital/story/20161028-native-english-speakers-are-the-worlds-worst-communicators (accessed 13 February 2018).

MRG (Minority Rights Group) (1994) *Education Rights and Minorities*. London: Minority Rights Group. Online. www.unicef-irc.org/publications/pdf/minorities_rights.pdf (accessed 18 September 2018).

Mullard, C. (1982) 'Multiracial education in Britain: From assimilation to cultural pluralism'. In Tierney, J. (ed.) *Race, Migration and Schooling*. London: Holt, Rinehart and Winston, 120–33.

Murakami, C. (2008) '"Everybody is just fumbling along": An investigation of views regarding EAL training and support provisions in a rural area'. *Language and Education*, 22 (4), 265–82.

Murphy, E. (ed.) (1990) *ESL: A handbook for teachers and administrators in international schools*. Clevedon: Multilingual Matters.

Murphy, E. (2000) 'Questions for the new millennium'. *International Schools Journal*, 19 (2), 5–10.

Murphy, E. (ed.) (2003) *ESL: Educating non-native speakers of English in an English-medium international school* (International Schools Journal Compendium 1). Saxmundham: Peridot Press.

NALDIC (National Association for Language Development in the Curriculum) (2014) 'The national audit of English as an additional language training and development provision: Report'. Online. www.naldic.org.uk/Resources/NALDIC/Research%20and%20Information/Documents/NALDIC%20-%20EAL%20Audit%202014%20FINAL%20FINAL%20YF%20Oct%2014.pdf (accessed 13 February 2018).

NALDIC (National Association for Language Development in the Curriculum) (2015) 'EAL and the initial training of teachers'. Online. www.naldic.org.uk/eal-initial-teacher-education/ite-programmes (accessed 13 February 2018).

Nieto, S. (1992) *Affirming Diversity: The sociopolitical context of multicultural education*. New York: Longman.

Nikula, T., Dafouz, E., Moore, P. and Smit, U. (eds) (2016) *Conceptualising Integration in CLIL and Multilingual Education*. Bristol: Multilingual Matters.

Nunan, D. (1999) *Second Language Teaching and Learning*. Boston: Heinle and Heinle.

OECD (2010) *Closing the Gap for Immigrant Students: Policies, practice and performance* (Reviews of Migrant Education). Paris: Organisation for Economic Cooperation and Development.

Ordóñez, C.L., Carlo, M.S., Snow, C.E. and McLaughlin, B. (2002) 'Depth and breadth of vocabulary in two languages: Which vocabulary skills transfer?' *Journal of Educational Psychology*, 94 (4), 719–28.

Ortega, L. (2013) *Understanding Second Language Acquisition*. London: Routledge.

Ortega, L. (2014) 'Ways forward for a bi/multilingual turn in SLA'. In May, S. (ed.) *The Multilingual Turn: Implications for SLA, TESOL and bilingual education*. New York: Routledge, 32–53.

Ortiz, A.A., Wilkinson, C.Y., Robertson-Courtney, P. and Kushner, M.I. (2006) 'Considerations in implementing intervention assistance teams to support English language learners'. *Remedial and Special Education*, 27 (1), 53–63.

Ostler, N. (2005) *Empires of the Word: A language history of the world*. New York: HarperCollins.

Ostler, N. (2018) 'Have we reached peak English in the world?' *The Guardian*, 27 February. Online. www.theguardian.com/commentisfree/2018/feb/27/reached-peak-english-britain-china (accessed 27 February 2018).

Ovando, C.J. (1998) 'Mathematics and science'. In Ovando, C.J. and Collier, V.P. *Bilingual and ESL Classrooms: Teaching in multicultural contexts*. 2nd ed. Boston: McGraw-Hill, 174–206.

Ovando, C.J. and Collier, V.P. (1998) *Bilingual and ESL Classrooms: Teaching in multicultural contexts*. 2nd ed. Boston: McGraw-Hill.

Özerk, K. (2001) 'Teacher–student verbal interaction and questioning, class size and bilingual students' academic performance'. *Scandinavian Journal of Educational Research*, 45 (4), 353–67.

Páez, M. and Rinaldi, C. (2006) 'Predicting English word reading skills for Spanish-speaking students in first grade'. *Topics in Language Disorders*, 26 (4), 338–50.

Pappamihiel, N.E. (2001) 'Moving from the ESL classroom into the mainstream: An investigation of English language anxiety in Mexican girls'. *Bilingual Research Journal*, 25 (1–2), 31–8.

Paulston, C.B. (1980) *Bilingual Education: Theories and issues*. Rowley, MA: Newbury House.

Peal, E. and Lambert, W. (1962) 'The relation of bilingualism to intelligence'. *Psychological Monographs, General and Applied*, 76 (546), 1–23. (Reprinted in Gardner, R. and Lambert, W. (1972) *Attitudes and Motivation in Second-Language Learning*. Rowley, MA: Newbury House, 247ff.)

Pearce, R. (ed.) (2013a) *International Education and Schools: Moving beyond the first 40 years*. London: Bloomsbury Academic.

Pearce, R. (2013b) 'Student diversity: The core challenge to international schools'. In Pearce, R. (ed.) *International Education and Schools: Moving beyond the first 40 years*. London: Bloomsbury Academic, 61–84.

Pedalino Porter, R. (1990) *Forked Tongue: The politics of bilingual education*. New York: Basic Books.

Pennycook, A. (2003) 'Global Englishes, Rip Slyme, and performativity'. *Journal of Sociolinguistics*, 7 (4), 513–33.

Perrenoud, P. (1998) 'From formative evaluation to a controlled regulation of learning processes: Towards a wider conceptual field'. *Assessment in Education: Principles, Policy and Practice*, 5 (1), 85–102.

Petitto, L.-A. and Dunbar, K.N. (2009) 'Educational neuroscience: New discoveries from bilingual brains, scientific brains, and the educated mind'. *Mind, Brain, and Education*, 3 (4), 185–97. Online. www.ncbi.nlm.nih.gov/pmc/articles/PMC3338206/ (accessed 13 February 2018).

Piccardo, E. and Aden, J. (2014) 'Plurilingualism and empathy: Beyond instrumental language learning'. In Conteh, J. and Meier, G. (eds) *The Multilingual Turn in Languages Education: Opportunities and challenges*. Bristol: Multilingual Matters, 234–57.

Pollitt, C. (1990) *Managerialism and the Public Services: The Anglo-American experience*. Oxford: Basil Blackwell.

Popham, W.J. (2008) *Transformative Assessment*. Alexandria, VA: Association for Supervision and Curriculum Development.

Purves, L. (2015) 'Gift of language is what migrants need most'. *The Times*, 12 October. www.thetimes.co.uk/article/gift-of-language-is-what-migrants-need-most-chf0pd7cl7c (accessed 13 February 2018).

Ramírez, A.G. and Politzer, R.L. (1976) 'The acquisition of English and maintenance of Spanish in a bilingual education program'. In Alatis, J.E. and Twaddell, K. (eds) *English as a Second Language in Bilingual Education*. Washington, DC: Teachers of English to Speakers of Other Languages.

Ramírez, J.D. (1992) 'Executive summary'. *Bilingual Research Journal*, 16 (1–2), 1–62.

Rampton, B. (1997) 'Second language research in late modernity: A response to Firth and Wagner'. *Modern Language Journal*, 81 (3), 329–33.

Reardon, S.F. and Galindo, C. (2009) 'The Hispanic-White achievement gap in math and reading in the elementary grades'. *American Educational Research Journal*, 46 (3), 853–91.

Rees, S. (1995) 'The fraud and the fiction'. In Rees, S. and Rodley, G. (eds) *The Human Costs of Managerialism: Advocating the recovery of humanity*. Leichhardt, NSW: Pluto Press Australia, 15–27.

Reeves, A. (1994) 'Developing bilingual theatre-in-education programmes'. In Blackledge, A. (ed.) *Teaching Bilingual Children*. Stoke-on-Trent: Trentham Books.

Richards, J.C. and Lockhart, C. (1994) *Reflective Teaching in Second Language Classrooms*. Cambridge: Cambridge University Press.

Richardson, S. (2016) 'The "native factor", the haves and the have-nots' [video], IATEFL conference, Birmingham, 14 April, https://iatefl.britishcouncil.org/2016/session/plenary-silvana-richardson (accessed 13 February 2018).

Rittel, H.W.J. and Webber, M.M. (1973) 'Dilemmas in a general theory of planning'. *Policy Sciences*, 4 (2), 155–69.

Robinson, P. and Ellis, N.C. (2008) 'Conclusion: Cognitive linguistics, second language acquisition and L2 instruction: Issues for research'. In Robinson, P. and Ellis, N.C. (eds) *Handbook of Cognitive Linguistics and Second Language Acquisition*. New York: Routledge, 489–545.

Rolstad, K. (2017) 'Second language instructional competence'. *International Journal of Bilingual Education and Bilingualism*, 20 (5), 497–509.

Rolstad, K., Mahoney, K. and Glass, G.V. (2005) 'The big picture: A meta-analysis of program effectiveness research on English language learners'. *Educational Policy*, 19 (4), 572–94.

Romaine, S. (2004) 'The bilingual and multilingual community'. In Bhatia, T.K. and Ritchie, W.C. (eds) *The Handbook of Bilingualism*. Malden, MA: Blackwell Publishing, 385–405.

Ruiz Zafón, C. (2013) *The Prisoner of Heaven*. Trans. Graves, L. London: Phoenix.

Rusbridger, A. (2015) 'Climate change: Why the Guardian is putting threat to Earth front and centre'. *The Guardian*, 6 March. Online. www.theguardian.com/environment/2015/mar/06/climate-change-guardian-threat-to-earth-alan-rusbridger (accessed 13 February 2018).

Sang, D. and Chadwick, T. (2014) *Breakthrough to CLIL for Physics*. Cambridge: Cambridge University Press.

Scanlan, M. and López, F. (2012) '¡Vamos! How school leaders promote equity and excellence for bilingual students'. *Educational Administration Quarterly*, 48 (4), 583–625.

Schecter, S.R. and Cummins, J. (eds) (2003) *Multilingual Education in Practice: Using diversity as a resource*. Portsmouth, NH: Heinemann.

Scheff, T.J. (1988) 'Shame and conformity: The deference-emotion system'. *American Sociological Review*, 53 (3), 395–406.

Schleppegrell, M.J. (2004) *The Language of Schooling: A functional linguistics perspective*. Mahwah, NJ: Lawrence Erlbaum Associates.

Schmidt, R. (1995) 'Consciousness and foreign language learning: A tutorial on the role of attention and awareness in learning'. In Schmidt, R. (ed.) *Attention and Awareness in Foreign Language Learning*. Honolulu: Second Language Teaching and Curriculum Center, 1–63.

Sears, C. (1998) *Second Language Students in Mainstream Classrooms: A handbook for teachers in international schools*. Clevedon: Multilingual Matters.

Sears, C. (2015) *Second Language Students in English-Medium Classrooms: A guide for teachers in international schools*. Bristol: Multilingual Matters.

Sennett, R. (2006) *The Culture of the New Capitalism*. New Haven and London: Yale University Press.

Sharifian, F. (ed.) (2009) *English as an International Language: Perspectives and pedagogical issues*. Bristol: Multilingual Matters.

Sharp, D. (1973) *Language in Bilingual Communities*. London: Edward Arnold.

Shaw, P. (2003) 'Leadership in the diverse school'. In Schecter, S.R. and Cummins, J. (eds) *Multilingual Education in Practice: Using diversity as a resource*. Portsmouth, NH: Heinemann, 97–112.

Shepard, L.A. (2000) 'The role of assessment in a learning culture'. *Educational Researcher*, 29 (7), 4–14.

Shepard, L.A. (2005) 'Linking formative assessment to scaffolding'. *Educational Leadership*, 63 (3), 66–70.

Shin, S.J. (2008) 'Preparing non-native English-speaking ESL teachers'. *Teacher Development*, 12 (1), 57–65.

Shohamy, E. (2006) *Language Policy: Hidden agendas and new approaches*. London: Routledge.

Singleton, D. (2014) 'How do people acquire the words of a second language?' In Cook, V. and Singleton, D. *Key Topics in Second Language Acquisition*. Bristol: Multilingual Matters, 37–54.

Skelton, M. (2002) 'Defining "international" in an international curriculum'. In Hayden, M., Thompson, J. and Walker, G. (eds) *International Education in Practice: Dimensions for national and international schools*. London: Kogan Page, 39–54.

Skutnabb-Kangas, T. (2000) *Linguistic Genocide in Education – or Worldwide Diversity and Human Rights?* Mahwah, NJ: Lawrence Erlbaum Associates.

Skutnabb-Kangas, T., Phillipson, R., Mohanty, A.K. and Panda, M. (eds) (2009) *Social Justice through Multilingual Education*. Bristol: Multilingual Matters.

Skutnabb-Kangas, T. and Toukomaa, P. (1976) *Teaching Migrant Children's Mother Tongue and Learning the Language of the Host Country in the Context of the Socio-cultural Situation of the Migrant Family*. Tampere: University of Tampere, Department of Sociology and Social Psychology (for UNESCO).

Smith, F., Hardman, F., Wall, K. and Mroz, M. (2004) 'Interactive whole class teaching in the national literacy and numeracy strategies'. *British Educational Research Journal*, 30 (3), 395–411.

Snow, C. (2008) 'Cross-cutting themes and future research directions'. In August, D. and Shanahan, T. (eds) *Developing Reading and Writing in Second-Language Learners: Lessons from the report of the National Literacy Panel on Language-Minority Children and Youth*. New York: Routledge, 275–300.

Sternberg, R.J. (2016) 'Testing: For better and worse'. *Phi Delta Kappan*, 98 (4), 66–71.

Stoller, F.L. (2008) 'Content-based instruction'. In Van Deusen-Scholl, N. and Hornberger, N.H. (eds) *Encyclopedia of Language and Education. Volume 4: Second and foreign language education*. 2nd ed. New York: Springer, 59–70.

Storti, C. (1997) The *Art of Coming Home*. Yarmouth, ME: Intercultural Press.

Stringer, E.T. (1999) *Action Research*. 2nd ed. Thousand Oaks, CA: SAGE Publications.

Swain, M., Kinnear, P. and Steinman, L. (2011) *Sociocultural Theory in Second Language Education: An introduction through narratives*. Bristol: Multilingual Matters.

Tam, K.Y., Heward, W.L. and Heng, M.A. (2006) 'A reading instruction intervention program for English-language learners who are struggling readers'. *Journal of Special Education*, 40 (2), 79–93.

Tangen, D. and Spooner-Lane, R. (2008) 'Avoiding the deficit model of teaching: Students who have EAL/EAL and learning difficulties'. *Australian Journal of Learning Difficulties*, 13 (2), 63–71.

Tharp, R.G. and Gallimore, R. (1991) *Rousing Minds to Life: Teaching, learning, and schooling in social context*. Cambridge: Cambridge University Press.

Thomas, W.P. (1992) 'An analysis of the research methodology of the Ramírez study'. *Bilingual Research Journal*, 16 (1–2), 213–45.

Thomas, W.P. and Collier, V.P. (1995) *Language Minority Student Achievement and Program Effectiveness: Research summary*. Fairfax, VA: George Mason University.

Thomas, W.P. and Collier, V. (1997) *School Effectiveness for Language Minority Students*. Washington, DC: National Clearinghouse for Bilingual Education.

Thomas, W. and Collier, V. (2002) *A National Study of School Effectiveness for Language Minority Students' Long-Term Academic Achievement*. Santa Cruz, CA: Center for Research on Education, Diversity and Excellence.

Thomas, W.P. and Collier, V.P. (2014) 'English learners in North Carolina dual language programs: Year 3 of this study: School year 2009–2010'. Fairfax, VA: George Mason University. A research report provided to the North Carolina Department of Public Instruction. Online. https://drive.google.com/file/d/0B5l6NsqrKtjRZG4tbzRpNkQ0Q1E/view (accessed 19 September 2018).

Thomas, W.P. and Collier, V.P. (2017) *Why Dual Language Schooling*. Albuquerque: Fuente Press.

Thompson, E. (1998) 'Editor's introduction'. In MacDougall, R. *The Emigrant's Guide to North America* (ed. E. Thompson). Toronto: Natural Heritage Books, vii–xxiv.

Thrupp, M. and Willmott, R. (2003) *Education Management in Managerialist Times: Beyond the textual apologists*. Maidenhead: Open University Press.

Tomlinson, S. (2001) *Education in a Post-Welfare Society*. Buckingham: Open University Press.

Torres-Guzmán, M.E. (2002) 'Dual language programs: Key features and results'. *Directions in Language and Education*, 14, 1–16.

Tosi, A. (1987) 'First, second or foreign language learning? Political and professional support for bilingualism in national and international education'. Unpublished PhD thesis, Institute of Education, University of London.

Tosi, A. (1991) 'Language in international education'. In Jonietz, P.L. and Harris, D. (eds) *International Schools and International Education* (World Yearbook of Education). London: Kogan Page, 82–99.

Toukomaa, P. and Skutnabb-Kangas, T. (1977) *The Intensive Teaching of the Mother Tongue to Migrant Children of Pre-School Age and Children in the Lower Level of Comprehensive School*. Helsinki: Finnish National Commission for UNESCO.

Troike, R.C. (1978) 'Research evidence for the effectiveness of bilingual education'. *NABE Journal*, 3 (1), 13–24.

Trowler, P. (2003) *Education Policy*. 2nd ed. London: Routledge.

Tucker, G.R. (1999) *A Global Perspective on Bilingualism and Bilingual Education* (ERIC Digest). Washington, DC: ERIC Clearinghouse on Languages and Linguistics.

Twing, J.S., Boyle, B. and Charles, M. (2010) 'Integrated assessment systems for improved learning'. Paper presented at the 36th annual conference of the International Association of Educational Assessment (IAEA), Bangkok, Thailand, 22–27 August.

Umansky, I.M. and Reardon, S.F. (2014) 'Reclassification patterns among Latino English learner students in bilingual, dual immersion, and English immersion classrooms'. *American Educational Research Journal*, 51 (5), 879–912.

UNESCO (1975) *Interactions between Linguistics and Mathematical Education: Final report of the symposium sponsored by UNESCO, CEDO and ICMI, Nairobi, Kenya, September 1–11, 1974* (UNESCO Report No. ED-74/CONF.808). Paris: United Nations Educational, Scientific and Cultural Organization.

UNESCO (2003) 'Education in a multilingual world'. UNESCO Education Position Paper. United Nations Educational, Scientific and Cultural Organization, Paris.

References

Useem, R.H. and Downie, R.D. (1976) 'Third culture kids'. *Today's Education*, 65 (3), 103–5.

Useem, R.H. and Downie, R.D. (1986) 'Third-culture kids'. In Austin, C.N. (ed.) *Cross-Cultural Reentry: A book of readings*. Abilene, TX: Abilene Christian University Press, 167–72.

Valdés, G. (1998) 'The world outside and inside schools: Language and immigrant children'. *Educational Researcher*, 27 (6), 4–18.

van Lier, L. (2004) *The Ecology and Semiotics of Language Learning: A sociocultural perspective*. Boston: Kluwer Academic.

Vaughn, S., Bos, C.S. and Schumm, J.S. (2006) *Teaching Exceptional, Diverse, and At-Risk Students in the General Education Classroom*. 3rd ed. Boston: Allyn and Bacon.

Vygotsky, L.S. (1962) *Thought and Language*. Cambridge, MA: MIT Press.

Wallace, C. (2003) *Critical Reading in Language Education*. Basingstoke: Palgrave Macmillan.

Wei, L. (2015) 'Complementary classrooms for multilingual minority ethnic children as a translanguaging space'. In Cenoz, J. and Gorter, D. (eds) *Multilingual Education: Between language learning and translanguaging*. Cambridge: Cambridge University Press, 177–98.

Wheatley, K.F. (2002) 'The potential benefits of teacher efficacy doubts for educational reform'. *Teaching and Teacher Education*, 18 (1), 5–22.

Whitty, G., Power, S. and Halpin, D. (1998) *Devolution and Choice in Education: The school, the state and the market*. Buckingham: Open University Press.

Wiley, T.G. (2008) 'Language policy and teacher education'. In May, S. and Hornberger, N.H. (eds) *Encyclopedia of Language and Education. Volume 1: Language policy and political issues in education*. 2nd ed. New York: Springer, 229–41.

Wiley, T.G. and Wright, W.E. (2004) 'Against the undertow: Language-minority education policy and politics in the "age of accountability"'. *Educational Policy*, 18 (1), 142–68.

Wilkinson, R. and Pickett, K. (2010) *The Spirit Level: Why equality is better for everyone*. London: Penguin Books.

Williams, C. (1994) 'Arfarniad o ddulliau dysgu ac addysgu yng nghyd-destun addysg uwchradd ddwyieithog' ['An evaluation of teaching and learning methods in the context of bilingual secondary education']. Unpublished PhD thesis, University of Wales, Bangor.

Willig, A.C. (1985) 'A meta-analysis of selected studies on the effectiveness of bilingual education'. *Review of Educational Research*, 55 (3), 269–317.

Wittgenstein, L. (2007) *Tractatus Logico-Philosophicus*. Trans. Ogden, C.K. New York: Cosimo Classics.

Wolf, M. (2008) *Proust and the Squid: The story and science of the reading brain*. Cambridge: Icon Books.

Wolff, D. (2003) 'Content and language integrated learning: A framework for the development of learner autonomy'. In Little, D., Ridley, J. and Ushioda, E. (eds) *Learner Autonomy in the Foreign Language Classroom: Teacher, learner, curriculum and assessment*. Dublin: Authentik, 211–22.

Wolin, R. (1992) *The Terms of Cultural Criticism: The Frankfurt School, existentialism, poststructuralism*. New York: Columbia University Press.

Wolin, S.S. (2008) *Democracy Incorporated: Managed democracy and the specter of inverted totalitarianism*. Princeton: Princeton University Press.

Wong Fillmore, L. (1983) 'The language learner as an individual: Implications of research on individual differences for the ESL teacher'. In Clarke, M.A. and Handscombe, J. (eds) *On TESOL '82: Pacific perspectives on language learning and teaching*. Washington, DC: Teachers of English to Speakers of Other Languages, 157–73.

Woolcock, N. (2014) 'All children will learn English as foreign language, says head'. *The Times*, 26 March. www.thetimes.co.uk/article/all-children-will-learn-english-as-foreign-language-says-head-nbtnf69pb99 (accessed 13 February 2018).

Woolley, G. (2010) 'Issues in the identification and ongoing assessment of ESL students with reading difficulties for reading intervention'. *Australian Journal of Learning Difficulties*, 15 (1), 81–98.

Wright, S. (2004) *Language Policy and Language Planning: From nationalism to globalisation*. Basingstoke: Palgrave Macmillan.

Yamamoto, M. (2001) *Language Use in Interlingual Families: A Japanese–English sociolinguistic study*. Clevedon: Multilingual Matters.

Young, A. (2014) 'Looking through the language lens: Monolingual taint or plurilingual tint?' In Conteh, J. and Meier, G. (eds) *The Multilingual Turn in Languages Education: Opportunities and challenges*. Bristol: Multilingual Matters, 89–109.

Zimmerman, B.J. (2000) 'Attaining self-regulation: A social cognitive perspective'. In Boekaerts, M., Pintrich, P.R. and Zeidner, M. (eds) *Handbook of Self-Regulation*. San Diego: Academic Press, 13–39.

Index